CLAIMING THE
ORIENTAL GATEWAY

A list of additional titles in this series appears at the back of this book

CLAIMING THE
ORIENTAL GATEWAY

Prewar Seattle and Japanese America

Shelley Sang-Hee Lee

TEMPLE UNIVERSITY PRESS ⊤ PHILADELPHIA

TEMPLE UNIVERSITY PRESS
Philadelphia, Pennsylvania 19122
www.temple.edu/tempress

Portions of Chapter 2 were originally published in Shelley S. Lee, "The Contradictions of Cosmopolitanism: Consuming the Orient at the Alaska-Yukon-Pacific Exposition and the International Potlatch Festival, 1909–1934," *Western Historical Quarterly* 38 (Autumn 2007): 277–302. Copyright by the Western Historical Association. Reprinted by permission.

Portions of Chapter 3 were originally published in Shelley Sang-Hee Lee, "'Good American Subjects Done through Japanese Eyes': Race, Nationality, and the Seattle Camera Club, 1924–1929," *Pacific Northwest Quarterly* 96 (2004–2005): 24–34.

Library of Congress Cataloging-in-Publication Data

Lee, Shelley Sang-Hee, 1975–
    Claiming the oriental gateway : prewar Seattle and Japanese America / Shelley Sang-Hee Lee.
        p. cm. — (Asian American history and culture)
    Includes bibliographical references and index.
    ISBN 978-1-4399-0213-4 (hardback : alk. paper) — ISBN 978-1-4399-0215-8 (e-book)
    1. Japanese Americans—Washington (State)—Seattle—History—20th century. 2. Japanese Americans—Washington (State)—Seattle—Social conditions—20th century. 3. Japanese Americans—Cultural assimilation—Washington (State)—Seattle—History—20th century.
    4. Seattle (Wash.)—Social conditions—20th century. 5. Seattle (Wash.)—Race relations. I. Title.
    F899.S49J348 2011
    305.894956'0730797—dc22
                                                                                    2010024878

ISBN 978-1-4399-0214-1 (paperback : alk.paper)

Printed in the United States of America

080913-P

To Miles and Kalea

⋊╟⊰

Contents

>|+|<

Acknowledgments

Many people played a role in the process of turning my doctoral dissertation into this book. Their input and influence have improved the final product, and any errors that remain are mine alone.

From my days as an uncertain graduate student at Stanford University through the completion of this book, I have sought, time and time again, the wise counsel of my dissertation advisers, Gordon Chang and Richard White. I deeply appreciate their continued support and generosity, and they remain for me models of how to achieve excellence in the profession without losing one's sense of humor and compassion. Also serving as a model of scholarly rigor and professional integrity is Estelle Freedman, who taught me so much of what I know about doing historical research. The lessons I drew from her graduate seminar have stuck with me for more than a decade and, I think, are evident throughout this book.

After graduate school, I followed a winding path that eventually led to Oberlin College, and in retrospect this was a fortuitous and enriching journey. At the University of California at Santa Barbara, Jim Lee, Steve Sohn, and Hung Thai extended their hospitality and good cheer. I briefly crossed paths with erin Ninh and am grateful for our enduring friendship. I am particularly thankful for the generosity of Celine Parreñas Shimizu, Xiaojian Zhao, and Paul Spickard, who dispensed their sage professional wisdom and read my clunky dissertation to give insightful comments on how to revise it for publication. A postdoctoral fellowship in the Asian American Studies Program at the University of Illinois at Urbana-Champaign (UIUC) afforded critical time and resources for work on this book. There, I met a terrific group of scholars who not only made the year pleasant but also, through reading my work, attending my talks, chatting over meals, and organizing sessions, helped me sharpen my ideas and rethink how to present them. They include Marcelo Bucheli, Diem-My Bui, Antoinette Burton, Adrian Cruz, Rachel Endo, Augusto Espiritu, Martin Manalansan, Victor Mendoza, Joel Miyazake, Lisa Nakamura, Kent Ono, Yoon Pak, Liz Pleck, and David Roediger. I also thank Viveka Kudaligama and Mary Ellerbe for their help in navigating the maze of UIUC.

I have been fortunate to work at Oberlin since 2007, where my students and colleagues are as extraordinary and engaging as they come. I am also fortunate to have as my colleagues such brilliant and accomplished scholars as Pawan Dhingra, Wendy Kozol, Pablo Mitchell, Gina Perez, and Meredith Raimondo, who also happen to be wonderful human beings and valued friends. Eric Estes, Mike Fisher, Jenny Fraser, Meredith Gadsby, Heather Hogan, Daphne John, David Kamitsuka, Maggi Kamitsuka, Clayton Koppes, Gary Kornblith, Carol Lasser, Anu Needham, Renee Romano, Ari Sammartino, Len Smith, and Steve Volk shared their time and advice on such matters as how to budget my time, where to find a decent cup of coffee, and everything in between. The students of my History/Comparative American Studies 260 and 246 classes have been joys to teach and inspirations for finishing this book. Their enthusiasm, curiosity, and commitment to antiracism remind me of why I went into Asian American studies and give me hope for the future. The prompt assistance of the staff at the Oberlin College library allowed me to complete my revisions and to obtain key images in a timely manner.

Over the years, many individuals helped push this project along by locating materials, commenting on drafts, and providing a space for presenting portions of it. The staffs at the University of Washington Libraries, Special Collections, and the Museum of History and Industry in Seattle, especially Nicolette Bromberg, Carolyn Marr, and Alan Presly, provided terrific assistance and knowledge, several times coming through for me in a pinch. Presenting chapters at meetings of the Western Historical Association, the Organization of American Historians, the Association for Asian American Studies, and a symposium at the University of Washington for the centennial of the Alaska-Yukon-Pacific Exposition allowed me to share preliminary ideas and to receive the astute comments of Albert Broussard, Kevin Leonard, Karen Merrill, and Vince Rafael. I also thank Moon-Ho Jung, Jonathan Sadowsky, and Judy Wu for inviting me to present chapters at the University of Washington, Case Western University, and The Ohio State University.

Early on, Eiichiro Azuma read the dissertation on which the book is based and gave incisive and thorough feedback that pushed me to pinpoint what it was I was trying to do and say. At various points in the process from dissertation to book, Magdalena Barrera, Stephanie Batiste, Ned Blackhawk, Matthew Booker, Birgit Brander Rasmussen, Rachel Jean-Baptiste, Karen Leong, David Martin, Gail Nomura, Carol Pal, Lise Sedrez, Kären Wigen, and Judy Wu brought their keen and discerning eyes to different parts of the project. Jon Okamura offered helpful guidance in navigating the world of book publishing, and Scott Wong provided crucial comments and much appreciated encouragement on the penultimate draft. I also thank Heather Wilcox, who copyedited the manuscript.

So much of what I learned about Asian American studies as an undergraduate and graduate student came from books in the *Asian American History and Culture* series at Temple University Press, which makes bringing this book to completion particularly gratifying and humbling. Janet Francendese's efficiency, good instincts, broad knowledge, and no-nonsense approach made her an ideal editor for this first-time author, and I thank her for seeing the potential in my project and for taking it on. Also at Temple, Courtney Davison, Gary Kramer, Matthew Kull, Emily Taber, and Joan Vidal kept me on point and gave invaluable support, and two anonymous readers provided thorough reports full of constructive suggestions.

I cannot adequately express my gratitude to my parents, Vicky Lee and David Leon, and my sister, Sandy, for their faith in me and unconditional support, without which I would never have completed graduate school, much less this book. My parents made extraordinary sacrifices to give my sister and me lives rich with love and opportunities, and I aspire to live my life with the spirit and resilience that they demonstrate every day. The past few years also brought into my circle a wonderful extended family that includes Anthony, Suzanne, and James Kim; Rich, Ryan, and Aimee Baldoz; and Holly Stalder. In my partner, Rick Baldoz, I found an intellectual companion, an emotional anchor, and a constant source of humor. Although he was working to finish his own book, he selflessly made time to read many drafts and to offer the right combination of criticism and encouragement. I look forward to the rest of our journey together.

CLAIMING THE
ORIENTAL GATEWAY

Introduction

In the opening scene of John Okada's 1957 novel, *No-No Boy*, the main character, Ichiro Yamada, descends from a bus that has pulled into his hometown of Seattle, Washington. World War II has recently ended, and along with nearly 120,000 other Japanese Americans, Ichiro has endured a most harrowing ordeal, memories of which haunt him throughout the novel. Over the last four years, Ichiro's travails included internment and jail time, and while in "camp," he broke with the majority of the Japanese American internees by refusing to pledge unqualified allegiance to the United States, an act of disloyalty leading to his imprisonment. After his time away from home, Ichiro returns to the streets of downtown Seattle, but he feels "like an intruder in a world in which he had no claim."[1]

A fellow resident of Japanese ancestry he encounters tells him, "The smart [former internees] went to Chicago and New York and lotsa places back east,"[2] suggesting that Seattle, although once home to many Japanese Americans, is no longer a place where they ought or want to be.[3] Exploring his old stomping grounds on Jackson Street, which runs through Japantown and is adjacent to the vice district and Chinese and black neighborhoods, only compounds Ichiro's feelings of alienation:

> The war had wrought violent changes upon the people, and the people, in turn, working hard and living hard and earning a lot of money and spending it on whatever was available, had distorted the profile of Jackson Street. The street had about it the air of a carnival

without quite succeeding at becoming one. A shooting gallery stood where once had been a clothing store; fish and chips had replaced a jewelry shop; and a bunch of Negroes were horsing around raucously in front of a pool parlor. Everything looked older and dirtier and shabbier.[4]

Jolted by the cacophonous sounds, unfamiliar faces, and air of inauthenticity he detects around him, Ichiro pines for the comfort of familiarity, but to no avail. Instead, a group of black residents heckles him to "Go back to Tokyo, boy," and later some whites also tell him to "Go back to Japan."[5] Though Ichiro was born in and grew up in America, his "Oriental" face marks him as a foreigner, and perceptions of his individual "otherness" are steeped in broader perceptions of Japan's cultural and geographic otherness, not to mention memories of the recently concluded war against Japan. In the context of war, the construction of Japan as an enemy nation and race whose people, values, and culture were vastly different from, even antagonistic to, those of Americans galvanized U.S. troops against the wartime foe. Domestically, however, this construction also established the impossibility of full American citizenship for persons of Japanese ancestry in the United States, even those who held legal U.S. citizenship. This impossibility was doubly so for those who would not commit their unqualified allegiance to the United States and renounce Japan during the war.

The taunts he endures to go "back to Japan" signal to Ichiro that, even in his hometown of Seattle, once the site of a bustling Japanese American community and major port of trans-Pacific commerce, he is out of place. *No-No Boy* only hints at his prewar life, and, in one such instance, a walk down Jackson Street sparks sobering realizations of how much he and his city have changed:

> Was it possible that he, striding freely down the street of an American city, the city of his birth and schooling and the cradle of his hopes and dreams, had waved it all aside beyond recall? Was it possible that he and Freddie and the other four of the poker crowd and all the other American-born, American-educated Japanese who had renounced their American-ness in a frightening moment of madness had done so irretrievably? Was there no hope of redemption?[6]

Although Seattle is the backdrop against which Ichiro's postwar odyssey plays out, it is also a reflection and projection of his angst. It is the home to which he returns, initially with hopes of losing himself in the familiar and forgetting the trials of the past, but the city offers no such solace and is anything but the setting of a happy homecoming. As noted above, it has changed too much, as has Ichiro. Furthermore, seeing and interacting with other persons of Japanese ancestry provide no comfort or sense of belonging, as he has internalized his outsider status as a racial "other" and "disloyal" subject. Yet memories of Ichiro's prewar life in Seattle haunt him and sustain his hope, however faint, that he might one day find redemption and restore his fragmented postwar self.

Although *No-No Boy* is a fictionalized account of the struggles of Japanese American resettlement in Seattle, the novel does, nonetheless, powerfully channel the sudden and tumultuous changes in fortune that West Coast Japanese Americans experienced over the first half of the twentieth century. Most of the memories Ichiro grapples with in the book come from the war years, but at various moments, Okada alludes to his prewar life, inviting the reader to speculate about what changed and what was lost to the tidal wave of mass removal and incarceration. When Ichiro wonders, for example, whether it was possible that the "hopes and dreams" he nurtured during his childhood had been swept aside by the tumult of internment, Okada alludes to, but gives little detail about, a time that the reader is left to imagine as only an idyllic prelude to the traumatic and dislocating war years.

Although they are relatively minor aspects of the book, these moments of reflection on the past, prompted by Ichiro's encounters with his urban surroundings, conjure up images of a pre–World War II Seattle when Japanese Americans' relationship with the city inspired much less dreary sentiments. For example, in 1930, the *Japanese-American Courier,* an all-English weekly targeted at members of the second generation (Nisei), depicted conditions in Jackson Street that contrasted greatly with Okada's bleak postwar visions. Rejecting then-dominant impressions of the area as a seedbed of vice and racial deviancy, Seattle Nisei lawyer and ethnic community leader Clarence Arai reclaimed the neighborhood's reputation and sought to instill residents' pride by describing it as a center of "international" culture that was enhanced—rather than degraded—by the presence of Japanese, Chinese, and Filipinos. Members of these ethnic groups, he said, so crucially defined that section that it might as well be called the "Far East of Seattle City":

> As one saunters down one of the main streets, one finds that a Japanese restaurant caters to the group by a prominent sign, "Philippine Dinners." Glancing thru the new phone book one will run across the word "Filipino" added to the firm name of one of the oldest Japanese

business firms. The South End is no longer Seattle's "Little Tokio" [*sic*] or "Chinatown" but Seattle's "Far East."[7]

In Arai's depiction, likely aimed at deflecting nativist and racist hostility toward Japanese people and assuring coethnic readers of their rightful place in the city, the Asian and Asian American presence is such as integral part of Jackson Street's landscape that the lines between the United States and Asia seem to blur. The moniker "Seattle's 'Far East'" confers upon people of Asian ancestry a special claim to the area while also calling forth an imagined geography in which the United States and East Asia are—contrary to the logic of Orientalism—neighboring, even overlapping, places.

That such Japanese Americans as Arai viewed and wrote about Seattle in such ways grew out of a set of historical dynamics that brought the American West Coast into close encounters with the "Far East" over the early twentieth century. Flows of goods, people, and ideas across the Pacific transformed coastal cities into crucial nodes in the emerging "Pacific world," which then made it possible for the residents of those locales to imagine themselves as inhabitants of an expansive space in which the United States and Asia came together. Furthermore, the Japanese government's encouragement of emigrants to promote the state's international and economic position by creating semiautonomous "New Japans" in the United States enhanced the perception among some Japanese settlers in North America that their immigrant communities were less transplants in Seattle and other West Coast cities than bridges between their countries of origin and settlement.[8] White American leaders also embraced visions of a Pacific-centered world that might serve their long-standing objective of reaching the markets of Asia and bolstering the geopolitical position of the United States in that part of the world. But this Pacific imaginary also threatened to destabilize the enduring Orientalist pillar of Western thought that the "twain" could never meet. According to Arai, in "Seattle's 'Far East,'" the East and West did more than just "meet"; the East had settled in the West and in the process became a critical part of it.

The experiences of Japanese Americans in Seattle, Washington, from their early settlement around the turn of the twentieth century until the outbreak of World War II, provide a window into this contradictory set of conditions, which, among this population, fostered flexible identities, fueled aspirations for belonging, and ultimately dealt crushing disappointment in a locality that was alternately and simultaneously American and Pacific. To focus this examination, *Claiming the Oriental Gateway* pursues two main questions: (1) What was the impact of U.S. Pacific expansion and Japanese migration on Seattle's urban development, and (2) how did Seattle's pursuit of status as a major Pacific port affect Japanese American experience? The title of the book underlines the city's pursuit of status as a "gateway to the Orient" as an ever-present backdrop to Japanese American history in Seattle. During the late nineteenth and early twentieth centuries, white commercial and civic boosters consistently promoted Seattle in these terms. Meant to encourage growth and to enhance urban prestige while supporting the nation-state's larger endeavor to become a major power in the Pacific region, this effort always hinged on the U.S. relationship with Japan, a key partner in trade and diplomacy and a major source of immigrants to the West Coast from the 1890s to 1920s. In this context, locals would also claim that Seattle embodied "cosmopolitanism," thereby framing domestic diversity as a phenomenon of international networks and a worldly embrace of difference. And to the extent that people endeavored to actualize this claim in concrete terms, Japanese Americans took up the mantle of cosmopolitanism, becoming highly visible in the urban landscape, participating in the local culture, and envisioning themselves as members of "cosmopolitan Seattle."

Although the city's bid for distinction as the "gateway to the Orient" and Japanese Americans' efforts to secure inclusion yielded significant forms of visibility for this minority group, Seattle—like other West Coast ports—remained a racially volatile place, so whatever acceptance Japanese Americans attained in white society was always tenuous and transitory. West Coast cities may have attached their priorities and identities to the Pacific and, thus, in meaningful ways, bound their destinies to Asia, but they were also the settings of—if not ground zero for—anti-Asian politics. Moreover, the societies that emerged within the boundaries of Seattle and other West Coast cities became more, not less, racially stratified through the early twentieth century. Although Seattle elites' claims of cosmopolitanism underscored collaboration and mutual interests among Pacific Rim nations as factors reflected in local conditions, the ups and downs in the relationship between the United States and Asian countries and on-the-ground anti-Asian racism belied those ideals and exposed their limits. A city touting its ties to the Pacific and claiming to be a "gateway to the Orient" was one thing; the symbolic appropriation of a people opening the way to substantive steps toward full inclusion and racial equality was quite another.

Mindful of the fact that Japanese Americans' inclusion was tenuous and stemmed from a view of them as stand-ins for their country of origin, conduits to trans-Pacific markets, or objects within a larger "cosmopolitan" mosaic, as opposed to self-determined actors and fully vested members of *American* society, this book also explores how Japanese Americans were resourceful and active agents in Seattle's sociocultural landscape. Specifically, the local discourse about Seattle as cosmopolitan, which entailed fetishizing differences, reifying groups of people as racial and cultural types, and glossing over entrenched racial hierarchies, nonetheless opened the possibility for Japanese residents to adapt the concept for their own ends and to make cases for their civic belonging. In addition to participating in city events and contributing in other ways to the "local color," Japanese Americans drew on the imaginings of Seattle as a cosmopolitan "gateway to the Orient" to reenvision and to make claims to spaces as small as city parks and as large as the Pacific world.

SEATTLE, THE PACIFIC RIM, AND THE TRANS-PACIFIC WEST

This book uses the "Pacific Era" as a broad historical frame for thinking about the relationship between Japanese American history and Seattle history during the early 1900s. As the turn of the twentieth century approached, the United States stretched its "empire of liberty" to the ends of the continent and, it seemed, conquered the wilderness in the West. Although for some observers, this territorial expansion spelled the closing of the frontier and, thus, the end of the first phase of American history, it also marked the beginning of a sustained period of U.S. imperialism and expansionism in the Asia-Pacific region. The Pacific Era thus captured this recognition of a phase in American history during which the United States would push further west beyond the continental border to realize its national destiny in the Pacific world. In this context, the notion of the "Pacific Rim" became salient. Expounding on this concept, Arif Dirlik argues that the Pacific Rim is less a fixed physical place than an ideological construction of Euro-American origin and design.[9] As he explains, the idea of the Pacific Rim has existed for scarcely more than two hundred years, stemming from and rationalizing the forward march of Western capitalism around the world. Deployed as an ideology, the Pacific Rim concept has served two main functions, explains Dirlik: "to set up a domain of economic activity and power for those who play a hegemonic role in the Pacific"; and "to contain within it relationships that in and of themselves are not confined to it."[10] In the last century and a half, the United States has played a leading role in this process, with its control of or involvements in Alaska, Hawaii, the Marianas, Guam, Wake, Midway, the Philippines, China, Taiwan, South Korea, and Vietnam.

Underscoring dynamics of U.S. imperialism and expansionism, the Pacific Rim concept also draws attention to Seattle's geographic position in a transoceanic region bounded by the U.S. West Coast and Asia. In the last few decades, scholarship emphasizing Pacific Rim and trans-Pacific approaches to the study of the American West and Asian American history has solidified our understandings of the West's ties to Asia and the Pacific.[11] Indeed, at one time or another between the mid-nineteenth century and the present, each major U.S. West Coast city has harnessed its future to the Asia-Pacific region and proclaimed itself the nation's "gateway to the Orient." Inklings of these aspirations were evident as early as the 1840s, when, during the Mexican-American War of 1846–1848, Captain John Fremont predicted that San Francisco would eventually become the nation's headquarters for Pacific military operations. A few years later, at the 1849 California constitutional convention, a delegate linked his dreams for the new state to the "resources of the East":

> No other portion of the globe will exercise a greater influence upon the civilization and commerce of the world. The people of California will penetrate the hitherto inaccessible portions of Asia, carrying with them not only the arts and sciences, but the refining and purifying influence of civilization and Christianity; they will unlock the vast resources of the East, and, by reversing the commerce of the world, pour the riches of India into the metropolis of the new State.[12]

Because access to overseas markets was a key factor in the capitalist development of the American West, the largest cities on the coast—San Francisco, Los Angeles, Portland, and Seattle—owe much of their growth to their historical orientation to the Pacific.[13] In the Pacific Northwest, major incentives for the early-nineteenth-century push into that region were the potential profits to be drawn from extending the fur trade into China. Subsequently, coal, lumber, and wheat joined the list of key regional goods extracted from the region and exported through Western ports.

Asian American historians have further illuminated the deep connections between the U.S. West and Asia. Gail Nomura, for instance, observed that as the United States moved beyond the continent to pursue its interests in the Pacific, "the Far East became the Far West," a statement that underscores how the transition from continental to extraterritorial expansion blurred the conceptual boundaries between the "East" and "West."[14] Nomura's remark also highlights a unique relationship between American culture and Orientalism. In their respective discussions of U.S. imaginings of China and India, historians John Tchen and Vijay Prashad have elaborated on how

Americans, although inheritors of European Orientalism, often had a more intimate relationship with the "Orient," showing, for instance, a willingness to emulate and to incorporate aspects of the "East" into their ideological sensibilities and cultural practices.[15] In the American imagination, the boundaries between the "East" and "West" were further challenged with large-scale Asian immigration from the mid-nineteenth to early twentieth centuries. These circumstances in effect modulated the East-West dichotomy, an enduring pillar of Western identity, but rather than leading to its disavowal, it was continually reconfigured and asserted through immigration restrictions, miscegenation laws, alien land acts, and other measures that maintained what in practice was a yellow-white color line in America. This simultaneous blurring and reasserting of the Orient-Occident boundary in American law and culture has been a striking paradox in Asian American history, and this paradox is reflected in Japanese American history in Seattle during the early 1900s. On the one hand, the city itself was deeply invested in relationships with Japan and sought to capitalize on the presence of residents of Japanese ancestry, yet racialized notions of citizenship and superficial interpretations and practices of cosmopolitanism limited Japanese Americans' lives and precluded their full belonging in the city and the nation.

The United States and New Internationalism

Toward explaining how and why Seattle's white elites embraced the "gateway to the Orient" idea, this book understands the city's urbanization against what diplomatic historian Akira Iriye has called the "new internationalism," which reached its apex just after World War I but had been several decades in the making. Around the turn of the twentieth century, American political and business leaders agreed on the need to expand beyond the continent, and the Spanish-American War of 1898 signaled a decisive shift in U.S. foreign policy in this direction. Justifying its actions abroad, however, required some ideological finesse, so by fusing the rhetoric of universalism with economic interests, the United States could export its commodities and ideas and extract the world's raw materials without assuming the explicit posture of a colonial power.[16] Framing the acquisition of the Philippines and China Open Door Notes, for example, in terms of spreading liberal capitalism, enlightened civilization, and self-determination allowed the United States to disavow nationalism and empire as motivations.[17]

With the end of World War I, a "new internationalism" reached its zenith, achieving perhaps its highest expression in the League of Nations and the foreign policy of Woodrow Wilson.[18] This outlook purported to replace the excessively competitive national rivalries of earlier times, encouraged extensive international contact and cooperation, and gestured a measure of equality among all nations.[19] The new internationalism fueled movements for cosmopolitanism and cross-national communication, which took on particular momentum during the 1920s and 1930s, as they were aided by technologies of modern communication and transportation. "It was widely recognized," states Iriye, "that ultimately internationalism must be built upon the education of more cosmopolitan, less narrowly nationalistic, individuals of all countries."[20] Accordingly, international relations encompassed a broader range of activities, such as academic and cultural exchanges and scholarly endeavors sponsored by nongovernmental organizations with the express purpose of building bridges and fostering intercultural understanding.[21]

Although internationalism and Pacific Rim ideology were deployed to cast U.S. expansion in a benign, even benevolent, light, these logics were rife with contradictions. For the United States, nationalism and internationalism were not distinct but intersecting, and "internationalism," particularly under the foreign policies of Theodore Roosevelt and Woodrow Wilson, was too often merely the projection of Americanism to other parts of the world.[22] As Charles Bright and Michael Geyer have noted, despite the long-standing official U.S. opposition to imperialism and regard for the sovereignty of nations, its foreign policy through the late nineteenth and early twentieth centuries could be aptly captured by the phrase "irremediable entanglement." They further observe that the United States was mired in an "unceasing effort to seek out the world and pull it in—people, territory, goods, knowledge—and the equally insistent efforts to put the world off and to negotiate a separation that would define the nation, its territory and its culture from and over against the world."[23] This was especially the case when it came to how the United States dealt with East Asia and Asian immigration. On the one hand, it aggressively pursued economic or political influence in Japan, China, and the Philippines during the late nineteenth to early twentieth centuries. On the other hand, it made strenuous efforts to severely limit, and eventually to prohibit, the migration of people from these parts of the world across its borders.

If delineating the Pacific Rim as a geographic domain rationalized and lent purpose to a global vision of discrete regional identities and enabled Europeans and Americans to justify their economic and military incursions abroad, this most certainly was the case during the U.S. expansion into the Pacific. This movement was incorporated into the nation's overarching narrative of spreading civilization and progress, but it disregarded, and at times openly disdained, the aspirations of the societies it encountered in the process. Returning to Dirlik's ruminations on the Pacific Rim, a striking but intentional blind spot in Westerners' conception of the Pacific was that Asian people had always been important to the region and its activities, not only in populating and traversing it but also in pursuing their own imperial designs. In the twentieth century, Japan was the most obvious contradiction and, thus, threat to the U.S. fantasy of Pacific domination. Around the turn of the twentieth century, Japan had made a dramatic and unexpected rise in the global arena, with its rapid economic and political modernization and military victories over China in 1895 and Russia in 1905. And as the world's attention shifted from the Euro-American Atlantic to the Pacific, it was clear that the United States and Japan would be the key players of the Pacific Era. Yet from the U.S. perspective, it was also growing evident that Japan would be a rival that commanded respect in the region rather than a complacent partner in trade and passive recipient of American influences.

CLAIMING THE ORIENTAL GATEWAY

Mindful of this international backdrop, of central concern to this study is explaining how intersecting dynamics of American expansion, Asian trans-Pacific migration, and internationalism manifested locally and impacted people's relationships with one another and their surroundings. A significant development of recent Asian American history has been the heightened attention to the ways that dynamics of international relations and trans-Pacific ties inform Asian American lived experience.[24] Although these transnational and international turns have expanded the scope of the field and recast a number of topics of long-standing importance, much space remains to examine issues of place and scale and to bring those considerations to our broader understanding. *Claiming the Oriental Gateway* focuses on the intersections of urbanization, ethnic identity, and internationalism, exploring how these factors gave rise to a distinct set of local practices and experiences in which Japanese Americans were integral. As a window into the dynamic and mutually constitutive dimensions of the broad, abstract "Pacific" and a smaller scale, more concrete locality, Seattle is a prime location for examination due to its self-proclaimed status as the nation's "gateway to the Orient" and its long history of Japanese settlement dating to the 1890s.

If the Pacific Era would be a defining theme of the twentieth century and a constituent element of the U.S. rise to global hegemony, this development certainly casts a new significance on the role of West Coast urban hubs. Their geographical location made them crucial points of contact between the United States and its Pacific possessions and partners. Furthermore, the cities themselves had much to gain from the economic and diplomatic relationships being forged between the United States and Asia. Enthralled by the possibilities of Pacific encounters in terms of local development as well as the broad sweep of human history, elites in Seattle would celebrate each stride that signified the closing of the distance between the United States and Asia. For example, in 1935, well into this process, Seattleites celebrated the completion of telephone lines between their city and Tokyo. Extolling the significance of this milestone, University of Washington Professor of Oriental Studies Robert Pollard declared that Rudyard Kipling's famous dictum "East is East and West is West and Never the Twain Shall Meet" had been "relegated to the ash heap."[25]

Such developments were also significant because they lent material legitimacy to Seattle's claim of being a "gateway to the Orient." Along these lines and toward the larger objective of modernizing the city, local elites touted Seattle as a "cosmopolitan" port. That they invoked this particular term is noteworthy. Historian David Hollinger offers a useful explanation of cosmopolitanism in which he differentiates it from closely related ideologies such as pluralism. Although pluralism and cosmopolitanism promote tolerance for ethnic diversity, they differ in their relationship to and investments in cultural heterogeneity and the possibility that a society can transcend the ethno-racial boundaries that otherwise divide it. "If cosmopolitanism can be casual about community building and community maintenance and tends to seek voluntary associations of wide compass," Hollinger says, "pluralism promotes affiliations on the narrower grounds of shared history and is more quick to see reasons for drawing boundaries between communities."[26] In short, a pluralistic outlook is more provincial and focused inward on the group than a cosmopolitan one, which embraces difference but works from a broader vantage point and is, thus, able to place a premium on thinking and relating across boundaries. In practice, this meant that "cosmopolitanism" carried a more sophisticated, worldly, and modern connotation than "pluralism."

We also tend to think of cosmopolitanism as a social/political philosophy and personal disposition, whereby "cosmopolitans" are people who regard themselves as "citizens of the world" because they travel, possess knowledge of and facility with different cultures, and/or think globally and expansively instead of locally and narrowly.[27] In political and philosophical discourse, the subject often prompts interrogations of the historical conditions by which this outlook becomes a possibility and the potential for geographically unbounded communities of obligation to emerge. Calling Seattle "cosmopolitan," however, focuses the dynamism and possibilities of international crossings explicitly on *place*. Additionally, Seattleites often folded the city's burgeoning ethnic diversity into this discourse; that is to say, as noted earlier, "immigrant Seattle," which included Europeans and Asians, was a phenomenon of "gateway Seattle." Such an imagining called on people to view the city as an entity that existed and functioned on several scales, which furthered its case that it was a modern urban metropolis of the twentieth century.

Nationally, interest in cosmopolitanism resurged with the expanding U.S. presence in world affairs and in response to the rise of nativism in America in the late 1800s to early 1900s. Early-twentieth-century cosmopolitanism is commonly associated with the American intellectual Randolph Bourne, who laid out its basic concepts in relation to debates about immigration to the United States in his 1916 essay, "Trans-national America," which appeared in the *Atlantic Monthly*.[28] Reflecting primarily on European migration to eastern cities, Bourne observed that foreign immigration had turned American centers in the United States into international communities writ small and argued that this was a development to be embraced, not feared. Rather than dividing Americans, ethnic difference ought to be valued as a resource that enlightens and strengthens the collective national body. Further, America's ethnic diversity was merely a mirror of a world whose people and components were becoming rapidly interconnected, and whether the United States could accommodate its demographic diversity would prove not only the soundness of its democratic principles and institutions but also its fitness to lead the modern world.[29]

In describing Seattle as cosmopolitan, boosters appropriated extant understandings of the term at the time but also gave it an unconventional, even radical, twist by including Asians and a West Coast city in the discourse. In several ways, they exhorted, Seattle was an exemplar of modernity and cosmopolitanism in the Pacific Era. As a West Coast port, it facilitated international trade and exchange, but it was much more than a mere transit point through which goods, people, and ideas passed en route to other places. The city itself embodied cosmopolitanism, in its spirit, heterogeneous population, and particular sites within its limits. To be sure, these were exaggerated claims that were not always supported by material conditions and, thus, better reflected the insecurities and desires of residents eager to shed the vestiges of the frontier past and to set their city apart from rival urban centers.

As offshoots from Japan and members of a sizeable local ethnic community, Japanese American residents of Seattle embodied cosmopolitanism in several ways. Large numbers of Japanese immigrants began settling on the

West Coast during the 1890s. By 1930, about nine thousand lived in Seattle, where they clustered in Jackson Street, a minority-concentrated neighborhood located just south of the downtown business district. Members of Seattle's Japanese American community understood that if international connections and a diverse population were the touchstones of the city's claims to cosmopolitanism, then they—as representatives of the Asian side of the Pacific Rim and a part of the fabric of American heterogeneity—could play a pivotal role in its development into a major urban center. They thus embraced aspects of cosmopolitanism to articulate their place in the city, to build relationships with other communities, and to argue for their local and national belonging. For example, local civic celebrations, such as the International Potlatch festival of the 1930s, brought Japanese cultural displays and Japanese American residents to the foreground of the urban landscape; schools with high Japanese enrollments were characterized as "cosmopolitan"; and Japanese artists who achieved international acclaim further bolstered Seattle's claims to world preeminence. Basketball competitions between second-generation Japanese and Chinese teams in the 1920s and 1930s became occasion to imagine Collins Fieldhouse as a battleground for Asian athletic supremacy. With their black, Chinese, and Filipino neighbors, Japanese Americans in Jackson Street, before and after World War II, adapted cosmopolitanism to defy negative images of minority enclaves and to argue that such multiracial areas exemplified true Seattle cosmopolitanism.

Cosmopolitanism was a powerful concept that appealed to Seattle's ambitions and resonated with broad forces transforming the nation and the world during the early 1900s. Although embraced by the city's elites and deployed in a top-down fashion, it still held out the possibility for Japanese Americans, an otherwise marginalized minority, to make arguments for their importance to the city at large and to thereby shore up their claims to belonging. However, it was also a very tenuous concept, and the advantages people drew from cosmopolitanism relied on its ambiguities. It capitalized on Seattle's geography, but cosmopolitanism was also constrained by it, for as much as Seattleites insisted that theirs was an international city, its location within U.S. national boundaries meant that cosmopolitanism would always have an American accent. It brought an international frame to discussions of racial and ethnic inclusion and explicitly eschewed crude expressions of cultural chauvinism, but in Seattle, cosmopolitanism was always linked to a national ambition for Pacific influence. The city's history, moreover, points out a general shortcoming in cosmopolitan thought during this period. The vision of a diverse society finding and embracing a common ground, which Bourne wrote so optimistically about, was not, in fact, the domain of the world, but of the United States, and it presumed that the United States was the center and guiding hand of transnational exchange and cross-cultural understanding.[30]

Also, as an outlook that embraced heterogeneity, cosmopolitanism implicitly relied on the maintenance and consciousness of group differences, thus engendering a curious situation in which Japanese Americans achieved a degree of local acceptance and membership but remained racialized "others" denied the full privileges of citizenship. Although elites pursued close relations with Japan and celebrated moments when local conditions manifested the closure of the distance between the "East" and "West," Orientalism maintained a stubborn hold on the city's politics. United States–Japan relations and Japanese immigration to the United States might have signified the breaching of the "Orient-Occident" divide, but the persistent framing of these developments as East-West encounters upheld underlying Orientalist assumptions. Further adding to the precarious position of Japanese Americans was that they came from a country that was important to Seattle's development yet was also a rival for power in the Pacific region. Their standing would, thus, depend on the acceptability of group differences and whether United States–Japan relations were alternately characterized by harmonious internationalism or nationalistic competition, a balancing act that decisively broke on December 7, 1941.

Examining the varied meanings of Seattle's claims to cosmopolitanism and pursuit of gateway status also underlines the significance of scale and how local and international dynamics intersect and shape each other. Although the city linked its growth and modernization to visions of an expansive Pacific world, legitimizing these global visions called for turning local sites and actors into embodiments of cosmopolitanism. In other words, the dynamics of international relations and foreign immigration were made concrete and meaningful at the local level, and this was evidenced, for instance, in discourses about Seattle public schools, neighborhood identities, and city celebrations. A consideration of the centrality of scale in the charting and conceptualization of Seattle's modernization also highlights fluid understandings of space that abounded among white and Japanese Seattleites. Spaces as confined as classrooms and baseball diamonds and as expansive as the entire city and the Pacific Rim became crucial terrains for negotiating national and ethnic identities and on which individuals inscribed meaning, exemplified, for example, in Arai's description of Jackson Street as "Seattle's Far East." Accordingly, this book considers how Japanese Americans channeled local and global concerns to understand and to articulate their surroundings and the particular roles they played within them. For

Japanese photographers in Seattle in the 1920s, accessing and traversing the Puget Sound terrain was a critical aspect of their artistry and legitimacy in the art world. Schools, parks, playgrounds, and streets became sites where Japanese Americans could argue for their vitality in Seattle's physical and social landscape. They also negotiated the meanings of invented and intangible yet equally meaningful spaces, such as the "gateway to the Orient" and the Pacific Rim. Indeed, these abilities to connect and to navigate between scales and to appropriately articulate space proved to be key aspects of Japanese American strategies for belonging in the decades before World War II, when internationalism and Americanism appeared to be complementary, and not conflicting, values.

As a contribution to Japanese American history, *Claiming the Oriental Gateway* urges for a greater consideration of issues of place and interethnic relations, which, with few exceptions, have largely elided the field. In the last few decades, scholarship on Japanese Americans has branched out beyond the traditional concerns of victimization and internment.[31] Reflecting a general shift in American ethnic history, scholars of Japanese America have rightly focused much attention on minority agency, yielding rich understandings of the multifaceted nature of ethnic communities and the choices that immigrants and their descendants made within the constraints of a society structured by racial, gender, and class inequalities.[32] Although such work has contributed nuanced perspectives on internal community dynamics, comparatively little scholarship has examined interethnic encounters and Japanese Americans' relations with the cities or communities in which they resided, leaving intact the impression, first argued by sociologist S. Frank Miyamoto in 1939, that Japanese Americans' most "conspicuous characteristic" was their unusually strong ethnic solidarity.[33] Miyamoto said this trait developed as a strategy for coping with their rejection by the dominant white society, although he also attributed it to a predisposition toward "group action." By studying the relationships that Japanese formed with groups and entities outside the local ethnic community, this book clarifies some of the ways that Japanese Americans, even with their strong group solidarity, were far from isolated from the rest of Seattle.

Scholars presenting Japanese American history in a transnational frame have persuasively emphasized the duality of ethnic identity among members of this group in terms of American and Japanese nation-building projects. "Dualism," "two-ness," and "in-betweenness" are common tropes in American racial and ethnic history, which speak to the immigrant's or minority's partial sense of belonging and feelings of being suspended between two cultures. As historian Eiichiro Azuma points out, Japanese Americans' dualism stemmed from their being in "between two empires"; in other words, the parallel—at times competing—nation-building projects of their countries of origin and settlement shaped and delimited their lives.[34] Although this condition of dualism afforded significant flexibility in the lives and identities of the Issei (first-generation immigrants) and Nisei, it also eventually made them vulnerable to accusations of being agents of Japan and subjected them to pressure to identify as either American or Japanese. *Claiming the Oriental Gateway* builds on the literature exploring Japanese American duality while bringing to the discussion a consideration of place, proposing that Japanese Americans residing in West Coast cities developed unique and pronounced investments in Japan's international standing while viewing themselves as inhabitants of and players in the Pacific world.

This book's interest in issues of place goes beyond concerns exclusive to Japanese American history, although, to be sure, its focus on Seattle addresses a deficit in regional perspectives in Asian American history, a field that generally remains steeped in research on California and Hawaii.[35] *Claiming the Oriental Gateway* also situates itself in relation to an expanding literature in American history that understands West Coast cities as paradoxes. On the one hand, for much of the last two centuries, these places have been viewed from within and without as "promised lands" boasting brighter opportunities and fewer obstacles compared to other parts of the United States. Yet they were also battlegrounds where struggles for racial privilege, economic resources, and social status took on a particular intensity. Finally, this book joins a growing corpus of works in American urban ethnic history that examines the historical experiences of minorities against the contingencies of geography and place, thereby yielding rich insights about the relationships between racialized communities and the development of particular cities. Recent works by historians Gabriela Arredondo, Coll Thrush, Robert Self, and Scott Kurashige, for example, not only provide new knowledge and perspectives on Mexicans in Chicago, Indians in Seattle, blacks in Oakland, and Japanese and blacks in Los Angeles, respectively, but also substantially recast how we view these cities' histories altogether.[36] In shedding light on the dynamic and complex relationships between the cities and some of their most disenfranchised inhabitants, they focus our appreciation of how the given configuration of urban space and politics have limited and created possibilities for racial minorities' civic engagement and broad visibility.

How people described, employed, and claimed space are underlying concerns through each chapter. As such, it should be emphasized that this book is not about "hidden transcripts" or what was deep in the hearts and minds of Japanese American people and somehow inaccessible to others. Rather, it examines what Japanese Americans in Seattle did and said in public, as public and semipublic actors. Admittedly, these interests make this book chiefly about white and Japanese American elites who had the privilege of engaging in public rituals and making public commentaries through newspapers, books, radio, and other media. Because of this, I make no claims about the broad representativeness of the ideas and statements of the individuals who appear in this book, although they often claimed they spoke for their communities. Most ordinary and working people, after all, did not have the time or inclination to dwell on such issues as urban identity, whether Seattle was truly cosmopolitan, or how best to position the city as a "gateway to the Orient." These sorts of questions are, as they would be in other times and places, preoccupations of elites. That said, they remain important perspectives, because the political, economic, or cultural authorities in the city—and those who had an audience with them—had the greatest power to set the terms and to shape the structures of life in Seattle. Accordingly, most of the sources used in this study come from agencies, organizations, and individuals representing the leadership strata of the city and its Japanese American community: city office records, school archival records, yearbooks and newspapers, city and ethnic newspapers, booster literature, and personal correspondences.

Chapter 1 describes Japanese American settlement in Seattle from the turn of the twentieth century to the 1930s and details the formation of Jackson Street. In this neighborhood, Japanese businesses clustered on streets crowded with Chinese, Filipinos, and, increasingly, African Americans. Members of these groups lived and worked in this small area, and, by the early 1920s, Jackson Street was widely regarded as Seattle's "ghetto." Jackson Street was not only a neighborhood where people of varied backgrounds encountered one another but also eventually a site of contested meanings; white Seattle called it a dangerous slum, while residents claimed that Jackson Street better represented Seattle cosmopolitanism than any other part of the city.

The rest of the book discusses various facets of day-to-day life to reveal the interplay of international and local dynamics in Japanese Americans' experience and their relationship to Seattle's urban development and identity. Chapter 2 discusses the political and commercial origins of Seattle cosmopolitanism and how it was performed in city celebrations, commenting on how a wide cross-section of the local population exalted the city's impressive ethnic diversity for the overriding purposes of urban boosterism. Chapter 3 describes the Seattle Camera Club, a small organization of amateur pictorial photographers active during the 1920s. Photography opened up wide networks of association spanning oceans and continents, and the visibility of Japanese immigrants whose work made an American city famous complicated and brought to the fore questions about race, nationality, and legitimacy in art. Chapter 4 concerns the Seattle public school system. Officials and outside observers touted the public schools as exemplars of cosmopolitanism and the ability of institutions to "Americanize" Japanese immigrants. Rather than being imposed upon by teachers and school officials, Japanese parents forged a two-way relationship as they frequently pressed their wishes upon teachers and school board members. Chapter 5 discusses the many roles that sports played in the Japanese American community during the 1920s and 1930s. Far from being mere vehicles of Americanism and Anglo-conformity, organized sports reinforced ethnic solidarity, heightened international consciousness, cemented Japanese Americans' relationships with other minority communities, and deepened respect in the wider community for their prowess and dedication on the baseball diamond, basketball and tennis courts, football field, and bowling alley. Chapter 6 describes life in the Jackson Street neighborhood immediately before and at the start of the U.S. entry into World War II. A brief epilogue discusses the return of Japanese Americans to Seattle and the revival of a neighborhood-based but still tenuous "cosmopolitan" coalition in 1946 with the formation of the Jackson Street Community Council, which was led by Japanese, Chinese, Filipinos, Jews, and African Americans.

1

Multiethnic Seattle

Two Views of Jackson Street

In two well-known works of Asian American literature—one autobiographical and the other fictional—that offer descriptions of life in pre–World War II Seattle, the bustling tempo and multiethnic character of urban life immediately strike the reader. In her 1953 memoir, *Nisei Daughter,* Monica Sone recalls an idyllic childhood preceding and contrasting starkly with the jarring experience of wartime Japanese internment. Born in 1919, she portrayed 1920s and 1930s Seattle, especially the working-class Jackson Street neighborhood, as an exhilarating place, pulsing with business activity and people from all walks of life. "Our street itself was a compact little world, teeming with the bustle of every kind of business in existence in Skidrow," writes Sone.[1] Aware that others derided the neighborhood she called home and where her parents operated hotel and laundry businesses as "skid row," she nonetheless recollects with fondness, "This was the playground where I roamed freely and happily."[2] Her daily treks to school were adventures in and of themselves:

> When I finally started grammar school, I found still another enchanting world. Every morning I hurried to Adams Hotel . . . and called for Matsuko. Together we made the long and fascinating journey—from First Avenue to Twelfth Avenue—to Bailey Gatzert School. . . . We meandered through the international section of town, past the small Japanese shops and stores, already bustling in the early morn-

ing hour, past the cafes and barber shops filled with Filipino men, and through Chinatown.[3]

In his 1946 semiautobiographical novel, *America Is in the Heart,* the Filipino American writer Carlos Bulosan makes Seattle a pivotal location in the odyssey of his protagonist, Carlos, an immigrant itinerant worker in the 1930s American West. The city was Carlos's (as well as the real-life Bulosan's) point of disembarkation from the Philippines and a place to which he periodically returns or seeks to return in the course of his circuitous life in North America. Following a series of harrowing encounters with racial violence in California and Montana, Carlos goes back to Seattle. During his bus ride, he remembers his initial journey there and ponders, "When had it been that this bright city had softened the sadness in my heart?" Upon arriving, however, he finds neither familiarity nor comfort, but a continuation of his despair:

> I left the bus and walked around the block, watching for Oriental signs on the buildings and stores. I found the hotel where I had stayed when I arrived in Seattle from the Philippines, but it was now under new management. I took a room for twenty-five cents and sneaked away with the sheets the next morning. I sold them in a Negro store down the block. That would be my first deliberately dishonest act.[4]

Although these passages paint very different pictures and evoke nearly opposite emotions, as Sone's conveys a child's wonder about her surroundings while Bulosan's illustrates an immigrant's isolation and agony, it is striking that both writers highlight the multiethnic character of the urban environs in creating their distinct impressions of life in the city.

Such dense and multiethnic settlements where Chinese, Japanese, Filipinos, blacks, and other minorities lived and worked could be found in pockets throughout the urban West Coast during the early twentieth century. These took shape from pull factors connected to the U.S. conquest and exploitation of the West as well as the forces of trans-Pacific and internal migration and racial segregation. Scholars have examined the unique social formations, identities, and challenges that emerged in these communities that were striking for their diversity as well as their isolation and marginalization from the white societies that neighbored them.[5] Reflecting the broader transnational turn in U.S. history and American studies, a significant portion of the literature—much of which focuses on Los Angeles—examines how the location of West Coast cities within global networks of people and capital contributed to not only the growth of a diverse population but also the ideological and imaginative meanings applied to urban space and the people making claims to it. As discussed in the Introduction, this book draws on recent scholarship that employs a "Pacific world" perspective to illuminate how the American West has historically been part of expansive systems of migration, politics, and commerce, thereby highlighting the salience of Asia and Asian people in the construction of the Pacific world and the history of the West.[6]

Toward explicating what it meant for Seattle and its Japanese American residents to be part of the Pacific world and exploring the relationship between Pacific-world dynamics and local racial formations, this chapter describes the emergence of the city's minority population between the 1870s and the 1930s, with particular attention on Asian and black settlement in the section that would become known as Jackson Street. Although Jackson Street was, by most accounts, a rough and seamy area from which "respectable" residents warily kept their distance, it was also a vibrant, ethnically and racially diverse place, and the landscape against which much of Seattle Japanese American history played out. Furthermore, for such individuals as Sone and thousands of other ethnic and racial minorities, these peripheral and derided places were their "America." This aspect of Seattle's history also speaks to a larger story about the American West and its cities, for multi-raciality and ethnic diversity have long been regarded as key distinguishing factors in the region's history.[7] From the gold-mining societies of the mid-nineteenth century, American conquest and development of the region simultaneously entailed the displacement of Indians and Mexicans and in-migration of whites, Asians, blacks, and Latin Americans.[8] Jackson Street's multiracial past also points to the need for an analysis of race in the West that employs an expanded lens that takes account of the presence of multiple, not just two, racial groups.

From the early to mid-1900s, "Jackson Street" referred to a part of the city south of the downtown business district. Its boundaries had always been amorphous, and by the early 1950s, the name had largely fallen out of usage by residents. Jackson Street emerged from a vaguely defined part of the city south of Yesler Way, and over the years its various subsections and areas with which it overlapped have gone by a multitude of names: Skid Row, "Skid Road," Jackson-Yesler, the Lava Beds, Chinatown, Nihonmachi, and the International District, to name a few. Despite its uncertain boundaries and changing monikers, what was clear by the 1920s was that Jackson Street bore the legacy of Skid Row's notoriety and was home to most of the city's nonwhite residents and other ethnic minorities. A product of successive migrations and settlements, Jackson Street's social makeup was also the result of the consolidation of white privilege; the city's racial minorities concentrated there in large part because they were not welcome anywhere else. By looking closely at this pocket of the city, which was also the site of Seattle's Japantown, this chapter seeks to bring out of the margins a neighborhood that we know little about and to assert its central place in Seattle's multiracial past.

From Frontier Town to Urban Revolution

Founded in 1851 and incorporated in 1869, Seattle was a modest "village town" through much of the second half of the nineteenth century and underwent its "urban revolution" between the 1890s and 1910s. Defying the image of westward-bound families in covered wagons seeking homesteads on which to farm and to subsist, Seattle's early Anglo settlers, who included Henry Yesler, Doc Maynard, and Arthur Denny, were a very enterprising group, arriving from such states as Ohio and Illinois and bringing with them dreams of commercial riches and visions of a future urban metropolis. In fact, the first settlers called their new town "New York-Alki" (New York by and by).[9] Although its deep-water harbors and nearby abundant natural resources encouraged settlers to imagine that their settlement would eventually become to the Pacific what New York was to the Atlantic, throughout its frontier period, Seattle struggled mightily to rival not coastal ports San Francisco and Portland, but rather nearby towns and hamlets such as Port Townsend, Olympia, Tacoma, and Mukilteo. With an early economy driven by supplying lumber, fishery products, coal, grains, and other exports to San Francisco and to various hinterland communities in the interior, by 1880, Seattle had developed a fairly sophisticated urban economy that included meatpacking, carpentry, furniture industries, and such services as law offices, banks, doctors' offices, and stores. The development of this diverse town economy along with a thriving export economy was key to its growing self-sufficiency and ability to eventually outstrip its regional competitors.

From its christening as "Seattle" in 1852, white Americans staked the city's future on trade.[10] Early white travelers to the Pacific Northwest were struck by the region's natural abundance and its potential to become a major world supplier of such raw materials as furs, skins, lumber, coal, and wheat. The land acquisitions from the Mexican-American War of 1846–1848 and resolution of the Oregon dispute of 1847 extended the United States to the Pacific and closer to the coveted markets of Asia, while the growth of San Francisco after the California gold rush of 1849 enlarged the market for northwestern lumber and drove Seattle's first major surge. Sawmills, mines, canneries, and other operations soon dotted the Puget Sound basin, and the completion of the Seattle & Walla Walla Rail Line in 1876 allowed for the quicker and cheaper transport of coal and minerals. Until the early 1890s, however, Seattle's trade relations concentrated in the Puget Sound basin and nearby hinterlands, with some exchange with San Francisco and southwestern Alaska. Until the city linked up with a transcontinental railroad and transoceanic steamship lines, it could not capitalize on its location and break into long-distance trade.[11]

By 1910, Seattle cemented its status as the premier city of the Pacific Northwest. Such key developments as becoming the Great Northern Railway's transcontinental terminus in 1893 and massive regrade projects that reduced the steepness of many of the city's hills allowed Seattle to further expand economically and physically. A national five-year depression beginning in 1893 slowed the pace of economic growth but had little impact on population growth; in the last two decades of the nineteenth century, Seattle's population mushroomed from 3,533 to 80,671. The Klondike gold rush of 1897 further secured its position as the main urban center of the region, as it served as a crucial supply station and stopping point for people en route to or from the gold mines. The city's population surged to 237,194 by 1910.

New in-migration fueled the population expansion, which achieved unprecedented levels in the late nineteenth to early twentieth centuries and turned Seattle once again into a society of newcomers. A greater proportion of women participated in the post-1880s migrations compared to earlier periods, and by 1890 the city's gender ratio was less than two males per female. Although most of the new migrants came from within the United States (the Midwest states being especially well represented), many more people arrived from other countries than they had in earlier decades; according to the 1910 census, about 28 percent of Seattle residents were born outside the United States. Particularly numerous among immigrants from Europe were Scandinavians, who in 1910 made up about a third of Seattle's foreign-born population. Settlers from Sweden, Norway, Denmark, or Finland typically arrived via other parts of the United States and stayed in Seattle, finding its climate and topography to be similar to conditions in their native countries.[12] Eventually Scandinavians dominated the local fishing and maritime industries, and to this day they maintain a distinct presence in the Ballard neighborhood.[13] A large foreign-born population in Seattle, however, did not make it the eclectic cultural melting pot we might expect to find, as most of these foreigners came from English-speaking nations such as Canada, England, and Scotland.

Reminding us of an obvious but frequently forgotten point, historian Coll Thrush states in his study of Indians in Seattle that "every American city is built on Indian land."[14] He details how the urban revolution swept away indigenous Seattle, although Indian people remained, albeit in the periphery and in greatly diminished numbers. Two years after Washington became a U.S. territory, the federal government began carrying out a reservation policy for Indians in Puget Sound with the Point Elliott treaty of 1855. From there, Indian removal proceeded violently and incompletely, with those deemed "friendly" being permitted to stay in the city limits, although an array of city ordinances highly circumscribed their movements.[15] Furthermore, as the physical city and its Anglo population grew, Indians' residential options were reduced to beach encampments and a few neighborhoods, such as the Lava Beds, located in present-day Pioneer Square and at that time considered a center of ill-repute where Indian women and white men cohabited. Indians were, however, enormously important as laborers and they participated in every sector of the urban economy. Without Indian labor, Thrush notes, urban Seattle would not have emerged, yet to white residents, Indians seemed more and more out of place in the modernizing city. One way that they stayed highly visible was in the local iconography; Indian place names (down to the city's name) and totem poles remain strikingly ubiquitous in Seattle and attest to the enduring appeal of imagined Indians over actual ones in American history and culture.

SKID ROAD RISING

Describing Seattle during its urban revolution in the 1890s, Roger Sale paints a dynamic picture:

> The most striking single fact about Seattle in 1897 is that, with the exception of First Hill, different land uses and economic classes everywhere were being mixed. This mixing had not been planned. . . . Instead, it had resulted from the great variety of work being done, which gave people mobility and opportunity, which mottled the economic scale with so many variations and changes that class lines could not easily form or harden, which perhaps just gave people so much to do that they could not afford the luxury of worrying or being contemptuous of their neighbors.[16]

In the midst of the city's rapid growth, it seemed that everything was in a state of flux, although Sale also concedes that class lines were becoming increasingly pronounced. By this time, the city's elite comprised the earliest settlers and their descendants, who were viewed more or less as old-fashioned defenders of capitalism and corporations. Newcomers who had arrived after

1880 made up a large and varied group, and although some quickly joined the economic elite, they also composed the ranks of the city's working class. The class divide in Seattle's population had spatial dimensions, and Yesler Way eventually became a boundary line between low-class, rootless, transients to the south and settled, "respectable" citizens to the north. Practically no single-family homes were in the area south of Yesler; instead, one found there residential hotels, shacks, and union housing facilities for sailors and longshoremen. By the 1890s, says Sale, "No one of prominence lived in this area" and "only the older firms were here, and new businesses were settling north of Yesler, away from the warehouses and flophouses and seamen's hotels."[17] Locals viewed this area as "another Seattle, more transient, lower in class, more openly or gaudily sinful" than rest of the city.[18] As the city grew out of its original boundaries, newer sections came to be regarded as the genteel neighborhoods, while the area south of Yesler would be seen as a self-contained section of urban disorder.

From the turn of the twentieth century onward, parts of Skid Row extended eastward and were increasingly racialized. The presence of Native Americans in the Lava Beds, an area known for its brothels, boardinghouses, gambling dens, transients, and mixed-race households, contributed to this racialization, as did the settlement of Chinese and emergence of Chinatown just to the east. Although Sale insists that Seattle's Skid Row at this time was "not a ghetto in the usual sense, because many gentile whites lived here," he acknowledges that " almost no minorities lived anywhere else, except the more affluent Jews . . . who had stores on First Avenue just north of Yesler."[19] As he further describes, this area had apparently become so isolated from the rest of the city that "the clerk or machinist who might come to know Judge Thomas Burke because the two lived and worked near each other might never even see a Jew, a Japanese, or a black, and so could feel free to think of them simply as types: Shylock, or sly and inscrutable, or lazy and shiftless."[20] Although Sale argues for a degree of fluidity across class lines among whites even as a nascent class system took shape, he acknowledges that the boundary between white and nonwhite Seattle was quite pronounced. Nonwhites made up just 1.8 percent of the overall population in 1890 and just under 5 percent between 1900 and 1920, but their concentration south of Yesler magnified their presence in that part of the city.[21]

The appearance of Chinese immigrants in the Lava Beds and establishment of Chinatown marked a new stage in Skid Row's development while cementing its association with nonwhites. Although it is not frequently acknowledged, Chinese people have been a part of Seattle's and Puget Sound's histories since the frontier period.[22] In 1860, the U.S. census counted about three hundred Chinese in King County, and it is believed that Chin Chun Hock, Seattle's first Chinese resident, also arrived that year.[23] By the following decade, a distinct Chinese enclave had emerged at Second Avenue and Washington Street, centered on Chin Wa Chong Company, which had been built in 1868 south of Yesler's mill and manufactured cigars, provided tailoring services, sold tea and sugar, and plied the opium trade. In 1876, Chinese constituted 7 percent of the population, or 250 of about 3,400, and an itinerant population likely numbering in the hundreds further boosted their presence.[24] After Chinatown was destroyed in a fire that consumed much of the downtown area in 1889, a new Chinatown was quickly rebuilt at Main Street between Second and Fourth Avenues, a few blocks east of the original location. On these blocks sat restaurants, laundries, rooming houses, merchant shops, and churches. Throughout the late nineteenth century, most of the residents were men who earned their livelihoods fishing and peddling as well as working in restaurants, hotels, and laundries in the city. Day-to-day life revolved around the general merchandising shops Quong Tuck Company, Wa Chong, and Ah King, run by the powerful merchants Chin Gee Hee, Chin Chun Hock, and Ah King, whom working-class Chinese greatly depended on for employment contacts, basic goods, mutual aid, and lodging.

Chinese settlement in Seattle must be understood in the context of large-scale trans-Pacific migration during the nineteenth century. Compelled by political and economic instability at home, hundreds of thousands left southeastern China for opportunities in North America, South America, Australia, New Zealand, the West Indies, Africa, and other parts of Asia.[25] Chinese were among the throngs of international gold-seekers to California after 1848. In the first large wave of Chinese migration to North America, from the 1840s to 1880s, the overwhelming majority of immigrants were single male laborers who intended to return to their homeland with their earnings. With San Francisco a main port of entry, by 1880, about 105,000 Chinese lived in the United States.[26] Although "Gold Mountain" was an initial lure, employment opportunities made the American West an attractive destination and sustained a steady inflow of Chinese until the 1880s. Seen by employers as a cheap, tractable, and plentiful labor source, Chinese participated in nearly all the major industries in the region, including the salmon canneries of Washington, the agricultural fields of San Joaquin Valley, and the mining communities of Wyoming. Perhaps most notably, Chinese workers made up 90 percent of the Central Pacific Railroad's labor force for the building of the western half of the first transcontinental railroad.[27]

In the Pacific Northwest, Chinese immigrants initially went to company towns in the interior of or just outside Seattle, where jobs were more plentiful than in the town itself. Their work as laborers, managers, and contractors in the key regional industries of mining, railroad, canning, fishing, and logging proved critical to the Northwest's development. Railroad construction also provided employment for many, and two-thirds of the Northern Pacific Railroad's workforce, or fifteen thousand men, were Chinese.[28] As a burgeoning regional urban center, Seattle eventually became the receiving point for laborers who had completed their work contracts for railroad companies or needed a place to go to while they awaited seasonal employment assignments. The city also offered entertainment, goods, and conveniences that could not be found in the hinterland work camps. Furthermore, like those in other cities, Seattle's Chinatown came to be a refuge from the anti-Chinese violence characteristic of the outlying rural areas.[29] Thus, the nature of work and the location of social options led many Chinese to merely pass through Seattle while others decided to stay for longer periods or even permanently.

One of the most notable Chinese immigrant success stories set in Seattle is the life of Chin Gee Hee (Chen Yixi), whose exploits have been described by historian Madeline Hsu. His rags-to-riches life inspired his veneration as a "hometown hero" in his native Taishan County nearly sixty years after his death.[30] Fleeing the poverty of his native village, Chin came to the United States around the early 1860s with very little. In Washington, he gained valuable experience and connections that he was able to parlay into becoming one of Seattle's most prosperous Chinese Americans. According to Hsu, he worked as a junior partner in a Chinese labor-recruiting firm in Port Gamble, dabbled in importing and exporting, and assisted railroad engineers. During the 1870s, he met Henry Yesler, who admired Chin's business acumen and convinced him to move to the new city of Seattle. Until his death in 1892, Yesler, who became one of Seattle's earliest economic and civic leaders, was a key associate and ally of Chin's, as was Thomas Burke, the civic booster, counsel for the Great Northern Railway, and judge on the Washington Territorial Supreme Court.

Burke and Yesler went on to become two of the most highly revered and celebrated pioneers in Seattle history, a distinction that eluded Chin due to his race and alien status, although his efforts were no less significant for the city's commercial growth in the late 1800s. In fact, Chin, Yesler, and Burke developed a strong professional camaraderie, which Hsu explains was "born out of recognition that regardless of race or country of origin those who contributed most to the building of Seattle were almost all immigrants who by dint of hard work and determination overcame humble origins to become influential men of business."[31] Chin's Quong Tuck Company was an enormously important local institution for the Chinese in Seattle, and through its contracting services for the Great Northern Railway and various steamship lines, it was also instrumental in facilitating the port's early trans-Pacific trade. Chin returned to Taishan around the turn of the twentieth century inspired; through an ambitious railroad construction project, the Xinning Railroad, he hoped to trigger the modernization of his native Taishan by applying the Western learning he had acquired as a participant in and witness to Seattle's remarkable growth in the 1870s to 1890s. Hsu notes that Chin's heroic return to Taishan might not have occurred had he not encountered the obstacles that he did in the United States owing to his status as an alien Chinese. Considerable as his success as a Seattle merchant was, his power and influence over the city and region's development never matched those of his white associates Yesler and Burke.

It is hard to say whether Chinatown was perceived as dangerous and immoral because it was in Skid Row or Skid Row's reputation for debauchery derived from being the site of Chinatown. In any case, Seattle's was not much different from other urban Chinatowns in this respect. From San Francisco to New York, Chinatowns might have been located within modernizing and bustling cities, but they were also isolated and popularly depicted as mysterious, dangerous, and unseemly places. As Mary Ting Yi Lui suggests in her book on early-twentieth-century New York's Chinatown, many of white Americans' negative perceptions of the area stemmed from their anxiety about the assertion and maintenance of racial and sexual boundaries, particularly between Chinese men and white women, which seemed especially unstable and malleable.[32] Likewise associated with dangerous forms of social fluidity, Seattle Chinatown's disrepute was further exacerbated by its association with working-class and transient men, proximity to Indians in the Lava Beds, and vice establishments.

From their arrival in the United States, Chinese were denied full participation in American life and were subject to intense racial antipathy. As the exclusion of Chinese was part of a broader movement to consolidate Anglo power in the West, their experience bore some similarities (as well as key differences) with those of Hispanics, blacks, and Indians.[33] The 1880s were especially tumultuous years, with anti-Chinese sentiment intensifying during a five-year economic depression that began in 1883.[34] Two years later, the completion of the Northern Pacific Railroad and Canadian Pacific Railway, which unleashed thousands of newly unemployed Chinese into the labor market, further fueled the scapegoating of Chinese "cheap labor" by working-class whites. Federally, the government responded to Western pleas to restrict Chinese immigration with passage of the 1882 Chinese Exclusion Act. This action did not, however, quell anti-Chinese resentments in the

West, and in 1885, violence reached a crescendo, with scattered outbreaks of vigilantism in mining and other work camps throughout the West. The most infamous incident occurred in Rock Springs, Wyoming, where a party of whites attacked a Chinese mining camp, killing twenty-eight, injuring fifteen, and causing more than $100,000 in damage.[35]

Meanwhile in Seattle, word of these disturbances prompted officials to brace for a riot in their town, where the anti-Chinese movement played out as a drama pitting raucous working-class and unemployed whites ("Sinophobes," as Murray Morgan calls them) against the established, capitalist, employer class of the city (the "Better Element").[36] In September 1885, anti-Chinese activists representing several communities and labor unions in western Washington met at Yesler Hall to form the Anti-Chinese Congress. It elected German-born Tacoma mayor R. Jacob Weisbach as its president and issued a November 1 deadline for all Chinese to leave western Washington. The notice struck enough fear to prompt some Chinese to leave voluntarily, but the deadline otherwise came and went. On November 3, members of the anti-Chinese Committee of Nine entered Tacoma and expelled the remaining Chinese from that town. By this time, the situation had attracted national attention, and the territorial governor, fearing that a forced expulsion in Seattle was imminent, asked Secretary of War William Endicott to send federal troops there to maintain order. This action as well as pleas by Mayor Yesler, Judge Burke, and other "law and order" advocates for peace and the prosecution of a group of seventeen men for conspiring to deprive the Chinese of their rights kept tensions below the surface, at least for a few weeks.[37]

Historians of Seattle have suggested that the end of the anti-Chinese movement was a turning point in the sense that it was one of the last instances when the troubles of Skid Row preoccupied the entire city. From there, it became a largely neglected neighborhood and faded from the attention of the city's powerful.[38] The final act in Seattle's anti-Chinese saga, occurring in February 1886, is a well-known part of the city's historical lore. The Sinophobe faction regrouped and devised a new plan to expel Chinese from the city for once and for all. They entered Chinatown, claiming that they were there to ensure that the city health codes were being followed. As Morgan describes the scene, "Once inside the leader would inform the Chinese that the building was condemned as a hazard to health and warn them that if they wished to avoid serious trouble they would get out of town at once. The steamer *Queen of the Pacific* was at the ocean dock, about to sail for San Francisco. Did they want to leave with her?"[39]

Nearly all the city's 350 Chinese residents agreed to leave, and members of the white mob assisted them in carrying their belongings to the dock. This went on for two hours before city and territory officials realized what was happening. Alarmed that what was playing out was an involuntary exodus, Judge Burke, U.S. Attorney W. H. White in Seattle, Mayor Yesler, and King County Sheriff John McGraw arrived at the scene. When it became clear that some of the Chinese were indeed being expelled against their will, the deportation was stopped. The next morning, the Chinese were brought to the courthouse at Third and Yesler and told that if they wished to stay, they would be protected. Faced with the hostility of white Seattle, only 16 stated that they wanted to stay, but, due to a shortage of room on the *Queen of the Pacific,* 185 Chinese remained in the city. Most planned on taking the next ship out of the city, but, in the meantime, the Home Guard, a volunteer law enforcement unit, was instructed to escort them back to their homes in Skid Row. This was a tense scene, as thousands gathered to watch the spectacle and to taunt the Chinese and Home Guard. A few shots were fired, resulting in the death of one man and the wounding of four others, and Governor Watson Squire briefly declared martial law, but otherwise the drama came to an end.

This climax of anti-Chinese agitation in Seattle occurred as the city entered its period of rapid growth and modernization. Although most people in the city in the 1880s were newcomers, the Chinese, as racial "others" from the "Orient," seemed more foreign and, thus, less entitled to available opportunities than others. Those who stayed after the traumas of that decade remained segregated in Skid Row along with the other "undesirables" in the city, and Chinatown endured.

By the turn of the twentieth century, Seattle's Asian population was on the rise, in part because Chinese were making a modest comeback (between 1900 and 1910, their population increased from 438 to 924), but more importantly because of the rise of Japanese immigration. In 1910, this group numbered 6,127.[40] Japanese immigrants filled labor needs left by Chinese exclusion, but they also came at a much different time in Seattle's history. As Morgan says, "[In 1896] the Orientals came back to Seattle in grand style."[41] James Hill of the Great Northern Railway had heard that a Japanese steamship line was about to commence regular service to the West Coast and that San Diego was going to be its port of entry. He sent an agent to Tokyo to convince the company to use Seattle instead. Hill prevailed, and on August 31, 1896, the *Miike Maru* of the Nippon Yusen Kaisha line sailed into Elliott Bay. Morgan continues, "With the arrival of the *Miiki Maru,* Seattle's attitude toward the Oriental came full cycle. Again the Asiatics were looked on, not as a menace, but as the solemn symbols of the wealth of the Far East. There was little objection among the townsfolk when some Japanese, and later Chinese, settled in Seattle; after the Spanish-American War, there was an influx of Filipinos."[42]

This claim is an overstatement to be sure, as Asian immigrants after 1896 faced their share of racism. Morgan's conjecture, however, does underscore the fact that Seattle was a much different place during the 1890s than it was in the 1860s when Chinese first arrived. Japanese immigrants settled in the midst of Seattle's urban revolution and were, thus, a part of the city's modernity. One thing that had not changed was racial segregation, and Japanese lived and operated their businesses in Skid Row.

The first significant wave of Japanese immigration to the continental United States began around the 1890s and consisted primarily of working-class males, many of whom were dispossessed farmers and casualties of modernization under the reforms of the Meiji regime, which came to power in 1868. Initially, they went to Hawaii in the 1880s, then under monarchical rule, as contract laborers to work in the booming sugar industry. Many came intending to stay temporarily, and, when they were able to do so, they returned to Japan or tried their luck on the North American continent. Between 1902 and 1906, 34,000 Japanese left Hawaii for Pacific ports, and from 1908 to 1924, that number exceeded 120,000.[43] The beginning of regular steamship runs between Japan and Seattle in 1896 facilitated direct migration to the city. As elsewhere, the curtailment of Chinese immigration created heightened labor needs in Pacific Northwest industries, so Japanese workers in this region eventually found employment in and became a significant part of the wage labor force in farming, mining, railroad construction, canning, and lumber mills.[44]

By the turn of the twentieth century, urban Japantowns, called Nihonmachis, and parallel farm communities dotted the West Coast, and, soon after, Japanese American settlements became less "bachelor" oriented and more nuclear family based. Compared to the earlier Chinese immigration, more Japanese entered the United States as family units. Furthermore, the greater proportion of Japanese women in this population allowed them to establish stable, organized communities and to successfully produce a second generation. The Gentlemen's Agreement of 1907 ended the immigration of male Japanese laborers to the United States, but it contained no stipulation on Japanese women, and their immigration actually increased in the years following the agreement. Many of them were "picture brides," married by proxy to Japanese bachelors in America who asked matchmakers or family members to arrange these marriages before sending for their new brides, whom they had never met. The immigration of picture brides was curtailed in 1920, when the Japanese government, responding to complaints by white Americans that it was an immoral practice, agreed to put an end to this migration. In turn, the number of Japanese women seeking entry dropped, but, by then, their numbers in the United States already exceeded thirty-eight thousand.[45] The rise of a second generation gave the Japanese American ethnic community certain advantages but also presented challenges. By the 1920s, the so-called "Nisei dilemma" preoccupied parents and Issei leaders, especially in matters of education and filial piety, and cultural rifts appeared over generational disagreements about the importance of individualism versus family and community loyalty.[46]

Residential options in Seattle, as in other cities, were limited, so Japanese immigrants settled in and around Chinatown, adding further to the multiethnic character of the area south of Yesler.[47] Their numbers increased between 1890 and 1920 from 125 to 7,874, and at their height in the 1920s and 1930s, they numbered just over 9,000.[48] As Japanese populated the blocks of Chinatown, the Chinese quarter turned into more of a pan-Asian section and spilled out of its original boundaries to Jackson and Weller streets between Maynard and Eighth. Although sharp lines never demarcated the sections within Jackson Street, the heart of the Japanese community was Sixth and Main. Over time, their residences migrated eastward toward First Hill, but Jackson Street remained the center of the Japanese American community due to the concentration of Japanese-owned businesses there.

Seattle native May Ota Higa, whose father worked as a hotel entrepreneur before World War II, spent much of her childhood in Skid Row. Eventually the family did well enough to move up to King and Eighteenth into a previously all-white neighborhood that was gradually transforming into an enclave for upwardly mobile Asians and other minorities. Initially, the Otas' neighbors were Italians, but this family soon left and was replaced by a Chinese family. Ota Higa recalled that not long after her family left Skid Row, other Japanese families joined the eastward migration: "the Hirades, Shigas, and Yanagimachis."[49] Growing up, her friends included Jews, Chinese, and blacks in addition to other Japanese, and, due to her mother's deep Christian faith, having Jewish friends could be a source of tension:

> [My mother] said, "Why do you have a Jewish friend?" "Because I like her." She says, "But the Jews killed Jesus." I said, "So what? Jesus was a Jew and you like Jesus." So my mother and I used to argue, and then they were about to sell their house and she said, she said she'd sell to anybody except a black or Jew. So I said to her, "Mama, you know, you're a Christian. Why do you talk that way?" I said, "God made the black people just like the Jews." But she would argue with me, and then, so then she went to see Reverend Tsai, you might have heard of him.[50]

Such Japanese Americans as the Otas who moved out of the area south of Yesler frequently encountered Jews in the eastern neighborhoods. Seattle's Sephardic Jewish community dated to the late 1860s, with most of the immigration occurring between the 1880s and the 1920s. Between 1885 and 1910, their numbers increased from two hundred to forty-five hundred. Although they were regarded as a distinct minority in the city, as a group, Seattle's Jews attained a significant degree of mobility and assimilation, signaled for instance in Bailey Gatzert's election as the city's first Jewish mayor in 1876.[51]

Entrepreneurship and participation in small businesses distinguished Japanese American life in Seattle. Among the most powerful businessmen was Masajiro Furuya, who ran multipurpose companies that provided services from labor contracting to mail delivery, but the small shop was the quintessential symbol of the Japanese American community and economic life. A 1924 survey of Japanese businesses in Seattle by Katherine Lentz, a graduate student at the University of Washington, found that in 1920, Japanese owned 1,462 establishments and engaged in 65 different kinds of businesses.[52] Among employed Seattle Japanese Americans, 46 percent earned their incomes from small businesses, a far greater proportion than the 5 percent in the United States as a whole.[53] Comprising just 2.8 percent of the city's population in 1920, Japanese operated about 26 percent of the hotels, 23 percent of the barbershops, and 26 percent of the dye works and cleaning businesses. To illustrate the rapidity with which they established themselves, before 1900, no more than 3 Japanese hotels and rooming houses existed in Seattle, but in 1925, according to Kazuo Ito, Japanese owned 127 hotels.[54] Capitalizing on the city's overall growth and the development of Japanese distribution networks throughout the region, their business activities also extended beyond the confines of Nihonmachi. For example, by World War I and through the 1930s, Japanese Americans ran 70 percent of the stalls at Seattle's bustling Pike Place Market.[55] These included Liberty Flower Shop, seen in Figure 1.1.

In his 1939 study of Seattle's Japanese community, sociologist Shotaro Frank Miyamoto attributes Japanese American business success to traditions of individual enterprise and mutual responsibility brought with them from the home country.[56] These values, buttressed by strong traditions of social responsibility and filial piety, he argues, ensured that Japanese American youths stayed out of trouble and equipped them for success as adults. Such organizations as the Japanese Commercial Club and the Japanese Chamber of Commerce, with membership rolls in the hundreds, promoted Japanese-owned businesses by regulating competition, providing mutual assistance, and sharing information. Miyamoto also cites *tanomoshi*, a system of kinship

Figure 1.1. Liberty Flower Shop at the Pike Place Market, Seattle, circa 1931. By the time this photo was taken, Japanese Americans were running the majority of stalls at Pike Place. *(Source: University of Washington Libraries, Special Collections, A. Curtis 59040.)*

connections and cooperative financing, as a major factor behind Japanese immigrant economic success.[57]

In addition to business groups, Seattle's Japanese formed an array of organizations serving various social and spiritual needs. Early on, mutual-aid associations based on immigrants' common region of origin played key roles in easing the adjustment to a new homeland. Reflecting the growth of the Japanese American community and the richness of members' lives beyond work and family, by the 1910s, Japanese in Seattle had established dozens of clubs for men and women to support their interests in art, photography, music, sports, flower arrangement, and cooking.[58] Religious institutions were also important among the first and second generations, and, by 1920, at least seven churches had been established for Japanese Christians and Buddhists. In addition to attending to the spiritual needs of their congregations, the churches maintained Sunday schools, nurseries, night schools, gymnasiums, and community centers. The establishment of a Japanese Language School in 1902, Kokugo Gakko, ensured that American-born children retained the ancestral language and roots, although the school's curriculum also consisted of American citizenship training.

Finally, organizations aimed at advancing the political interests of Japanese in America and improving their group standing in mainstream American society were formed in Seattle. These included the Japanese Association of America, the Japanese American Citizens League (JACL), and the Japanese Women's Progressive Club. The Japanese Association of America was an umbrella organization serving an array of needs for Seattle's Japanese until the 1940s. Formed in 1900 and spawning chapters throughout the West Coast, it provided a wide variety of services in the areas of immigrant adjustment, Americanization, legal aid, education, charity, and employment. Members of the small but emerging second generation demonstrated their organizational capabilities with the JACL, formed in 1929. This organization performed many of the same functions as the Japanese Association of America but specifically served Japanese who were born in the United States, urging members to assimilate to American culture and to demonstrate their good American citizenship.[59] Other groups, such as the Japanese Progressive Women's Club of Seattle, had Japan-born and American-born members, with an aim of promoting closer relationships between native and foreign-born women through discussions and social gatherings.

Impressed by Japanese Americans' evidently remarkable capacity for organizing and providing mutual support, Kazuo Ito argues that the Japanese community in Seattle stood out among others in the American West. He says that, more than Japanese Americans elsewhere, Seattle's community exhibited "outstanding" qualities, perhaps stemming from its high rates of literacy and esteemed social backgrounds, compared to its counterparts in Hawaii or California. Ito believes the uniqueness of the Seattle Japanese community could be explained by its early leaders, many of whom were "members of the intelligentsia who were skillful both with tongue and pen, orators and aspiring politicians who were in the forefront of the community."[60] In surveying the pre–World War II Japanese American population, Ito counted at least nine former Diet members and surmised that their influence accounted for the community's unusual level of interest in politics and publishing, which, as he observes, exceeded its interest in the arts and other more typically "popular" amusements.[61] "In Seattle there was an air of freedom," remembered one resident, "and many newspapers and magazines were published in Japanese and sold well. It was a society where one could make a living easily by publishing a small magazine."[62]

Although white Seattleites did not carry out an organized expulsion of Japanese similar to what they mounted against Chinese in the 1880s, Japanese Americans did endure racism in various forms.[63] At the height of Japanese migration to Hawaii and North America, the United States was pursuing diplomatic relations with Japan, and U.S. officials' general concern with diplomacy with the country acted as a check on the tone and severity of anti-Japanese politics. The Gentlemen's Agreement of 1907 was, in effect, an exclusionary measure pushed by American nativism, although it allowed Japan to save face through its concession to restrict the issuing of passports to laborers wishing to go to the United States. To deal with the Japanese already within the nation's borders, California, Washington, and seven other states passed alien land laws prohibiting land ownership and restricting the lease rights of "aliens ineligible to citizenship." These land laws dealt a serious blow to Japanese farmers, but many continued to farm as tenants or with land held under the name of a U.S. citizen, often a Japanese relative born in the United States. Japanese immigrants were also denied full political rights, with the U.S. Supreme Court decision in *Takao Ozawa v. United States* in 1922, which ruled that Japanese were not Caucasian and therefore were ineligible for naturalization. The Johnson-Reed Act of 1924, with its ban on the immigration of "aliens ineligible to citizenship," was the final and most sweeping act in the Japanese exclusion saga.

Japanese Americans were also vulnerable to economic discrimination through their exclusion from labor unions and business associations, often based on their ineligibility for citizenship. At various points, Japanese in Seattle were excluded from the Teamsters as well as unions for barbers, laundry workers, and cleaners, among other organizations.[64] Furthermore, Japanese business owners expended as many resources and as much energy fighting economic harassment as they did in building their businesses, as their success frequently drew outside resentment and attacks. In 1919, for example, a coalition of white business owners formed the Anti-Japanese League, which obtained the support of the City Council and American Legion. And during the 1920s and 1930s, at the Pike Street Market, white vendors tried to squeeze out their Japanese competitors by invoking a rule that sellers could sell only what they grew, realizing that this would be impossible for immigrant Japanese subject to the state's alien land law.[65] Among the common strategies that Japanese business owners turned to in order to protect themselves against these and other forms of economic harassment was to organize their own associations, such as the Japanese Pike Place Market Corporation, Japanese Barbers' Association, and Japanese Dyework Association. They also took to the legal system to protect their interests, especially in fighting pernicious attempts by King County prosecutors to undermine Japanese-owned businesses by citing the alien land law. According to Ito, Japanese business owners successfully contested many of these challenges, although at high financial and emotional costs.[66]

Aside from these legal and economic forms of harassment and exclusion, Japanese in Seattle, as elsewhere, experienced racism as part of their ordinary everyday realities. In Kazuo Ito's compilation of Issei life histories, for instance, sources provided copious examples of day-to-day encounters with racism and remembered the 1920s as particularly harsh years. Seemingly random forms of harassment, such as tire slashings, window breakings, and verbal taunts, when directed at Japanese Americans, served as sobering reminders of their minority and outsider status.[67] As a result, very mundane kinds of daily activities would be fraught with uncertainty and potential danger. Japanese residents could never be sure, for example, if they could walk the streets without being heckled or if they would be allowed into a business or entertainment establishment where they had never been before.[68] Remembering one such incident, Sentaro Tsuboi described an evening in which he took his wife and friends out for a night on the town at a theater located on Third Avenue. Although they were let in, they were promptly instructed to sit in the segregated second-level balcony along with the black patrons.[69]

Such an encounter recalls the conditions of Jim Crow America, which must have been especially disconcerting for newly arrived blacks from the South. Historically, African Americans came to Puget Sound and the American West along with others drawn by gold, jobs, and land. Their presence in Seattle dates to the 1850s, although their numbers were minuscule until the 1910s, and, even during this decade, their growth was modest compared to the rapid expansion occurring throughout the city. In 1900, the U.S. Census counted just 406 blacks in Seattle, and by 1910, there were 2,296. From there, Seattle's black population grew slowly, reaching 3,789 in 1940.[70] Historian Quintard Taylor calls the West a "racial frontier" for African Americans. Indeed, black homesteaders who went to such places as Kansas, Oklahoma, and Texas during the 1860s and 1870s saw the West as a promised land where they could escape the harsh racial orders of the Southeast and Northeast. Although Kansas held a particularly powerful place in the black imagination with respect to westward migration, Taylor explains that during the late 1880s, more westward-bound blacks went to the burgeoning cities rather than to rural areas.[71]

As did Chinese, Japanese, and Jews, blacks initially settled south of Yesler. One attraction of this area was the available work as porters, cooks, or waiters as well as the low rents and proximity to the railroad station. The East Madison area also became a common location of black settlement. Their concentration in these neighborhoods and exclusion from others intensified as their numbers grew and restrictive covenants became more commonplace, especially by the 1930s. Despite these concentrations, the number of blacks in Seattle did not achieve the levels allowing for the emergence of predominantly black blocks or neighborhoods until the 1940s.[72]

For a small community, Seattle's blacks were remarkably well organized. Much of the leadership in this regard came from the middle class, whose roots in the city stretched to the mid-1800s. This black middle class was highly literate and entrepreneurial, and individuals from its ranks owned barbershops, saloons, and other businesses or worked in self-employed trades. Horace Cayton, Sr., a former slave who settled in Seattle during the 1880s, began publishing the *Seattle Republican* in 1894 and went on to become one of the city's most prominent African Americans from the late nineteenth to early twentieth centuries. Cayton extolled civic engagement, mainstream political participation, and self-help among other African Americans in Seattle. Members of the black middle class also led local branches of the Young Women's Christian Association (YWCA), Sojourner Truth Home, National Association for the Advancement of Colored People (NAACP), and African Methodist Episcopal (AME) Church and formed their own fraternal lodges. The church was an especially important center of community and social life. Blacks in Seattle also participated in state and local politics—mostly within the Republican Party—seeking influence by joining clubs and pressing elected officials for appointments in exchange for votes.[73]

Among working-class African Americans in the city, severely restricted economic opportunities characterized their lives before World War II. This lack of options and mobility hampered the prospects of all black workers to achieve economic stability and independence, but it was especially detrimental for the newly and recently arrived. As elsewhere in industrial and urban America, racial prejudice among white employers and unions engendered and perpetuated this highly disadvantageous economic landscape facing African Americans, but in Seattle and other West Coast cities, these problems were compounded by the presence of Asian workers in many of the occupations that blacks might have otherwise filled. World War I brought some limited opportunities, as blacks were commonly employed as strikebreakers in shipyards and mines, but generally, until World War II, working-class blacks would remain concentrated in unskilled, low-paying jobs, such as construction, janitorial service, and waiting tables.

As recent works examining race in western cities have illustrated, one of the most striking aspects of African American history in these areas, which significantly distinguishes it from African American history in the South and the North, is how this group's racialized experiences were forged within multiethnic and multiracial settings.[74] In West Coast cities, such as Los Angeles, San Francisco, and Seattle, the presence of Asians has been a particularly significant part of the racial landscape and should, thus, be taken into account in examinations of the black experience. Furthermore, although life in Jackson Street was highly segregated, observations of daily life there from the early 1900s indicate that encounters across ethnic and racial lines were the norm rather than the exception. Because of her father's social gregariousness and her mother's work managing an apartment in Jackson Street, Aki Kurose, who was born in Seattle in 1925, constantly encountered people from various backgrounds and walks of life: "My dad loved to bake, so every Friday evening he'd make jellyroll and then all the neighbors would come in to have jellyroll and we'd just have a good time, listening to music and just being social. . . . And the neighborhood was very diverse. And there were many Jews and a Chinese family, and several black families, and we went in and out of each other's homes all the time."[75]

An especially interesting detail from Kurose's memories of Japanese-black relations in early 1900s Seattle was that one of the smaller Japanese language schools in Seattle employed a black teacher. Information about this teacher, Evelyn Whistler, is scarce, and Kurose did not know how Whistler even came to learn Japanese, speculating that the couple who ran the school, Mr. and Mrs. Ishii, took her under their wing and taught her the language.[76]

A unique cultural scene in Jackson Street also reflected the diverse mixture of the local population. This mixing was especially true of Seattle's jazz scene during the 1920s and 1930s, which was associated with such clubs as the Alhambra, Ubangi, and the Black and Tan. Jazz in Seattle at this time relied on extensive camaraderie between Asian business owners and black musicians; such establishments as the Chinese Gardens and Hong Kong Chinese Society Club also served as major local venues, while the Tokiwa Hotel provided lodging for musicians, who would eat at Japanese and Chinese restaurants.[77]

Although camaraderie and friendship characterized one aspect of Asian-black relations in Jackson Street, other aspects, especially economic relations, could be competitive and antagonistic. Quintard Taylor explains that the success of Nihonmachi "doomed black business success" and was a persistent obstacle to black economic self-sufficiency.[78] Japanese Americans not only developed structural advantages by creating regional distribution networks connecting wholesalers, grocers, and farmers; they also expanded their clientele to include non-Japanese patrons, forcing black business owners to compete with Japanese for black customers.

Like blacks, Filipinos in Seattle did not develop a substantial ethnic economy and were reliant on services that Japanese American businesses provided.

Due to already entrenched patterns of racial segregation and limited availability of housing, services, and social options elsewhere, Filipinos, who numbered about sixteen hundred in the city in 1930, ended up settling in three main areas: Jackson Street, Capitol Hill, and the University District. Within the neighborhood, they tended to occupy the space between the black area and the "Asian ghetto," and, as they settled in, Chinese gradually spread along Yesler and Jackson streets and clustered around Twelfth and King streets. Barred from land ownership in Washington until 1940, Filipinos' employment options were limited, and, throughout the 1920s and 1930s, they were largely relegated to seasonal jobs that paid little. In other parts of the Pacific Northwest, Filipinos filled the migratory labor circuit in canning and agriculture. They became involved in salmon canning as early as 1918, joining an already multiethnic workforce that included Chinese, Japanese, and Native Americans, and they constituted nearly 30 percent of the cannery workforce by 1930, the peak year of their involvement in the major regional industry.[79]

Because of the migratory and seasonal nature of the jobs most Filipinos held, Filipino America was a physically fluid community in constant motion that encompassed much of the far West from San Diego to Alaska.[80] Such cities as Seattle, however, became critical nodes within Filipino America, where individuals could rest and play, obtain leads on future jobs, or settle permanently.[81] The city was also a common point of disembarkation for trans-Pacific travelers from the Philippines and was the main regional dispatching point for migrant workers en route to the canneries of Alaska, British Columbia, and Puget Sound. At the end of cannery season during late summer/early fall, workers would typically go to Seattle to spend their money on entertainment, meet with friends, and find new work. In the city, they could also secure jobs as houseboys for middle-class families and busboys in restaurants. Finally, education was a compelling pull factor for Filipino immigrants to the United States, and to Seattle in particular. With U.S. rule of the Philippines after the Spanish-American War of 1898, colonial officials encouraged Filipinos to go to the United States to obtain an education and then to return to the home country for high-status bureaucratic and government positions.[82] In terms of higher education, the University of Washington in Seattle became a common destination for Filipinos migrating for this purpose. During the 1920s and 1930s, it had the largest enrollment of Filipinos of any university in the United States, with their numbers peaking at nearly one hundred in the 1919–1920 academic year.[83] Although many Filipinos came to Seattle with hopes of obtaining an education, completing school proved to be very difficult. Once in the United States, many had to obtain jobs, often joining the seasonal migratory circuit, and the demands of work posed major obstacles to finishing their studies whether at the high school or college levels. As a result, many Filipinos gave up on finishing school altogether. These challenges were evident, for example, in the struggles of Filipino student groups to remain active at various Seattle schools. In 1924, the Garfield High School yearbook reported that although the Filipino Club started out with several members, some would leave town during the school year for jobs or go away during the summer and never rejoin the club.[84]

Jackson Street, Skid Row, Melting Pot

Chinese American Ken Louie, who was born in New York in 1927 and moved to Seattle in 1938, fondly remembered Jackson Street as a place of great diversity, fluidity, and possibility. As he recollected, "In the old days, you don't have that many people in Chinatown to start out with. The Japanese people on one side of us, and the Filipino people sort of intermingle with both sides. And you walk down the street, you say hello to everybody."[85] The majority of white Seattleites, who by the 1930s largely regarded Jackson Street as Seattle's ghetto, did not quite appreciate the multiethnic character of the neighborhood. In this sense, it had inherited Skid Row's historical reputation. In 1933, the *Northwest Enterprise,* a local black newspaper established in 1920, acknowledged that the area was "one of the most abused streets in Seattle," not to mention "the butt of jokes" and a place "sneeringly referred to by residents of other sections of the city."[86]

Although they were aware of how outsiders viewed their neighborhood, Jackson Street residents held different impressions of the area they called home. Yoshisada Kawai, who had come to the United States in 1918 at the age of sixteen with his father, remembered, "I couldn't help being astounded at the vigorous liveliness of those Japanese who could hardly speak English and yet had brought their businesses to success."[87] As a site of urban paradoxes, Jackson Street was prosperous and poor, foreboding and convivial. Although there were the success stories of such businesses as Furuya Company and the modest but impressive achievements of smaller business owners, there were also young Issei who struggled for work and lived in poverty. It was a place where Miyoshi Yorita went as a young girl to watch lavish productions at the Nippon Kan Theater but also where dead bodies were occasionally found in alleyways.[88] In other words, Jackson Street was like any urban neighborhood at the time, with its attractions and its problems. Outsiders may have neglected or failed to appreciate it, but its residents felt and expressed a strong connection to the place.[89]

One of the most common observations made about Jackson Street's population was its bustling heterogeneity, and images of diverse peoples intermingling with ease represented a powerful counter-narrative to the dominant, disdainful perceptions of the neighborhood. Such depictions suggested that the characteristics of Jackson Street that marginalized it in some people's minds were to others what made it unique and attractive. In other words, its purported weaknesses were actually its strengths. A newspaper column called "Down Main Street," which appeared in the *Japanese-American Courier* during the late 1920s and early 1930s and was authored by Kinue Okamura and another writer known as "The Wag," asserted Japanese Americans' presence and roots in the neighborhood, while providing an informal portrait of daily life in Jackson Street. The column depicted the area as a lively and colorful place animated by the sounds of traffic, trains, and music, and whose streets were filled by people of different ethnicities, ages, and occupations engaging in a variety of activities. The contents of "Down Main Street" also suggested the presence of a close-knit Japanese American community. The authors noted the antics of such locals as Shizuko Harada, the "personality girl of Main Street," and reported on such sightings as Kelly Yamada playing her saxophone on her way to school, Ralph Ochi carrying his photography equipment down the street, "Mouse" Hoshide showing off his new Ford, and Yoshito Fuji working on his tennis game at the court on Eighth and Washington.[90]

The column also provided a glimpse of the multiplicity of cultures and ethnicities in the relatively small space of Jackson Street. As the writers remarked, a common street scene included Filipino "dandies" in town from the canneries, "swarm[ing] over the sidewalks of Jackson Street and by avenues, nattily attired in the 'latest' balloon pants, collegiate"; a Hebrew, "wearing a black skull cap and a long flow of beard stands in front of his shop. He . . . nods his head approvingly and rubs his hands in gleeful anticipation as he smiles benignly at paserby [sic]"; and a black man changing a flat tire at the corner of Maynard and King.[91] In another description of the sights and sounds of Jackson Street, this one invoking the unique local jazz scene, the author observed, "A wild southern symphony combined with the tenor of a colored jazz singer emanates from a tea shop below the Kin Ka Low Restaurant. A bit of Southern philosophy mixed in with that of the Orient."[92]

Local African American writers depicted the area in similar terms, although in their observations, they sometimes drew comparisons to other American cities so as to underscore to black readers Seattle's uniqueness. The *Northwest Enterprise* pointed out that in Jackson Street, it was commonplace to see a white man sitting between two blacks at a breakfast counter, a serious transgression of local racial mores in the Jim Crow South. As the major thoroughfare of the south business section, Jackson Street drew all kinds of people, but, echoing the Japanese American writers, this diversity was an enriching, not negative, aspect of the neighborhood: "Jackson Street might well be called the 'Poor Man's Playground.' Here all races meet on common ground and rub elbows as equals. Filipinos, Japanese, Negroes and whites mingle in the same hotels and restaurants and there is an air of comradeship. They address each other as 'buddy,' 'brother,' and 'pal.'"[93]

Visitors to the area, explained the *Northwest Enterprise,* would find a scene of rich ethnic and cultural diversity and witness easygoing social interactions among the residents. "Japanese merchants open their doors and sell without apparent molestation by authorities," it remarked. "Wearing apparel may also be obtained and the stores are well patronized by Negro and Filipino sheiks."[94] Sundays were the most pleasant day of the week, as church days found people looking their sharpest and on their best behavior.

A history of disenfranchisement, violence, and segregation in the United States shaped blacks' expectations in the West, but, when it came to addressing the obstacles they faced in the multiracial setting of Seattle, they were pushed to think beyond black and white. As described above, the presence of Asians as well as the intransigence of white prejudice shaped blacks' employment and other economic prospects. And although friendships across ethnic lines formed with ease among some, for others, tension and distrust characterized black-Asian relations. For instance, although Aki Kurose remembered her relationships with black neighbors and friends in thoroughly positive terms, she acknowledged that not all Japanese were so accepting of people who were different from them. When asked how other Japanese Americans responded to her family's close relationships with blacks, she said, "I'd hear like some of the parents saying, 'Well, they shouldn't bring a black to the house,' or something like that. Or, 'So-and-so is going with a black,' and it was very, like almost a shame kind of thing, you know."[95]

Wishing to forge a community that would be a "promised land" for blacks around the country, some local African Americans were curious about whether Asian Americans would be their friends or foes in their struggle for racial equality. For this reason, the *Northwest Enterprise* occasionally printed stories about Asian-black conflicts in Seattle and elsewhere, such as one article with the headline, "Chinese Help Jim Crow," about a Chinese merchant in Phoenix, Arizona, who gave $150 toward supporting a white family's effort to evict two black families from a tract of land.[96]

The objective of racial uplift among African Americans shaped their attitudes toward their Japanese neighbors, and these encounters, in turn, informed blacks' ideas on how their community might uplift itself in Seattle. One type of contact came in the form of black readership of the local English-language Japanese American media. In 1934, Reverend John Carr, an African American resident of Seattle, wrote to the *Japanese-American Courier* to express his thanks for what he described as the newspaper's sincerity and conciseness. He believed the paper could be a source of inspiration for all blacks, saying, "I am of the Negro Race; and as an American who loves the spirit of the principles of this government as expressed in the constitution and the progressive forward steps in governmental righteousness and strength; am alive to the constructive influence of such a publication as your excellent paper."[97] Carr conveyed his wish to share the *Japanese-American Courier* with black newspaper editors in the Eastern and Southern United States and asked for back issues.

In other ways, Seattle African Americans looked to Japanese Americans as models. For instance, in 1941, the *Northwest Enterprise* extolled local Japanese high school students for the numerous honors they earned over the previous school year, singling out five Nisei who were named valedictorians and salutatorians. This "naturally studious race" set an example for African Americans. "We have strained our eyes to see a member of our own race winning a coveted honor. Our only hope is the honor roll."[98]

Japanese and blacks' physical proximity in Seattle, their common status as nonwhites, and opportune circumstances gave rise to nascent efforts at interracial coalition building. In 1928 and then in 1933, an African American and Japanese American, respectively, ran for seats in the Washington state legislature, and, out of necessity, sought votes outside their ethnic and racial communities. When Horace Cayton, Sr., ran for office in 1928, he courted Japanese Americans for their support, perhaps recognizing how this population had grown into a significant force with the rise of the Nisei generation. He reached out to this community with a statement that was reproduced in the *Japanese-American Courier:*

> I have always been proud to consider *The Japanese-American Courier,* as well as many other individuals in your group as my friends, . . . As a member of the State Legislature I will at all times fight for the rights and privileges of all minorities. . . . I have lived in this district for the last eighteen years and have grown up and gone through school with many of the members of your community. They, I am sure will not feel you have misplaced your confidence by supporting me to this office.[99]

In 1934, Nisei Clarence Arai ran for a seat in the state legislature and looked to African Americans for electoral support. During his campaign, he spoke to the King County Colored Republican Club, the Colored Progressive Club, and the Colored Mt. Zion Baptist church and won key endorsements from the Colored Republican Club and John E. Prim, the attorney and president of the Seattle NAACP.[100] The *Northwest Enterprise* threw its support behind Arai, announcing that he could count on his "colored friends."[101] Cayton and Arai both lost their elections, but their campaigns revealed the growing recognition among blacks and Japanese of the importance of cross-racial connections in pursuing shared and individual objectives.

CONCLUSION

This chapter traces the history of Jackson Street in terms of the minority experience to establish the centrality of multiraciality as a facet of daily life in the neighborhood. An area disregarded by some as the city's ghetto and celebrated by others as a bustling and dynamic quarter, it embodied to some the best and to others the worst of growing Seattle. As shown in preceding pages, Jackson Street's residents drew a sense of pride from the neighborhood's qualities. To them, the mix of people, active pace of life, and assortment of activities in the public spaces made it the most interesting part of the city. Meanwhile, as white elites worked to build Seattle's economy and prestige, they frequently claimed that their city was a cosmopolitan "gateway to the Orient." Residents of Jackson Street could look at their own surroundings and argue that their neighborhood best embodied those claims. As discussed in the Introduction, Clarence Arai's declaration that Jackson Street was the "Far East of Seattle" exemplified this perception.

If a city calls itself "cosmopolitan," what are some of the specific ways that its residents can solidify the claim? The following chapter explores this question and finds that Japan and Japanese people in the city were crucial in Seattle's bid for urban distinction as a cosmopolitan location and the nation's "gateway to the Orient." The results would be uneven, often contradictory, and leave Seattle's Japanese with a mixed bag. For Seattle, cosmopolitanism might have brought the city's Japanese Americans to great visibility, and members of this group did not shun the spotlight, but they would also learn that the space between cultural visibility and racial equality in early-twentieth-century America was very wide.

2

꒦꓄꒷

Making Seattle "Cosmopolitan"

COSMOPOLITAN SEATTLE

In September 1936, the Seattle cultural journal, the *Town Crier,* began publication of a series called "Cosmopolitan Seattle." Written by Lancaster Pollard, a local historian and also the journal's publisher, the series consisted of installments respectively profiling the city's German, Chinese, and Japanese communities. Pollard was impressed by the findings of the 1930 Census, which had counted in the city nearly 73,000 foreign-born whites, 8,448 Japanese, 3,303 blacks, and 1,347 Chinese out of a total population of 365,583, and believed that the urban diversity represented by those numbers called for some appreciation in the pages of the *Crier.*[1] He also sought to repudiate the impression, still held by many, that Seattle was a backwater, and, along with other members of the small cultural elite, he worked to replace this perception with a more worldly and sophisticated image. He lamented that most residents did not appreciate the exciting ethnic scene, with its art exhibits, concerts, dance recitals, and plays, and bemoaned what he viewed as their "annoying complacency" toward their own ignorance. One area that seemed to especially enthrall Pollard was the city's culinary offerings: "There are in Seattle restaurants where one can eat the food of almost every race and nation, some of it celebrated by gourmets throughout the world, all of it interesting to anyone with any gustatory curiosity."[2] By introducing readers to some of the local ethnic communities, he aimed to "do something toward correcting the attitude, which is held by many persons elsewhere and by not a few Seattleites, that Seattle is the most provincial city of its size in the United States."[3]

Toward promoting an exciting and modern image of the city, the "Cosmopolitan Seattle" series celebrated ethnic minorities in a pluralistic society but glossed over the decidedly unglamorous details of their histories and recent experiences. Pollard argued that the "cultural communities" of Seattle enhanced the city and urged readers to pay a visit to Chinatown and Nihonmachi, but he neglected to note that these neighborhoods' physical isolation from most white Seattleites was a legacy of racism and segregation. He showed little interest in Chinese and Japanese people outside their contributions to cuisine, the arts, and other aspects of "local color." Yet when it came to boosting the city as a cosmopolitan locale, he gave them a disproportionate amount of attention, which is all the more curious considering that Asians at the time made up only about 3 percent of the city's population. Nonetheless, in the installment on Japanese, Pollard said that Nihonmachi, with its art societies, playhouse, and other cultural establishments, "had become an integral part of Seattle and a center combining both Oriental and Occidental features."[4] Japanese were Seattle's largest nonwhite group, but they were only the fourth-largest national group behind several European nationalities. Pollard could, for instance, have also written about the city's Swedes, who in 1930 numbered about ninety-six hundred, more than each of the major nonwhite communities.

Pollard and the *Town Crier*'s decision to tout Seattle's cosmopolitan credentials by invoking its Asian population exemplifies what by the 1930s was a curious, but common, strategy among white cultural and economic elites to promote the city as a modern metropolis. Highlighting proximity to and association with the "Orient," in terms of transoceanic access to Asia and Asians living in the city, brought attention to Seattle's open, inclusive, and international disposition, which yielded it unique commercial, social, and cultural advantages. This chapter examines such efforts to promote Seattle as a "cosmopolitan" city vis-à-vis its relationship with Asia and Asians through discussion of two events, the Alaska-Yukon-Pacific Exposition of 1909 (A-Y-P) and the International Potlatch festivals of 1934 to 1942, focusing on the involvement and appropriation of Japan and Japanese Americans. Throughout the country, such events, large and small, advanced the visions of local boosters, brought people out to celebrate, and created collective memories. They were also more often than not tightly controlled vehicles of elite and middle-class whites seeking to promote municipal improvements, distribute patronage, bolster local economies, and deploy ideologies in concert with their aspirations. In Seattle, the booster-driven claim of cosmopolitanism served the larger objectives of modernizing the city and integrating it into the dynamic world of Pacific Rim trade and diplomacy. Seattle was cosmopolitan, it went, because it drew people, commodities, and ideas from other parts of the world, and, as Pollard pointed out, one needed only to look at the racial and ethnic makeup (especially in the Yesler-Jackson area) for evidence. As long as their interests remained tied to Asian commerce and their conception of cosmopolitanism extolled an image of worldly inclusiveness, boosters would continue to make their case for Seattle's distinctiveness by conspicuously incorporating Japan and the city's Japanese American residents in urban celebrations.

Attentive to the contradictions between cosmopolitan discourse and the persistence of anti-Japanese prejudice, this chapter argues that cosmopolitanism was chiefly a consumer idea, which neither brought substantive steps toward equality for Japanese Americans in Seattle nor challenged boundaries regulating access to power and civic status. Cosmopolitan discourse offered the Japanese "colony" symbolic inclusion and at times even great prominence, but it did so by fetishizing them in the local imagination. In some respects, such appropriation resembled how Hispanics, for example, were embedded into the urban iconographies of southern California cities around the turn of the twentieth century.[5] Yet the appropriation of Japanese in Seattle was different, because they were not a defeated or conquered people subject to the nostalgic, romantic fantasies of Anglos. By linking their urban imaginary to Japan, Seattleites embraced modernity, internationalism, and a place in Pacific Rim commerce and affairs.

Examining the symbolic inclusion of Japan and Japanese in Seattle public celebrations also highlights some of the unique dimensions not only of Japanese Americans' experience in this city but also of Asian Americans in the urban West Coast more generally. That is, although Asian immigrants have experienced harassment and discrimination at the hands of the white majority, factors stemming from the Asia-Pacific orientation of West Coast cities worked against their complete invisibility and exclusion in the Western urban landscape. As historian Phoebe Kropp has observed in her book about the appropriation of the Spanish and Mexican past in California culture, throughout American history, a dialectic of disdain and desire, or the impulse to possess and to reject nonwhite peoples, has been a "central method Americans have used to express race and nation."[6] This chapter also comments broadly on the dynamics of urban development and culture in the West. Growing up in the shadows of the eastern metropolises, western cities struggled not just for economic vitality but also for status and respectability. Seattle's proclaiming itself the "gateway to the Orient" was a key strategy toward pursuing those ends. In this regard, the chapter also highlights awareness of scale as a key aspect of urban modernity. Seattleites commonly thought and talked about their city in terms of its relationship to distant lands and its place within larger geographic areas, such as the Northwest and the Pacific world. This conceptual negotiation of scale proved to be an enduring and critical aspect of articulating Seattle's rise as a modern metropolis and "gateway to the Orient."

A PACIFIC CITY

During its first few decades, Seattle developed with its gaze eastward, northward, and southward and, from the turn of the twentieth century, increasingly westward across the Pacific. Founders proclaimed their settlement to be a future New York of the Pacific, and, as many other western settlers did, they looked to the East for their urban models. The early economy relied on sending exports to San Francisco and Portland, and Seattle's position as a gateway to Alaska proved pivotal in its ability to surpass its regional rivals. But the prize of commerce in and across the Pacific increasingly preoccupied Seattle and the West Coast's leading capitalists. In 1902, ruminating on the fantastic possibilities of this commercial frontier, *Northwest Magazine,* a Tacoma-based journal, said that American merchants were now "awakening to the fact that 800,000,000 people in Asia, Africa, and Australia as well as in the Pacific archipelagoes are commercially worthy of sharing the attention heretofore given wholly to 200,000,000 in Europe."[7] Advantageously situated to conduct trade in the Pacific, West Coast ports captured increasing shares of Asian commerce over the 1890s, illustrated in the rising number of steam vessel clearances between the U.S. Pacific Coast and Asia during that decade from 40 to 599.[8]

Historians cite the completion of the Great Northern's transcontinental terminus in 1893 and the 1897 Klondike gold rush as the main turning points opening the way to Seattle's premier status in the Pacific Northwest, but if we examine how locals remembered the past through public celebration, it was the beginning of regular steamship service between Japan and Puget Sound that elicited the greatest collective excitement during this decade. To be sure, much emotional and financial investment went into Seattleites' efforts to bring to their city a transcontinental terminus, beginning with territorial governor Isaac Stevens's miscalculated 1854 promise that a railroad from east of the Cascades would come to Puget Sound within five years.[9] And when gold was discovered along the Klondike River in the Yukon, the Seattle Chamber of Commerce, eager to capitalize on its location as the northernmost American rail-port to Alaska, launched a national publicity blitz led by Erastus Brainerd aimed at linking Seattle with Alaska in the public consciousness and then reaping the economic rewards.[10] The gold rush would be duly commemorated, although twelve years later, and a ceremony for the Great Northern Railway's completion was planned but canceled due to the financial panic of 1893 and the inability of important Eastern financiers to make the trip out west.

Great hoopla and fanfare did, however, greet the arrival of the *Miike Maru* into Elliott Bay on August 31, 1896. This moment, discussed briefly in the previous chapter, resulted from the handiwork of Great Northern president James Hill, who, upon learning that the Nippon Yusen Kaisha (NYK) steamship line of Japan was planning to start service with the West Coast and intended to use San Diego, dispatched an agent to Tokyo to convince the company to use Seattle instead. The choice offered considerable advantages, such as a shorter distance between it and Yokohama (about 4,150 nautical miles) than between Japan and any other major U.S. West Coast port. Using Seattle would, thus, trim days off the trans-Pacific journey compared to traveling from San Francisco or Los Angeles.[11] The NYK agreed to work exclusively with the Great Northern, and Hill promised to build a new terminal, warehouses, and grain elevators on the waterfront. According to Murray Morgan, as the *Miike Maru* docked, "the churchbells and firebells clanged, the bands began to play, and tens of thousands of Seattleites flocked to the waterfront to cheer as she was made fast to the dock. . . . The dream of Seattle as the gateway to the Orient was coming true."[12] As Morgan's description conveys, this event was more than a party celebrating a business deal; it was a signal achievement in Seattle's quest to become a modern, global city, a dream that would be deeply attached to the "Orient."

Once transportation links were established, the volume of goods flowing in and out of Seattle and to and from Asia rose dramatically. Seattle commerce experienced an eightfold expansion between 1895 and 1900, and Asian countries became the port's most important customers. The value of imports from Japan doubled between 1895 and 1896 and then tripled between 1896 and 1897, reaching more than $8 million by 1899.[13] Asian countries exported tea, raw silk, curios, camphor, and matting for American consumption, while importing American lumber, flour, cotton, machinery, and heavy hardware.[14] In 1909, raw silk alone accounted for more than $14 million of the total $21 million in goods imported from Japan and China.[15] The Spanish-American War of 1898 proved beneficial for Seattle, as suppliers shipping through its port negotiated contracts with the U.S. Army to send oats, hay, flour, groceries, and other supplies to American soldiers in the Philippines.

The arrival of the *Miike Maru* and Seattle's celebration of the event solidified the city's association with the "Orient," commercially and imaginatively.

Civic boosters and business leaders enthusiastically embraced the notion that Seattle was the nation's "gateway to the Orient" and repeatedly brought up this idea in their pursuit of modernization and cosmopolitan status for decades to come. To be sure, insisting that Seattle any time before World War II was a modern cosmopolitan city was dubious and spoke more of people's aspirations than actual conditions. Nonetheless, the refrain of "Seattle, gateway to the Orient" alluded to connections and relationships that were being forged across the Pacific, and, in the early 1900s, no country loomed larger in these developments than Japan, having emerged dramatically on the world scene following the Meiji Restoration of 1868 and its military victories over China in 1895 and Russia in 1905. Americans viewed the nation as a valuable trading partner and potential gateway to the Asian continent, and toward cementing their "gateway to the Orient" claims, business leaders and boosters followed two strategies with respect to the Japanese. One was to reach out directly to Japan by way of exchanges and hosting visiting dignitaries and trade commissioners. The second involved overtures to the local Japanese community, which was the largest in the Pacific Northwest and had established a vital economic presence in the city through ethnic enterprise. These strategies came together at the Alaska-Yukon-Pacific Exposition of 1909, Seattle's first world's fair.

SEATTLE "COMES OUT" AT THE
ALASKA-YUKON-PACIFIC EXPOSITION

With the A-Y-P Exposition, dubbed Seattle's "coming-out party," the city made its boldest bid yet to being America's "gateway to the Orient."[16] Three other West Coast cities—Portland, San Francisco, and San Diego—hosted world's fairs between 1905 and 1915, and together, these four expositions underscored the important place that the Pacific region held in the national imagination in the early twentieth century. Whereas earlier American world's fairs had celebrated the milestones of the nation's past, the West Coast expositions emphasized the future, particularly as it related to recently acquired territories in the Pacific and relations with Asian and Latin American countries. The expositions also made the case that the West Coast—as the U.S. continental gateway to its Pacific territories and trading partners—would be the site of pivotal national and global developments in the new century. In addition to arguing for the ascendancy of the western United States over the east, Seattle's fair sought to bring worldwide attention to the Northwest's abundant lumber, mineral, agricultural, and other resources and to educate the public about the nation's new territories in the Pacific.[17]

Hosting a world exposition suited Seattle at the time, because it was trying to promote itself as a city of international consequence. With its rapid growth and dizzying pace of construction and earth-moving projects under way, it certainly appeared to be a metropolis on the rise. As George E. Dickson, the president of the Washington State Commission for the A-Y-P, said, the fair would give Washington its "proper place among the great states of the republic."[18] From 1906 to 1909, members of a newly formed exposition corporation led by the president of Seattle's Scandinavian Bank, John E. Chilberg, planned and promoted the A-Y-P, eventually raising about $10 million and persuading hundreds of cities, states, and foreign governments to sponsor exhibits. The initial plans were to focus the exposition on the resources of Alaska and the Northwest, but more ambitious plans to include the entire Pacific Rim soon replaced this idea. Driven also by a spirit of urban competitiveness, the exposition corporation hoped that a successful fair would take attention away from Portland, which had hosted the Lewis and Clark Centennial Exposition in 1905, and help Seattle overtake San Francisco's share of foreign commerce.

The University of Washington campus was selected as the fair's venue. Two hundred and fifty-five acres of the grounds were transformed into a maze of buildings and thoroughfares representing the world in miniature. Visitors were impressed by such structures as the Spanish-style California Building, which showcased arrangements of produce from the state, and the renaissance-inspired Foreign Palace, where participating European nations displayed such fineries as Austrian crystals. Some of the European exhibits actually relied on local contributions, such as the Swedish and Norway Day programs, which members of Seattle's Scandinavian community helped organize. Attractions from the Pacific Rim included a display of Asian silks in the Oriental Palace and Klondike gold in the Alaska Building. In the Forestry Building, visitors viewed local and regional varieties of wood and demonstrations of the latest mechanical processes in lumbering. The A-Y-P also offered much for the fun-seeking, somewhat lowbrow visitor, from performances at the Music Pavilion to the carnivalesque attractions of the Pay Streak.

Although presented to the public as educative and celebratory of humankind's progress, the A-Y-P, like other European and American world expositions in the nineteenth and early twentieth centuries, was a spectacle of Western imperialism that affirmed white civilization's mastery over the globe and reduced nonwhite and non-Western peoples to crude human exhibits and quaint displays. Furthermore, exhibits with Filipinos and Native Americans underscored America's participation in imperial conquest. Native

Americans, by this time deemed a disappearing people yet culturally visible through white appropriation, held particular interest for spectators and organizers. In his analysis of Native people at the A-Y-P, Coll Thrush says, "Virtually every exhibit included some sort of ethnographic display, and the message was clear: these Indians were our people—not in the sense of being *us*, of course, but in the sense of being *ours*. Like other world's fairs, the AYPE was intensely didactic, brazenly ambitious, and thoroughly racist."[19] An Eskimo Village and a group of Indian school children from Tulalip purportedly educated visitors about primitive peoples and the possibilities of their uplift under the tutelage of white Americans. Other displays were more overtly entertainment driven, such as a Wild West show featuring Great Plains Indians and canoe races in Lake Union between members of British Columbia and Puget Sound tribes. Additionally, other Indians were given free entrance to the grounds and camping sites, but, in exchange, they had to live in tepees and wear their native costumes for the viewing entertainment of visitors.[20]

In addition to affirming the U.S. conquest of Natives and Filipinos and white Americans' rightful possession of the Northwest and Alaska, A-Y-P organizers shored up a vision in which Seattle linked up with Asia to lead the way to national prosperity in the twentieth century. As the *New York Times* described, "the citizens [of Seattle] believe . . . they can bring the Asiatic people into personal contact with the Americans by an interchange of the products and manufactures necessary to each."[21] Although other expositions held in the United States sought to bring attention to the rising significance of the Pacific to national interests, one A-Y-P official insisted Seattle's fair would be the first to show the *true* potential of Asian trade. Indeed, it featured what was then the most comprehensive showcase of goods from Asia and the Pacific Rim seen in the United States.[22] "Seattle has an unparalleled opportunity," wrote the fair's chief of publicity Frank Merrick, "to render the United States and the Orient an inestimable service in increasing the commerce of the Pacific by teaching the merchants and manufacturers of each section of the needs of the people of their respective markets, and how to secure and hold the business."[23]

The official seal of the A-Y-P is an illuminating window to how these aspirations—not to mention gendered and racialized ideas of nation—were deployed at the fair (see Figure 2.1). Created by West Coast artist Adelaide Hanscom and selected from an open competition, the design showed three women representing the Orient, the United States, and Alaska seated together and holding a steamship, locomotive, and gold nuggets, respectively. The feminization of national symbols was commonplace in U.S. political culture

Figure 2.1. The seal of the Alaska-Yukon-Pacific Exposition, 1909. This presentation of three female figures, representing Asia, Alaska, and the United States, expresses the fair's ethos of bridging Seattle and the "Orient" and the importance of Alaska to the city's urban growth. *(Source: University of Washington Libraries, Special Collections, Nowell x236.)*

by this time, and here, the gathering of women conveyed American expansion as an endeavor of peace, friendship, and mutual interests. Also striking was the seal's presentation of race. Predictably enough, a Japanized figure with black hair wrapped in a bun and dressed in a kimono sits in for Asia, and a Caucasian for the United States. More telling is Alaska's depiction as a Caucasian, indicated by the stark whiteness of her skin and clothing and blonde hair, a contrast with the darker shades we see on the Asia and U.S. figures. The living reproduction of the seal staged at the fair, featuring two white women and one Asian, further reinforced this conceptualization of the Pacific world in which the East and West were brought together yet still differentiated by clear racial markers.

Of the Pacific Rim nations participating at the A-Y-P, Japan was the most active and visible, in part by its own design. A rising international power, it had been accepting invitations to take part in European and American expositions since 1873 to strengthen its diplomatic and commercial ties with Western countries and thereby prove itself worthy in the "full fellowship of the family of nations."[24] By most indications, it was succeeding; during the 1904 Louisiana Purchase Exposition in St. Louis, *Success Magazine* declared it one of the "first nations of the world," and a reporter praised the government's exhibit as "the sensation" of the entire exposition.[25] The planners of Seattle's exposition, thus, had high expectations, with one committee member remarking, "No nation has a stronger reason to take part in a Pacific Exposition than has Japan."[26] The *Seattle Times* echoed these sentiments and elaborated that the shared commercial interests of Japan and the United States would be emphasized at the A-Y-P:

> Above all, [Japan's participation] was strikingly significant of the rising power of Nippon and strongly accentuated the fact that the Island Empire whose commercial interests are so closely identified with those of Westernmost America, are in the game of world politics and trade to stay and that they regard the United States as the most promising field, because of ties of sentiment and cold-blooded business reasons, in which to most extend their operations.[27]

Playing off the theme of trans-Pacific unity was the fair's decorative style, called "Jap-Alaskan" and evident in the totem poles connected by strings of Japanese lanterns in the Pay Streak. As far as its meaning, "Jap-Alaskan" architecture was ambiguous; on the one hand, it could read as symbolic of a coalescing Pacific world and shared United States–Japan interests, but, by the same token, it could also be regarded as an expression of America's view of Japan and Asia as its next frontier.

Indeed, throughout the exposition, Japan was treated as an honored guest. Upon accepting the A-Y-P's invitation to participate, the Japanese government supported the formation of a Japan Exhibits Association by leading businessmen and granted subsidies toward the construction of an exhibits building, which was formally dedicated on the fairgrounds on July 21, 1909 (see Figure 2.2). An impressive, visually imposing structure intended to be a representation of typical Japanese architecture, it came complete with curved pagoda roofs and tea gardens. Inside, dozens of exhibitors represented nearly all branches of Japanese government and industry. The Japanese Exhibits pamphlet distributed at the fair catalogued the array of fine commercial goods on display, such as pearls, silks, woolen carpets, wood cabinets, bronze lanterns, ornaments, embroidery, porcelains, dolls, and swords. In a speech given at the building's dedication ceremony, Thomas Burke praised Japan for its stunning military rise at the expense of China and Russia:

> What happened to Japan at the close of her victorious war against China? Nearly the whole world believed that China by the mere brute force of her overwhelming numbers would crush Japan. When however, by steady and persevering courage, great efforts and great sacrifices Japan came off victorious, one of the most powerful nations of Europe with the tacit consent of the rest, stepped in and, taking

Figure 2.2. The Japan Building dedication at the Alaska-Yukon-Pacific Exposition, Seattle, July 21, 1909. In this photograph by Frank Nowell, the formality and scale of the dedication ceremony indicate Japan's elevated position at the fair. *(Source: University of Washington Libraries, Special Collections, Nowell x2913.)*

advantage of Japan's weakness and exhaustion at the close of a great war, compelled her to give up the fruits of her well earned victory.[28]

Also in the course of the fair, the Japanese government presented U.S. President William Taft with an Ando vase worth $5,000. This vase was reportedly the most valuable gift given to the president by a foreign government at the A-Y-P, another noted distinction for Japan at the exposition.[29]

Other highlights included the four-day visit of a forty-six-member delegation of Japanese business and civic leaders who attended the fair as guests of the federal government and Associated Chambers of Commerce of the Pacific Coast. Their visit gave concrete expression to the exposition's "bridging" the United States and Japan (see Figure 2.3). Great fanfare marked the delegation's arrival aboard the *Minnesota* into the Great Northern Steamship Company dock on September 1. Thousands of greeters—"both Occidental and Oriental"—including the mayor of Seattle, the president of the Seattle Chamber of Commerce, a reception committee of Seattle Japanese, and about one hundred students from the local Japanese school, jubilantly welcomed the visitors, cheering and waving American and Japanese flags.[30] Throughout its visit, the delegation was honored during receptions hosted by the Chamber of Commerce, the Mayor's Office, and key Seattle industrialists. The head of the Japanese delegation, Shibusawa Eiichi, the president of the First National Bank of Japan, concurred with the exposition committee that Seattle, thanks to its prime geographic location and "wonderfully progressive and enterprising" qualities, had become a "gateway between the United States and Japan."[31]

September 4, the last day of the Japanese delegation's visit, was designated Japan Day, further signifying the nation's elevated position at the exposition. According to the *Seattle Star,* this day was to be the climax of the entire fair: "No event touching the future good of the Pacific Northwest, with Seattle in particular to share in it, has been arranged in the scheme of ceremonies and entertainment at the Alaska-Yukon-Pacific Exposition to compare with that which will occur when Japan Day, next Saturday, is observed on the event of the arrival here of the most distinguished party of Japanese that has ever visited these shores."[32]

Figure 2.3. The Japanese trade delegation's arrival at the Great Northern Steamship Company dock, Smith Cove, Seattle, September 1, 1909. *(Source: University of Washington Libraries, Special Collections, UW21813z.)*

The *Seattle Times* described Japan Day as "by far the greatest demonstration of the land of the chrysanthemum yet made on the Western continent," and the *Los Angeles Times* remarked, "never outside of Asia have so many Japanese been assembled as were gathered in the Alaska-Yukon-Pacific Exposition grounds today to celebrate Japan Day."[33] The program included two parades—one through Nihonmachi and one on the fairgrounds—consisting of fourteen floats, members of the delegation from Japan, and Japanese merchants and children from Seattle. Seemingly unaware that many of the Japanese people in the parade were long-time Seattle residents, the *Los Angeles Times* observed, "The city parade was led by a mounted Samurai warrior in a suit of mail and a white bandage about his head, looking like a picture from the Middle Ages. Close upon his heels came dozens of automobiles carrying dignified brown men wearing frock coats and high hats. The young women in automobiles that followed the commissioners were dressed and acted like American girls."[34] The procession included celebrations of United States–Japan relations and Japan's military rise, such as a mini-replica of Commodore Matthew Perry's flagship, the *Powhatan,* and a float commemorating Japan's conquest of Korea. Other festivities included a lunchtime lawn party outside the Japan Exhibits Building, musical performances, and a fireworks show that promised to "eclipse in grandeur all of the American fireworks displays."[35]

It is worth pausing to reflect upon this curious assembling of symbols that simultaneously celebrated aspirations of American and Japanese empire (i.e., Perry in Japan, Japan in Korea). In utilizing the framework of empire to examine American world's fairs, scholars have clarified our understanding of these events' relationship to the arrival of the United States as a global player, the expansion of American power abroad, the rationalization of territorial conquest, and the consolidation of white national identity during the late nineteenth and early twentieth centuries.[36] Explaining Japan's participation at American world's fairs, however, calls for some modification of this framework, because Japan was seeking to advance economic and political interests of its own in the Pacific. Historians Akira Iriye and Eiichiro Azuma have pointed out how the parallel, at times competing, imperialisms of the United States and Japan significantly shaped diplomacy in the Pacific Rim and social patterns in the American West during the early twentieth century.[37] In light of these conditions, Japanese immigrants in America negotiated an unusual, delicate, and impossibly complex position as a people "between two empires."

Indeed, Japanese American participation at the A-Y-P demonstrated the opportunities and dilemmas of being "between two empires." The publicity for the fair put a spotlight on Seattle's Japanese "colony," and members of the local Japanese American community actively contributed to helping their country of origin make a strong showing. According to the fair's official guidebook, Japan's presence was bolstered by the fact that "Seattle has the largest Japanese population in any city in the United States." Furthermore, "the Japanese merchants," of Seattle and Japan, "are taking a deep interest in the Alaska-Yukon-Pacific Exposition, and propose that the Japanese exhibit shall be one of the most interesting on the grounds."[38] Additionally, the *Seattle Times* stated that Japan Day was a proud moment for "the Japanese of two hemispheres," referring to the "distinguished members of the Imperial Japanese Commission" and "the up-and-coming sons of the Mikado who now make this city and this Coast their home."[39] "It is a safe assumption," related the paper, "that most of them were in the fair, Japanese government officials who have traveled all over the world say that there has never been such as assembling of their people outside Japan."[40]

Aware that an impressive showing by Japan would rely on the participation of local Japanese, the exposition corporation secured the cooperation of Japanese American business leaders, the Japanese Association, and other organizations more than a year before the fair's opening. Issei business leaders played especially important roles, seizing the chance to work toward the interrelated goals of boosting Japan's reception, promoting their own interests, and cultivating a positive image of Japanese in America. The A-Y-P board appointed businessman Tatsuya Arai as a trustee and charged him with getting local Japanese to contribute to and to attend the fair. A committee consisting of Japanese small business owners, bankers, labor contractors, the consul general, and a representative of the Japanese government and led by Charles Tetsuo Takahashi, vice president of the Oriental Trading Company, organized the entire Japan Day celebration. Like Arai, Takahashi hoped to persuade local Japanese to "take an interest in the exposition and do their best to give Japan a splendid representation by their exhibits."[41] Additionally, Masajiro Furuya, Takahashi, and Arai, three of the most powerful Japanese businessmen in Seattle, joined forces to build the "Streets of Tokio" on the Pay Streak. In nearly all aspects of Japan's participation at the A-Y-P, local Japanese were involved, from sponsoring parade floats and hosting receptions for visiting dignitaries to being the visionaries and planners of Japan Day, the Streets of Tokio, and other popular attractions.

Japan's reception at the Seattle exposition and other world's fairs contrasted greatly with the treatment that other Asians endured. The Philippines' Igorot Village was a very popular attraction at Seattle's and previous world's fairs, but the inclusion of "these strange head-hunting, dog-eating people" clearly catered to visitors' curiosities about "primitive" people while affirming the American mission of "benevolent supremacy" in the Philippines.[42] Nor did China elicit respectful treatment or rhetoric. The Chinese government declined to participate in the A-Y-P, in protest of immigration exclusion and the poor treatment of Chinese employees at earlier expositions. As a result, Chinese immigrants from the Seattle area had to go it alone in organizing and financing representation for their country of origin.[43] For the A-Y-P, the Seattle Chinese merchants Goon Dip (who was friendly with John Chilberg and was an honorary consul to Washington, Idaho, and Alaska) and Ah King, stepped up to put together a China Village, to plan China Day celebrations, to set up concessions, and to bring in performers from Shanghai. However, without a government's official backing, the Chinese at the A-Y-P were limited to such amusements as acrobat shows, juggling acts, and rickshaw rides.[44]

Such contrasting receptions reflected differences in the size and makeup of Asian American communities as well as the international standing of the countries from which they came. Throughout the American West, Chinese, Japanese, and Filipino immigrants had all been subject to "cheap labor" accusations, disfranchised by racially discriminatory laws, and targeted by negative stereotyping. Yet by 1909, Japanese Americans were enjoying comparative class advantages over Chinese and Filipinos due to their larger numbers and higher rates of entrepreneurship. In terms of the international context, Japan was regarded by Western nations as a modernizing Asian country on the verge of catching up to them and was, thus, accorded more respect than China and the Philippines. Trying to explain the nation's economic and military progress, a reporter at the 1904 St. Louis World's Fair speculated that Japanese people must be more racially complex than other "Orientals."[45] Already deemed a declining civilization, China found its international esteem suffering further when thousands of its settlers in the United States became targets of ridicule and mistreatment during the late nineteenth century. Emigration from Japan to the continental United States occurred on the heels of Chinese exclusion and coincided with Japan's rise in international politics. Determined not to repeat China's experience, the government carefully regulated emigration and maintained consular offices near immigrant settlements. Furthermore, when an anti-Japanese movement intensified in the United States during the first decade of the twentieth century, Japan was able to avoid the indignity of a legislative ban on its nationals by the receiving country by preemptively restricting the emigration of male laborers through the Gentlemen's Agreement of 1907.

The lavish spectacles and feel-good rhetoric of the A-Y-P glossed over the underlying but ever-present issue of white racism toward Japanese people in the United States. This tension was particularly relevant given the negotiation of the Gentlemen's Agreement just two years before the fair. The spirit of the fair was one of celebrating United States–Japan relations and the important facilitating role being played by Seattle's Japanese, but this celebration was contradicted by numerous instances of anti-Japanese racism on the ground and in the local memory. Members of Seattle's white working class were especially active and visible in anti-Japanese politics. In 1906, the Asiatic Exclusion League of North America, one of the largest and most virulently anti-Japanese groups at the time, held its first international convention in Seattle. A-Y-P organizers, already well under way with their work, worried the event would undermine their efforts to secure strong Asian participation, so the Seattle Commercial Club, a key organizing body of the A-Y-P, urged residents to "[show] their civilization and good manners at all times in dealing with our transpacific neighbors" and to "[frown] upon any expression of blind race prejudice, and . . . promote good feelings, confidence and extensive trade relations."[46]

Although at the fair and elsewhere Japanese were attributed advantages over the "declining" Chinese and "primitive" Indians and Filipinos, the qualification that they were mere "little brown men" tempered appraisals of their positive qualities. As shown earlier, the *Los Angeles Times* even described the distinguished Imperial Japanese Commission in these terms. The underlying assumption that Japan's impetus to modernize came from the United States certainly diminished its achievements, and although Japan ranked high as an Asian power, it would presumably always lag behind white nations. Descriptions of Japan and its people, such as "Children's Paradise" and "Yankees of the Pacific," were patronizing and referential to the United States. And lest Japan's treatment and local Japanese Americans' presence at the A-Y-P be interpreted as evidence of white Seattle's acceptance of Japanese people as potential full-fledged members of American society, J. H. McGraw, the exposition's vice president, clarified, "While we all admire the Japanese, we cannot for a moment approve of their becoming citizens of the republic."[47]

The lack of public discussion of salient issues such as immigration restriction and racial prejudice also indicated Japan's desire to avoid embarrassment and to maintain the fair's focus on international friendship. Shibusawa Eiichi tried to put a positive spin on immigration restriction as enforced by the Gentlemen's Agreement, telling a group of Seattle businessmen at the A-Y-P that the measure allowed Japan to retain crucial labor for its own industrialization.[48] That the agreement was negotiated in the wake of a controversy surrounding an order by the San Francisco Board of Supervisors to place

Japanese children into a racially segregated Oriental school was nowhere acknowledged. Although the fair established Japan's importance as a consumer of American goods and possible gateway to Asia and showed that Japanese in Seattle were symbols of Seattle's cosmopolitanism, these conditions would not translate to equality for Japanese Americans, nor were Japanese officials willing to publicly point out and to protest this contradiction.

These issues aside, the A-Y-P was a breakthrough for Seattle. Attended by an estimated 3.7 million people and occurring over 138 days, it heralded a new Pacific Era and showcased Seattle as the premier city of the Northwest and the "gateway to the Orient." It demonstrated Seattle's unique blending of urbanity and nature, which distinguished it from eastern cities.[49] The fair also clarified Seattle's relationship with Japan by emphasizing the city's determination to be a critical staging ground of United States–Japan commerce and diplomacy. It furthermore stressed that local Japanese Americans would play central roles in these relations. By placing focus on the Japanese "colony," the exposition showed that, in addition to facilitating international relations, the city itself was being transformed by international relations. A description in the *American Review of Reviews* of the A-Y-P's opening captured this transformation, which surely must have pleased fair officials and other local boosters: "Opening day found a cosmopolitan gathering in Seattle to see the fair. A seaport on the Pacific is always cosmopolitan. Seattle on June 1 was strikingly so." As to what gave the scene its cosmopolitanness, the article continued:

> They were all on hand, slant-eyed Chinamen, gazing about always in their child-like innocence of manner, turbaned Hindus, dusky natives of the Pacific islands, unassuming gentlemen from the South American coast, and predominating among them all the sturdy little brown men of Japan, neatly dressed, courteous, intelligent, seemingly more thoroughly American in manners and tastes than many an American who gazed curiously at them. These foreigners of the Pacific, sprinkled freely among the crowds, gave to the exposition opening half of its uniqueness.[50]

The passage conveys ambivalence about the pronounced international character of seaports on the Pacific, and this ambivalence represents a central tension in cosmopolitan discourse in Seattle. The claim of cosmopolitanism here points to the presence of "foreigners of the Pacific," which implies the seaport's accessibility to foreign lands. Because Seattle was part of a nation where whiteness was a normative requirement for full membership and that, as an "Occidental" power, defined itself in opposition to the "Orient," cosmopolitanism, as it was depicted at the fair, was workable only at a very superficial level; for the city to be truly cosmopolitan, it would have to integrate these "foreigners" into the social fabric so they were no longer foreigners. This would make the city less white and hence less American, an unacceptable outcome. As long as Japanese people and "gateway to the Orient" status were central to Seattle's pursuit of growth and modernization, these tensions and contradictions would remain.

After the Fair

In the decades after the A-Y-P, Seattle continued its economic and demographic expansion, although at more modest rates compared to the previous twenty years. As an increasingly physically spread out and socioeconomically stratified city, it also confronted a new set of growing pains and tensions. World War I provided a boost to the shipbuilding industry and to the Seattle economy as a whole, but, with the war's end, the momentum dissipated, and the city sank into a depression. Additionally, social and economic fissures beset the city in the 1910s and 1920s, manifesting as moral-reform campaigns, class conflict, radical politics, and populist discontent against "the Interests." A labor movement drawing on moderate and radical energies harnessed rising worker discontent during the mid-1910s and culminated in the Seattle general strike of 1919. However, the volatility associated with the movement as well as the onset of the postwar depression strengthened the resolve of employers and anti-Red forces, who succeeded in crushing the power of labor until the 1930s.[51]

Throughout this period, waterborne commerce with Asia was a crucial pillar of Seattle's economy, and by the mid-1920s the city could, with legitimacy, claim "gateway to the Orient" status (see Figure 2.4). In 1922, according to the Port of Seattle, it was the fifth busiest port in the country in terms of the value of imports and exports handled, and in 1928, the port agency claimed Seattle was the second busiest behind New York.[52] International trade had long been key to the local economy, and, by the early 1930s, some twenty-three steamship lines berthing in Seattle provided service to Asia, Europe, South America, and Australia. In terms of Asian trade, imports from China and Japan in 1916 were worth $117 million, jumped to $168 million in 1919, and continued an uninterrupted growth into the 1920s.[53] Toward the end of the 1910s, Asian trade made up about 40 percent of the value of all waterborne commerce in Seattle (California and Alaska remained crucial), but of foreign trade, Asian trade accounted for 90 percent.[54] As far as the

Public Terminals Connected with all Transcontinental Rail Lines

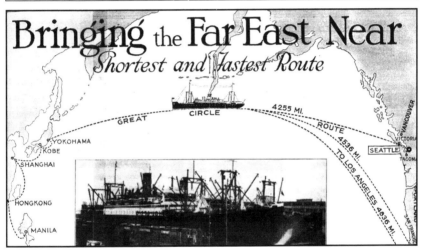

Figure 2.4. Advertisements from the *Port of Seattle Bulletin* illustrating how the city attempted to bolster its share of foreign trade by identifying with the "Far East" or "Orient." The routes to Asia from Seattle and other West Coast ports are compared to convince American manufacturers to use Seattle's facilities. *(Source:* Port of Seattle Bulletin, *July–August 1924 and November–December 1925.)*

Japan trade, the bulk of imports from the Island Empire reached the United States via Seattle, an estimated 80 percent in 1924.[55] Furthermore, between 1922 and 1931, Japanese imports—much of which was silk—made up 80 percent of Seattle's foreign waterborne commerce, while nearly 40 percent of goods shipped from Seattle were en route to Japan.[56] The height of the Japan trade was in 1925, when imports were valued at $241 million.[57] During the Depression years, United States–Japan trade dropped precipitously, hitting a low in 1934, although the value of imports remained in the tens of millions, Japan was the third-largest U.S. trading partner, and the United States was Japan's largest.[58]

As Seattle and Japan developed and strengthened these commercial ties, whites and Japanese in the city also formed connections with one another, often in the guise of promoting trans-Pacific relations and Seattle's continued prosperity. As the *Town Crier* explained in 1918:

> [The Japanese of Seattle] are an ever increasing element in our commercial life and our trade relations with their country is one of the most important factors with which Seattle has to reckon. No less is the existing good relationship with our Japanese corporations one of the essentials that will reap for Seattle to the practical exclusion of other ports, the benefits of the tremendous trans-Pacific trade.[59]

Although forged on large-scale visions of commerce and prosperity, these relationships also resonated locally. Contacts between business and civic organizations were important sites where white-Japanese relations in Seattle played out, with such groups as the Japan Society and the Chamber of Commerce on the Anglo side, and the Japanese Association, Seattle Japanese Chamber of Commerce, and the JACL on the Japanese side.

Among white Seattleites, leading capitalists, internationalists, social progressives, and cultural elites advocated positive relations with local Japanese, viewing this connection as an important part of maintaining good relations with Japan. Furthermore, this link between trans-Pacific and local concerns was reflected in the urban social and cultural landscape well into the 1930s. Established in 1923 with the goal of promoting economic and diplomatic relations with Japan, the Japan Society included such prominent members as E. G. Anderson of Western Dry Goods (and first president); Herbert Gowen, the Episcopal minister and first professor in the University of Washington's Oriental Studies department; and Thomas Burke, the judge and former counsel for the Great Northern Railway. A steadfast friend of Japanese business, the society coordinated and participated in activities aimed at boosting Japan's presence in Seattle, such as throwing a celebration to honor Emperor Hirohito's coronation in 1930.[60]

Such groups as the Japan Society and the Chamber of Commerce helped ensure that United States–Japan relations would be linked to Seattle's economy and civic identity. They also worked to maintain good public relations between the city and its Japanese residents. The activities and explicit goals of these organizations assured local Japanese of some measure of visibility in

the urban landscape and inclusion in various public celebrations. This visibility grew over time, as in the decades following the A-Y-P, representations
of Japan in local celebrations were increasingly the efforts of local Japanese
Americans, not the Japanese government. For example, in 1930, on behalf
of the Japanese American community, the Seattle Japanese Chamber of
Commerce ceremoniously presented thirty-five hundred cherry trees to the
city.[61] At the Federation of Business and Professional Women convention in
Seattle in July 1935, whose theme was "international amity," conventioneers
were treated to a Pacific Rim banquet as well as an entertainment program
coordinated by the Japanese Cultural Center, which included a group of
Nisei girls performing traditional dances and a tea ceremony.[62] Also, the
city's annual Commodore Perry Day commemorations celebrating United
States–Japan relations invariably involved the participation of local Japanese
American performers, whose corporeal presence presumably brought at least
a visual authenticity to the proceedings.[63]

Implicitly and explicitly, the promotion of Seattle as a "gateway to the
Orient" nurtured a sense of civic belonging among Japanese Americans and
gave validation to the view that they were important to citywide affairs.
Certainly this appeared to be the case when Chamber of Commerce officials
attended Seattle JACL conventions. The contacts between the Chamber of
Commerce and JACL were especially strong and enduring from the late
1920s to 1930s. Voicing the common view in the Seattle business community that promoting United States–Japan trade, Seattle's economic well-being, and positive inroads with the local Japanese American community were
interrelated goals, the president of the Seattle Chamber of Commerce, Wylie
Hemphill, stated in 1931, "As a city, Seattle is particularly charged with this
pleasant duty [of contributing to the mutual understanding of the Japanese
and the American people], because of the closeness to the ports of Japan,
and because of the excellent citizenship of our own Japanese people, who are
so responsive to all movements for the common good in this community."[64]

A later Seattle Chamber of Commerce president, King Dykeman, held
a regular subscription to the *Japanese-American Courier*. He corresponded
with the publisher, James Sakamoto, and on one occasion praised the paper
for being an important conduit between the business community and the
city's Japanese Americans. "I am hopeful and confident," wrote Dykeman
in a letter to Sakamoto, "that the reading of your newspaper will afford us
still further basis of understanding and therefore will be helpful in carrying
out our constant desire to maintain and increase the friendly and pleasant
relationships of the Japanese and American peoples."[65]

Nisei leaders appropriated the rhetoric of white business leaders and boosters to make a case for their ethnic community's importance to Seattle and United States–Japan relations. Chief among them was James Sakamoto, who advocated that Nisei could and should be "pure Americans" *and* "bridges of understanding" between the United States and Japan.[66] As late as 1938, the *Japanese-American Courier* belatedly predicted that Seattle would become the "Queen City" of the Pacific Coast, with its future greatness built on trade and commerce: "The fact that this city is the nearest Coast port to the Orient will soon play an important part in building and development of a coming metropolis."[67] Of course, nothing was new about such pronouncements in the history of Seattle, but Sakamoto and the *Courier* added their own perspectives to the discourse by suggesting that if U.S. interests in commerce and diplomacy had indeed shifted to the Pacific, then Japanese Americans in Seattle could play crucial roles in brokering international and intercultural relationships.[68] "There on the opposite rims of the Pacific basin standing face to face are the two great nations upon which the future of the Pacific era largely depends," remarked the *Courier.*[69]

This coming civilization, in which Japan and the United States would be the leaders, "would hold within its cultural confines the veritable propensities of a melting pot, of civilizations, cultures and peoples."[70] As the paper also pointed out, signs of progress were already evident on the West Coast and in Hawaii, where the Orient and Occident were "fusing": "The substantial number of Japanese-Americans, Chinese-Americans, and other Americans of this category right here on the coast and in Hawaii prove [that the international day] is coming."[71] In another article in the *Japanese-American Courier,* lawyer and prominent Nisei Clarence Arai pointed out that they operated one-third of the hotels in the city, 150 grocery stories, 100 fruit stands, about 50 dye works, 45 restaurants, and about 20 butcher shops. These activities gave them a stake in the city at large and validated their claims to Americanness. Arai asserted, "Assimilation means, 'Participation of the immigrant in the life of the community in which he lives'; and the Japanese, like all other immigrants, have also become a 'part of American life.'"[72]

Such expressions of goodwill did not reflect the outlook of everyone in the city, and it is important to note that the rhetoric regarding Seattle's cosmopolitan qualities and "gateway to the Orient" status was largely confined to the elites of the city. Seattle and the rest of the American West experienced a revived anti-Japanese movement during the 1910s and early 1920s, in which business owners, farmers, and laborers all joined the fray. In Washington, this movement culminated with the passage of an alien land law in 1921, and nationally the 1924 Johnson-Reed Act proscribed Japanese immigration based on this group's status as "aliens ineligible to citizenship."

Beginning with Japan's invasion of Manchuria in 1931, the nation's increasingly aggressive maneuvers in Asia contributed to anti-Japanese feelings in the United States, escalating in the Pacific war.

Yet, as Izumi Hirobe has shown, evidence suggests that internationalist and pro-Japan sentiments persisted in Seattle and elsewhere, countering some of the energy and arguments of anti-Japanese forces.[73] In pockets along the West Coast, civic, business, and religious groups advocated continued friendship between the people and governments of the United States and Japan from the 1920s right up until 1941. In Seattle, the Chamber of Commerce was one of the sole voices that opposed the alien land act as the Washington legislature debated the proposed legislation.[74] After the 1924 Johnson-Reed Act was passed, the Seattle Chamber of Commerce joined up with other West Coast chambers of commerce to argue for the modification of the law by granting Japan a quota. The Seattle Chamber of Commerce, along with the Japan Society, supported this movement, no doubt, because of members' vested economic and political interests in continuing positive relations with Japan. Although the movement to modify the 1924 Immigration Act was initially coordinated among several chambers of commerce, ultimately, the Seattle Chamber stood alone among West Coast cities in passing a pro-quota resolution in 1930.[75]

The International Potlatch

By the mid-1930s, as the nation was mired in the Great Depression and was confronting uncertainty in the Pacific with respect to Japan's intentions in Asia and the prospects for peace in the region, business leaders in Seattle were thinking about how to pull their community out of the doldrums while promoting their own interests. The idea to revive an annual summer festival called the Potlatch came from the Seattle Chamber of Commerce, which hoped the event would stimulate the local economy, raise residents' morale, and bring in tourist dollars. Held from 1934 and 1942, it became Seattle's largest annual celebration during these years.

As an annual civic celebration, the Potlatch festival actually originated in 1911, when it was called the Golden Potlatch and was held to commemorate the 1897 Klondike gold rush. Though tightly coordinated by the Potlatch Association, the event was portrayed as a mass undertaking, an opportunity for "all Seattle to stand together."[76] The florid rhetoric of the Potlatch's promoters was typically grander than the event itself. Locals claimed it would rival New Orleans's Mardi Gras and Portland's Rose Festival, and, before the 1911 Golden Potlatch, the *Town Crier* challenged San Francisco, stating,

"Seattle is the Golden Gate in fact."[77] In a "royal ceremony" opening the first Potlatch, the "King of Alaska," played by Charles Heifner, predicted: "Within the span of our own lives we confidently expect to behold . . . a city equaling, if not surpassing, in wealth, beauty, power, and influence the famous principalities of Paris, Vienna, and Berlin."[78] A riot fomented by labor unrest at the 1913 Potlatch hastened the hiatus of the affair until the 1930s.

As an annual event reflecting the city's image and economy, the Potlatch, like the A-Y-P, was a window into Seattle's image-making process and aspirations. Representing Seattle as a metropolitan center of refinement and social and cultural activity was of highest importance to the organizers. For instance, a pressing debate before the 1913 Potlatch involved whether to include a cattle roundup, which some residents felt was too crude and unbecoming of a city with refined aspirations. The *Town Crier* editorialized about the issue and agreed that a cattle roundup was a brutal spectacle incongruous with the spirit of the Potlatch.[79] In describing what made Seattle unique, the Potlatch's 1934 pamphlet touted the "genius" of the city's "vigorous, urbane youth, sufficiently sophisticated by the old embroidered civilizations of the Orient to have a distinct and rare cosmopolitan charm."[80] Organizers would also carefully consider parade float entries to reflect the city appropriately.

In this second incarnation, it was renamed the International Potlatch and conceived to be more lavish, inclusive of a wider variety of programs and venues, and, as the new name suggested, international. Some of the perennial attractions at the International Potlatch were sporting tournaments, a pet parade held at Woodland Park, the crowning of a Potlatch queen at Sick Stadium, a powwow at Seward Park, fireworks shows, historical commemorations (such as the dedication of a Totem Pole in Pioneer Place during the 1941 Potlatch), and a street parade.

Like the A-Y-P, the International Potlatch invoked Seattle's past by drawing on Native imagery and looked to the future with references to trans-Pacific commerce. The following quotation from the official program for the 1934 Potlatch provides an example of the rhetorical finessing that accompanied white Seattleites' appropriation of Native American practices and images:

And now in 1934, we white men and women of Seattle and the Pacific Northwest have decided to adopt the old, really cultural *intertribal* Indian idea and to extend it to *international* proportions. . . . Yet our real purpose is to hold open house, to extend invitations to our Potlatches, not only up and down this Pacific coast and inland, as the Indians did, but to send them also across the seas of the world to nations of other continents than our own—that we may come to know them better than we do, and that by joining our hands with theirs in friendship they may come to have an understanding and affection for us.[81]

By claiming to remain true to the original spirit of the Indian potlatch while expanding its reach from a regional practice to an international one, whites in Seattle neutralized a troubled and violent history of white-Indian encounters in the Pacific Northwest to extend their gesture of urban hospitality to the world. Drawing on the local Native American heritage, the Potlatch aimed mainly to promote the contemporary interest of international trade, and the Native practice's connotations of goodwill to neighbors suited this goal:

> For "excuse" for its Potlatch, if such be needed, Seattle harks back to the "gold days"; more particularly to that day in 1897 when the steamship Portland made her way up Elliot Bay with the first of the cargoes of riches with which the great Northland has since endowed the world. The foundation of Seattle's perennial prosperity is laid literally in the gold of the North and the Potlatch is the expression of Seattle's appreciation of the debt it owes Alaska.[82]

The name "International Potlatch" was in itself incongruous for many reasons. By the 1930s, the Seattle Indian population had virtually disappeared, and since the mid-1800s, with the arrival of white American missionaries, the Northwest Coast potlatch practice had been under attack and was very much on the decline.[83] As Coll Thrush has shown regarding the 1910s potlatch, white participants used Indian imagery to "sell the city."[84] This use was not new or unique to the Potlatch, but the brazenness of the cultural appropriation in this example is particularly notable. Perhaps the most striking instance was the Tilikums of Elttaes, a fake Indian tribe made up of white men that appeared annually at the Potlatch festival. A classic example of what Phil Deloria terms "playing Indian," the Tilikims took part in one Potlatch parade in canoes that were aloft on floats, and another year, they marched in white gowns and with totem poles atop their heads. Such performances and appropriations as well as place names throughout the city, says Thrush, expressed residents' "love with its Native American heritage," but not with Native American peoples.[85]

The "international" gaze of the Potlatch was fixed upon Asia and the

Pacific, and the "gateway to the Orient" remained a prominent theme in the 1930s Potlatches, even though over that decade, United States–Japan trade was on the decline and diplomatic relations were increasingly strained. Despite these conditions, Japanese trade remained an important part of Seattle's economy, and local business and civic leaders were still wedded to the ideal of United States–Japan friendship. Drawing a baffling parallel between Native American practices and Seattle's commerce with Asia, the program for the 1934 event stated:

> We shall show them what safe anchorages we have for the greatest of modern liners, and by tracing on maps, as the Indians did on sand, draw attention to the fact that we are 1,200 miles closer to the Far East than other Pacific harbors of the United States. For we of this Northwest face Asia's billion people, just across the Pacific from us, who are casting aside all old superstitions and medieval ways and commencing to demand countless modern products that are made right here in America in prodigious quantities. For while *we* know that Seattle and Puget Sound is America's most logical Gateway to the Orient, the rest of the world will not know it until we make it— very clear.[86]

Such rhetorical grandiosity was by this time common practice in Seattle promotional literature and underscored how the city continued to anchor its identity to the "Pacific world" concept. The International Potlatch would highlight the "genius" of the city's "vigorous, urbane youth, sufficiently sophisticated by the old embroidered civilizations of the Orient to have a distinct and rare cosmopolitan charm."[87] Toward realizing this vision of urban sophistication and "cosmopolitan charm," the Potlatches of the 1930s sought to better represent the city's ethnic communities. In 1934, for example, the downtown area at University between Fourth and Fifth avenues was transformed into "Orient Square," and members of the Scandinavian and Japanese "colonies" were on hand to perform their national folk dances in front of the Metropolitan Theater.[88]

The bestowing of a 26-foot-tall Japanese torii, or entry gate to a Shinto shrine, to the city during the 1934 Potlatch brought into focus the ways in which the interests of urban boosterism, Japanese trade, and the Japanese American community had become deeply intertwined. Potlatch organizers cast this moment as signal of United States–Japan friendship, even though the torii was a gift from the Seattle Japanese Chamber of Commerce and was designed and built by Seattle Japanese Americans; the Japanese government played no role. An inscription on the structure spelled out the city's long sought-after identification: "Seattle Gateway to the Orient." The torii was said to symbolize "Seattle's wonderful geographical advantages in the gigantic future trade of the Pacific" and the "bond between the Potlatch and the Seattle Japanese Chamber of Commerce and the entire Japanese community of this City."[89] Clifton Pease, the executive secretary of the Seattle Chamber of Commerce, affirmed, "The fine and generous gift of the beautiful Torii will remain a permanent and striking testimonial of the fine spirit of the Japanese people of Seattle."[90] Put on permanent display at Seward Park, the torii, which Monica Sone described as "a bit of Oriental heaven which the Seattle Japanese had helped to create," stood as symbols of the Japanese presence in the city as well as United States–Japan friendship.[91]

Judging from the letters that were exchanged between Potlatch officials and Japanese American participants, the presence of Japanese people and representations of Japan were vital to the event's success each year. Further, organizers' hearty expressions of gratitude to the Japanese American community following the potlatches validated members' quest for local belonging. Pease said that Japanese Americans' participation affirmed their importance to the entire city, stating in a 1934 letter to Seiji Hara of the Japanese Chamber of Commerce, "I am more than happy that . . . Seattle citizens in general and our guests had the opportunity to more fully recognize the prominent part played in this Northwest by the Japanese people."[92] Mayor Charles Smith, moreover, said that Japanese Americans' presence at the Potlatch was critical for making the event "broadly representative" and "truly [a] community celebration"; after the 1934 Potlatch, the president of the Seattle Chamber of Commerce, Alfred Lundin, stated, "In going over the affairs of the recent Potlatch celebration, no feature stands out more conspicuously than the participation of the Japanese people of this city."[93] To ensure the presence of Japanese people at the festival, letters would go out each year from the Seattle Chamber of Commerce, the Mayor's Office, and the Potlatch committee to the Seattle Japanese Chamber of Commerce, inviting Japanese Americans to attend and to send submissions for various parts of the program. As preparations for the 1935 festival got under way, Dorothy Snowden, the director of the Potlatch pageant, requested that local Japanese participate, recalling their performance at the 1934 pageant. "Remembering the wonderful cooperation of the Japanese American citizens in the past," wrote Snowden, "we have written a special sequence into the 1935 script for your colorful dancers and musicians."[94]

Through appearing at the annual Potlatch, Japanese Americans proved to be crucial players in the embodiment of Seattle cosmopolitanism, and,

Figure 2.5. The Japanese Chamber of Commerce float in the Potlatch parade on Second Avenue in Seattle, 1939. The Potlatch festival opened on July 25 and ran for five days. *(Source:* Seattle Post-Intelligencer *Collection, Museum of History and Industry.)*

through their participation, they could make persuasive claims to belonging in the city. This point was made especially concrete in the Potlatch street parades, which would usually proceed down Second Avenue toward Yesler Way. Tens of thousands of people, both locals and visitors, would turn out for these spectacles, which featured marching bands, drill teams, mounted cowboys, Washington National Guard batteries, the Potlatch queen and her princesses, the Seattle mayor and other public officials, and flowered floats submitted by various companies, towns, and civic and commercial organizations.[95] During the planning for the 1935 festival, a writer for the Japanese American newspaper the *Great Northern Daily News* boastfully predicted that Seattle's Japanese would "again take the spotlight" with a "magnificent" float.[96] Created by such organizations as the Japanese Chamber of Commerce, Japanese Boy Scouts, and Japanese Campfire Girls, these floats were major attractions and perennial prizewinners frequently noted for their size and creativity (see Figure 2.5). They often depicted events from Japanese history, such as a 1935 entry with historical figures from the Kamakura period, which was also awarded a silver cup.[97] A 1939 entry depicting United States–Japan amity won a cash prize of $25 in the noncommercial category.

Members of Seattle's Japanese community would each year greet the International Potlatch with eager anticipation, and they were not shy about expressing their desire to be the center of attention. In 1935, for instance, the *Great Northern Daily News* declared that Seattle's Japanese would make that year's Potlatch the "greatest ever held in this city."[98] The Japanese Chamber of Commerce usually took the lead in raising funds and designing a program. In 1935, when the Seattle JACL made its first contribution to the Potlatch, a group of Japanese girls in a *bon odori* for the pageant finale, many saw the significance of this involvement as the arrival of the Nisei generation and their chance to stake a place as *American-born* Japanese in the urban culture: "For the first time in the Potlatch celebration the members of the second generation, as an organized group, will be taking part in a city-wide celebration. The events of the coming week mean a few more gleams of the dawn of participation by the second generation in the community life of the city in Seattle."[99] Japanese Americans interested in the event approached the Potlatch with a spirit of competitiveness, as was the case when a columnist for the *Great Northern Daily News* chimed in on the debate over who should get to ride on Japanese floats in the parade, urging for "young bloods" over "seasoned products who lack springing life."[100]

CONCLUSION

To describe Seattle as cosmopolitan evoked the presence of "every race and nation" within the limits of the city and a particular intimacy with Asia and the Pacific. Yet with respect to race relations between white and Japanese Americans, Seattle cosmopolitanism rarely offered anything beyond "cultural browsing" experiences and symbolic appropriations. As discussed in the Introduction, during the early twentieth century, "cosmopolitanism" was an evocative concept that spoke to the internationalization of American society through foreign immigration. As it was conceived in Seattle, it placed primacy on the urban environment and the imagery of culturally diverse peoples coexisting in harmony, but it was also distinguished by its commercial, Asia-Pacific orientation and distinct Orientalist flair. When discourse about Seattle cosmopolitanism emphasized ethnic heterogeneity, as in Lancaster Pollard's essay discussed at the beginning of the chapter, Japanese people often figured prominently, but this form of inclusion was a strictly top-down formulation, informed and chiefly driven by white, elite commercial interests.

Efforts to make Seattle a cosmopolitan "gateway to the Orient" tell us more about the aspirations of its elites than it does about actual conditions there. To return to Pollard's "Cosmopolitan Seattle" series, his insistence on the city's cosmopolitan characteristics could not conceal aspects of life that remained decidedly uncosmopolitan, and beneath his and other boosters' celebratory claims of Seattle's sophistication and urbanity lurked insecurities rooted in the reality that the city had far to go before catching up to New York or Paris. Pollard himself revealed an inherent contradiction in the cosmopolitan formulation by admitting that Nihonmachi "was, and is, self-contained to a remarkable extent" and that the general public did not appreciate Japanese contributions to the cultural landscape.[101] Self-containment seemed to contradict the core of cosmopolitanism; after all, how cosmopolitan could a city really be if one of its main cultural communities was "not enjoyed as it well might be"?

Despite these contradictions, Japanese Americans found in cosmopolitan rhetoric, as problematic and limiting as it was, ways to mold their identities and to frame their activities in ways they found productive and affirming. The following chapter describes how a small but ambitious group of Japanese immigrant art photographers tapped into broader trends that not only brought together pictorialists from different nations but also celebrated the globe-trotting, genre-fusing artists to achieve—for a brief but exhilarating moment—a degree of international fame. It is an illustration of how the top-down cosmopolitanism could become a bottom-up resource for those very individuals objectified by its original aims and workings.

3

꛰꛱꛲

Making Local Images for International Eyes

Race, Nationality, and the
Seattle Camera Club, 1924–1929

A KIND OF PARADOX

In July 1927, following the Twenty-first Paris Salon, an exhibition of international photographic art, a French reviewer named Jean Chantavoine commented on the entries from a group of American artists whose work he found to be the most intriguing on display. He stated, "It is to America that we are indebted again for one of the most interestingly lighted landscapes in the Salon."[1] This was not the first time this group had been singled out for praise, as in the last few years the artists about whom Chantavoine wrote were known as active participants in the national and international photo exhibition circuits. They especially drew notice for their distinctive way of melding different cultural influences. Of this unique style, Chantavoine said:

> [It was] a kind of paradox, born of the mixture of races which America owes to immigration—one wishes that the United States would send an entire series of Japanese work. Distinctive and detached, even artificial, motivated not only by the desire to present the image of an object, but also the quality of pure design or of fantasy . . . all evoke here the traditions and above all the esthetic principles of Japanese art. In this group, attention is attracted by several other contributions which are American also, but which in spite of their place of origin, are from Japanese composers.[2]

As the quotation above reveals, these American artists were also Japanese; specifically, they were immigrants who belonged to the Seattle Camera Club (SCC).[3] Because pictorialism, the genre of art photography they were a part of, was a Western field that white Americans and Europeans dominated, discussion of the SCC members' racial ancestry and immigrant backgrounds often factored into appraisals of their work, which was noted for its combining of "Japanese treatment" with "American composition."[4] The SCC was the first pictorial organization in Washington, and, in its brief period of activity from 1924 to 1929, it became one of the most respected and renowned camera clubs on the West Coast. And because few other pictorialists worked in Seattle during the 1920s, art photography there was nearly synonymous with the exploits of the Japanese members of the SCC.

As unexpected as it may have been for a group of Issei photographers to be singled out at a Paris salon in 1927, for Seattle to be the home city for the production of such refined works of art was an equally an unlikely distinction. In the 1930s, Seattle and the Pacific Northwest enjoyed its first cultural heyday with the emergence of the Northwest School of art, but the 1920s, by contrast, are remembered as a relatively uneventful period when the city as a whole focused on recovering from the post–World War I economic depression, leaving broad-based local support for the fine arts wanting. Despite these conditions, and Seattle's place on the margins of attention when it came to the arts (and other areas), the 1920s were nonetheless formative years for the later emergence of a vibrant local art scene. For instance, Mark Tobey, who would come to wide attention as a member of the Northwest School of painting, moved to Seattle during the early part of the decade to teach art. Also, such establishments as the Seattle Symphony and Cornish School, although struggling throughout these years, maintained a presence and impetus for the fine arts.[5] The SCC was a part of this nascent yet dynamic creative scene, and a consideration of its place within Seattle's social and artistic landscape sheds light on key cultural aspects of urbanization. These are salient issues, because, for many cities, the pursuit of urban refinement and the cultivation of a local arts scene have often gone hand in hand.

This chapter examines the rise, success, and demise of the Seattle Camera Club from 1924 to 1929, with particular attention on how dynamics of race, place, and the international scope of pictorialism influenced the group's impact and legacy.[6] The pursuit of pictorialism, which anchored members locally while encouraging them to cross geographical and social boundaries, enabled them to negotiate racialized constraints of space and social relations that otherwise circumscribed the lives of all of Seattle's Japanese Americans. On the one hand, their achievements were locally significant, as their work contributed to a visual historical record of Seattle and the Puget Sound region, and they themselves often expressed desires to enrich art production and appreciation in the city. Taking pictures demanded observation and movement, and the pursuit of their craft took SCC photographers out of Nihonmachi to traverse the Puget Sound's urban and natural landscapes. The images they produced and the awe with which they regarded the area underlay their own claims to belonging and challenged their marginalization. Yet SCC members were also ambitious and creative artists with big dreams and hopes of impacting photographic art outside Seattle. Through their participation in national and international pictorial exhibitions, where images of their adopted city could be seen and appreciated, they advanced themselves as artists and helped boost Seattle's profile as a "world city." They also joined a diverse and gregarious pictorialist community, which was sustained by networks of camera clubs that extended across the globe.

However, as "Orientals" practicing a Western art form, SCC photographers faced a difficult predicament. On the one hand, being Japanese was key to their notoriety and status, but on the other hand, this heightened attention on their ancestry racialized and circumscribed them in ways that did not hinder their white counterparts. Their prominence in the field revealed the complex and intertwined meanings of race and nationality in America, and their Japanese-ness elicited perplexed discussions about what exactly determined an artist's national identity and constituted "American" art. At worst, it provoked racial chauvinism among the predominantly white artists and patrons in the local and global art communities. Because their popularity derived from their association with Japan and blending of Eastern and Western influences, the Issei pictorialists of Seattle were rarely identified or credited with helping develop an American artistic tradition. Further, the cosmopolitan ethos that underlay the pictorial movement may have permitted a prominent place for the Japanese photographers, but it ultimately failed to foster the sufficient local interest and heightened membership necessary to sustain the club into the 1930s and beyond.

Pictorialism and Art: A Background

To provide some background on pictorialism, this genre of art photography—the first art photography movement—emerged in Europe in the 1840s, although it did not become popular until the end of the nineteenth century.[7] Early pictorialists claimed that they were very much like painters in that their work incorporated aesthetics and represented interpretations of nature, but instead of paints and brushes, their creative tools were soft-focus lenses, lighting tricks, and careful composition. Artists and critics alike initially shunned photography and dismissed the notion that cameras, being machines, could generate authentic works of art. As cultural historian Lawrence Levine has explained, "Photography was a . . . serious threat to those who were sacralizing art [because] the camera could disseminate art among the masses. . . . [I]t could give a wide spectrum of people the very means of *creating* art."[8] It was not just the idea of using a machine to make art that irked traditionalists but also photography's association with amateurs and the masses—as cameras were relatively inexpensive and widely available by the turn of the twentieth century—and the fact that being a photographer did not require any formal training. These conditions would impede photography's entry into the ranks of "highbrow" art, but it did attain general acceptance as a legitimate art form by the early 1900s.

In the United States, the pictorialist movement spanned the turn of the twentieth century to the 1950s. Early American pictorialism is widely associated with Alfred Stieglitz and the small, elite, New York–based Photo-Secession movement.[9] As for the style and aesthetics of pictorialism, it initially retained its original Victorian influences and was characterized by sentimental, softly focused images, especially of "old-world" European locations and other traditional settings. Around the 1920s, modern elements became more commonplace in pictorialist compositions, in part due to the decline of the Photo-Secessionists, which opened up the field to a broader base of photographers and more diverse perspectives, influences, and styles. Presentations were still predominantly sentimental and softly focused, but works increasingly incorporated the use of sharp focus and contemporary subject matter, such as skyscrapers and automobiles.

A growth in the number of camera clubs in the United States after 1920 reflected the social and stylistic diversification of pictorialism as well as the growing popularity of taking pictures as a form of recreation and a way to spend one's time. *Photo-Era Magazine,* the national journal and booster of photography, estimated that some three million cameras were in use in America by 1927.[10] Camera clubs, independently formed and sponsored by companies and schools, typically consisted of twenty-five to fifty members and provided amateur photographers with outlets to share their work and to learn more about photography. In the 1910s and 1920s, fifty to seventy camera clubs existed nationwide, but in the 1930s, the number of clubs increased tenfold. Most cities of any size had at least one camera club, and large cities, such as New York and Chicago, boasted several.

One of the reasons for this significant spread of camera clubs in the early 1900s is what has been noted as a populist impulse that initially defined the field of pictorial photography. The field lacked a strong, central organization of national scope, and few professional training schools disseminated or controlled artistic standards for photography. Although the field of photographers was by and large white, middle-class, and male, amateurs dominated it, and it included more women than did the older, more traditional fine arts. For example, Imogen Cunningham, Clara E. Sipprell, Doris Ulmann, and Alaska-Yukon-Pacific Exposition seal designer Adelaide Hanscom were a few of the women who achieved notice through pictorial photography. The main arena of display, the photographic salon, was also a somewhat egalitarian institution in that anyone could submit entries for consideration, and the events were open to the public, usually free of charge.[11] Hosted by local camera clubs or photography organizations, salons might still be very selective and sometimes display as little as 10 percent of the works submitted. They could also be quite popular, as a single salon might draw tens of thousands of visitors. During the 1920s in the United States, about ten salons per year occurred on a regular basis, with many more being held in other parts of the world.

Art and Photography in Seattle

Because the Pacific Northwest was considered by many to be a visually stunning place that was sadly and woefully underappreciated by people outside the region, photographers there during the early 1900s spoke of a special responsibility they held: to share with the outside world the area's aesthetic beauty, for the sake of advancing art and for their regional and local pride. Appealing for its pristine natural scenery and modern cityscapes, the Northwest drew photographers Imogen Cunningham and brothers Edward and Asahel Curtis, who all spent time living and running studios in Seattle. By the 1910s, several pictorial clubs were formed in the region, one of the first being the Oregon Camera Club in 1895. In 1926, its president, C. L. Perkins, discussed the organization's mission, invoking the trope of "Manifest Destiny" and suggesting that photographers could help complete America's continental expansion by cultivating art and culture in the western reaches of the United States. "As the course of civilization has moved westward," said Perkins, "so also has the course of art and culture. Considered in the light of this movement, the Pacific Northwest is youthful in its development. Whatever our group can do toward the promotion of this intellectual expansion, is, we feel, of eminent value."[12]

We can also use the description "youthful in its development" to characterize the fine-arts scene in Seattle during the interwar years, although this description may be overly generous. In his history of Seattle, Roger Sale states of this period, "By the most obvious measurements of high culture Seattle was in those days impoverished and not just when compared with London but with some other provincial cities in America," and as late as 1941, Thomas Beecham, the director of the Seattle Symphony, derided the city as an "aesthetic dustbin."[13] Indeed, forging an art scene in Seattle and elsewhere in the Northwest must have felt like an epic and precarious effort until the mid-1930s, when artists there began generating positive national and international attention. The Seattle Fine Arts Society, founded in 1906, tried to drum up local interest, but, as historian Richard Berner explains, it was, through most of the 1920s, for all intents and purposes, a "small club."[14] The Cornish School, which had been established in 1914, promoted the creative arts in the city, recruiting painters, dancers, and musicians from all over the world and offering classes to locals, but its financial struggles during its early years were a constant problem.[15] Without a small handful of wealthy patrons that included Agnes Anderson, Margaret Fuller and her son Richard, and railroad builder Horace Henry, little, if any, support for local artists and art appreciation would have existed.

Outside the elite circle of arts patrons and its purview, but no less enthusiastic about the creative potential that existed in Seattle, was a group of immigrant Japanese pictorialists who emerged on the scene in the early 1920s. Initially, they had few outlets in which to display their work. In the early 1920s, the only major venue in the city for pictorialists to show their images was the Fredrick & Nelson Salon, held at the upscale department store downtown. In 1923, the *Great Northern Daily News* began sponsoring its own photographic exhibition to support the budding pictorialists. Established photographers with strong catalogs, such as Frank Kunishige and Hideo Onishi, occasionally held their own one-man exhibitions.[16]

Despite these activities, the photographers were still very limited without the support of a formal pictorial organization, so in 1924 a group of fifty-eight mostly Japanese pictorialists came together to establish the Seattle Camera Club (see Figure 3.1).[17] Kyo Koike, the club's chairman, discussed the circumstances around its formation for *Photo-Era Magazine*. Explaining why so few pictorialists lived in Seattle, he said, "There was no leader to awaken the average person from his long sleep and it is our mission to open the new route."[18] Koike insisted that Japanese pictorialists did not seek to lead other Seattle art photographers but felt compelled to do so simply because nobody else would. "We waited patiently for a long time thinking that some

Figure 3.1. The Seattle Camera Club, circa 1925. According to a handwritten note on the verso of the image, the individuals pictured are Mr. F. A. Kunishige, Dr. K. Koike, Mr. H. Ihashi, Mr. C. A. Musgrave, Mr. Y. Morinaga, Mr. Nilke, Mr. I. Kambara, Miss Ella E. McBride, Mrs. D. J. Ruzicka, Dr. D. J. Ruzicka, and Mrs. C. A. Musgrave. *(Source: University of Washington Libraries, Special Collections, UW14539.)*

Americans might organise a society for the friends of photography," "he explained, "but no light appeared on the dark sea. At last we Japanese determined to establish one by ourselves."[19] The club's purpose, as its bilingual newsletter, *Notan,* outlined, was to "promote, foster, and advance by every honorable means Photographic Art." Its headquarters were located in the Empire Hotel at 422½ Main Street, also the site of Koike's medical practice. There, the club maintained a reading room stocked with books, magazines, bulletins, and salon and exhibition catalogues. It held monthly meetings at Gyokkoken Café in Nihonmachi, where each member was required to bring one or two pictures for review and exhibition. Occasionally, it hosted guests from nearby universities and art schools as well as from abroad to speak on photographic techniques. It also organized picture-taking excursions to nearby landmarks, such as Mount Rainier and Mount Baker.

Koike emerged as the central figure and driving force of the SCC. A medical doctor and fine-arts enthusiast who had immigrated to Seattle in 1917 from Japan at age thirty-nine, he became a devotee of photography soon after arriving in the United States. His subjects were varied, but he considered himself foremost a landscape photographer (see Figure 3.2). Koike first came to local attention in 1920, when his work was displayed at the inaugural Fredrick & Nelson Salon, and his work was first seen in print in 1922 in *Photo-Era Magazine*. He was by far the club's most prolific and renowned member; during the 1927–1928 season, a total of thirty-six salons displayed his work, and in 1929, he was declared the most exhibited pictorialist in the world.[20] Koike also earned dozens of awards in national and international photo competitions and periodically wrote for national photography magazines as a critic and columnist. Such prestigious organizations as the Associated Camera Clubs of America and the Royal Photographic Society of Great Britain (RPS) accepted him as a member in recognition of his work. Koike's induction into the RPS is especially noteworthy, because, at the time, he was the only Japanese person admitted to the organization, one of the oldest photographic societies in the world.[21] His status was further solidified in 1928, when *Photo-Era Magazine* commissioned him to contribute to its new series titled, "Why I Am a Pictorial Photographer." Only the nation's most accomplished pictorialists were asked to write for the series, in which they shared advice and insights about practicing their craft.[22]

The SCC was part of a broader phenomenon of Japanese American pictorialism, and, as Japanese photographers in Seattle and elsewhere in the United States became increasingly visible, observers sometimes remarked on

Figure 3.2. Kyo Koike, "Landmark—Colman Dock." This photo was awarded an honorable mention prize in a *Photo-Era Magazine* contest in 1925. *(Source: University of Washington Libraries, Special Collections, UW23468z.)*

a "Japanese invasion" of the pictorial world. Los Angeles and San Francisco were other key sites of Japanese American pictorialism. Los Angeles was the home base of photographers Toyo Miyatake and Harry Shigeta.[23] Shigeta would move to Chicago in 1924 and join the Fort Dearborn Camera Club. In 1923, a group of mostly Los Angeles–based photographers formed the Japanese Pictorialists of California. Critics generally wrote positively about the work of the Japanese pictorialists and frequently pinpointed "notan" as the key to their distinctive compositions. In 1925, for instance, Henry Hall, of the Newark Camera Club, praised the sublime, distinctly non-Western quality of their work:

> The Japanese artists have coined in one word, what Westerners have been able to say only with several—and that word is *Notan*. Our painters took it up and we less trained pictorialists, or it may be, would-be pictorialists, have wrestled with that word for many an hour, and I am not sure that most of us have yet the meaning, as there is so little of our work that seems to show what I have in mind as Notan. We learned quite readily that the "picture" was a space to be filled—as a space, and so full that there was no picture there. We learned something of Elimination, and Principality, and Balance, and we did a little better, but most of us have still to learn how to fill the picture space with a pleasing combination of light and shade, and, telling but little, suggest a story that fills our picture space with meaning, and with pleasure to the beholder.[24]

Notan, a combination of Japanese characters roughly translated as "light and shade," came to be a common catchall term for the "Japanese style" of pictorialism, connoting space filling, flatness, and decorativeness.

Leaving aside issues of aesthetic form and content, examining the social aspects of pictorialism among SCC members opens new windows on how we might think about the functions and significance of art and recreation among racial and ethnic minorities in America during the early twentieth century. Historians of American immigrant communities have highlighted how recreation served a variety of purposes, including introducing newcomers to the customs and values of the host society, maintaining old-world practices and a sense of cultural continuity, and insulating them from outside rejection or hostility.[25] Communal and cultural amusements have been particularly important in minority communities when other avenues of mobility, through the workplace or political participation, for example, were closed off. In his 1939 thesis about Japanese in Seattle, S. Frank Miyamoto argued that among the Issei, recreation by and large reinforced ethnic solidarity, and the most popular activities reinforced immigrants' identification with Japan.[26] Furthermore, even activities that were "American" tended to affirm Japanese social solidarity, because they would usually participate in them only with other Japanese.[27] To some degree, these insights held true for SCC members, because in addition to finding in the club an outlet for pursuing their artistic interests, they sought in it social support and camaraderie.

In other ways, however, photography among the Issei members of the SCC defied many generalizations about recreation and social solidarity among Japanese Americans. For one, the activity may have strengthened personal and emotional bonds among individual members, but it did not necessarily foster a broad ethnic solidarity or consciousness. Many SCC members were lifelong bachelors, which marginalized them in the strongly nuclear family–oriented Japanese American community of Seattle.[28] Furthermore, that American pictorialism came into its own as an art form and avocation in the United States at the same time that the SCC was an active part of it suggests that the Japanese photographers did not merely pick up an American pastime and give it a "Japanese flair," but rather helped create and mold the American pictorial tradition, thus calling into question its "cultural purity."

The pursuit of pictorialism in Seattle also encouraged SCC members to reach out to non-Japanese photographers and to forge an interracial community based on a shared passion for art photography. The SCC, it should be emphasized, always defined itself as an interracial organization, although it did not have much success in drawing non-Japanese members. "Most of the contributors [to *Notan*] are Japanese," stated Koike in 1925, "but there is no limitation and our gate is always wide-open for everybody. If some Americans or others intend to tell their opinions to us, we will listen to them with much pleasure." Equating "American" with *white* American, he continued, "I eagerly desire Americans to help us, or to co-operate through the societies which they themselves may sooner or later organize."[29] Koike frequently went out of his way to welcome white Americans to the SCC. Some whites did join, as members included "Americans" Ella McBride, Mr. and Mrs. Charles Musgrave, H. G. McManus, and R. M. Lewis. During the 1920s, McBride was one of the most exhibited photographers in the world. She developed such close relationships with the members that she was once described in an issue of *Notan* as one of the club's fellow "Japanese artists."[30]

The club's acquaintance with noted local photographers and artists facilitated members' interaction with and influence over some of the Northwest's most acclaimed artists. Edward Curtis, known for his photographs of Native American subjects, ran one of the largest studios in Seattle from about 1900 to 1920. Ella McBride was a protégé of Curtis and had come to Seattle from Oregon in 1909. She eventually ran her own studio and served as the chief photographer at the Cornish School. Frank Kunishige came to know McBride and Curtis while working at their studios, and it is likely that other Japanese pictorialists encountered them also as studio employees or through Kunishige. The club's association with the Cornish School spawned connections with other Seattle artists and visiting performers. It may have been the basis of its relationship with Mark Tobey, who taught at Cornish during the early 1920s and attended an SCC meeting at least once to speak about art.[31] Beyond local ties, the club also forged links with pictorialists and other clubs around the world through photographic journals, which served as a medium of communication and exchange among camera clubs, and salon participation, which required sending works across long distances to be evaluated by peers in other countries.

Being part of the art photography world worked against not only the Japanese pictorialists' social isolation but also their physical seclusion in Seattle's Nihonmachi, both significant because much of what we know of Japanese American history tends to emphasize this group's (especially the Issei) insulation from mainstream life and other communities. The pursuit of interesting outdoor subjects in particular required photographers to leave their immediate physical and cultural confines (see Figures 3.3 and 3.4). Stressing the importance of venturing out for the sake of one's art, Kyo Koike once opined, "The harder the trip, the better the pictures." He pointed out, however, that good subjects could be found anywhere and did not require one to journey far from home. A keen eye was the most important tool a photographer possessed: "For finding my photographic subjects, I like to walk about leisurely. . . . [P]hotographic subjects exist everywhere when we are observing. Very often a noted place furnishes no picture, but from time to time we find an admirable subject just in front of our home."[32]

Koike's remarks suggest that he held an open and unrestricted perception of space, which was a key ingredient in his success as a photographer. Yet his comments also provide a glimpse of how he and other Japanese photographers were able to maneuver within and across a variety of spaces in their daily lives, thus revealing the physical and social fluidity of the Seattle and Puget Sound landscapes. At a time when the forces of urbanization, immigration, and class formation led whites in power to divide and to imagine the city terrain in terms of "moral" and "immoral" and "white" and "non-white" spaces, the pursuit of photography enabled the Japanese American

Figure 3.3. Kyo Koike, "Beyond the Cliffway," circa 1930. Mount Rainier was a favorite subject of Koike's. This photo was probably taken after the SCC had already disbanded.
(Source: University of Washington Libraries, Special Collections, MPH369.)

Figure 3.4. Kyo Koike, "Shadows on Snow," circa 1928. *(Source: University of Washington Libraries, Special Collections, MPH388.)*

artists to live out at least part of their lives in defiance of such measures aimed at containing them. Mary Ting Yi Lui has discussed the policing of space and enforcement of spatial boundaries as a strategy for maintaining racial and social order amid turn-of-the-twentieth-century New York's rapid urban transformation, a process accompanied by great anxiety about the porousness of Chinatown's borders and the futility of trying to contain the movements of Chinese immigrants.[33] Among the Seattle Japanese photographers, not only did they move about with relative ease throughout the city but they also constantly observed and commented on their surroundings, thus engaging dynamically with the spaces they inhabited and crossed.

SUCCESS AND THE CITY

Between 1924 and 1929, the SCC made a major impact on the national and international pictorial scene. With their entry into the art photography world, the Issei pictorialists joined a dynamic and diverse community of international artists. In addition to displaying their work and encouraging locals to appreciate and to take up photography, members actively participated in the worldwide scene of pictorialism and garnered the respect of critics and fellow artists. In a review of the 1925 season, *Notan* remarked that members "tried hard not to miss any chance and have kept in touch with the pictorial photographic exhibitions. They sent their works to the numerous salons because they well knew that it was helpful; for their future advancement, but not because they wished to make names for themselves alone."[34]

In 1927, *Camera Craft* magazine asserted that the Japanese pictorialists' influence on photographic art was growing evident throughout the western United States, seen in the acceptance of their pictures to some of the most important salons.[35] The following year, as the club prepared for its Fourth International Exhibition, *Camera Craft* declared that Seattle was now the "Northwest American center of photography," thanks in large part to the Japanese pictorialists of the SCC.[36]

Additionally, the SCC pictorialists built a formidable record of achievement with their consistent presence in salons all over the world. Members diligently submitted works to salons near and far, in such American cities as Buffalo, Fort Wayne, Chicago, Los Angeles, San Francisco, New York, Pittsburgh, Portland, Dallas, and Boston, and in such international cities as Paris, London, Liverpool, Glasgow, Brussels, Antwerp, Lucknow, and Montevideo. In 1925, members displayed a total of 367 prints in salons in the United States and abroad. That year, the club was also admitted to the Royal Photographic Society of Great Britain, a high honor that cemented its international profile. Member Hideo Onishi was awarded a ninth-place prize at the 1925 Los Angeles Japanese Daily News Exhibition for his portrait "Returning." Also that year, he achieved international distinction when his photo "Morning Calm" took first place at the Montreal Salon, and his "In the Canal" won a bronze medal at the Midland Salon in Birmingham, England. At the 1925 Portsmouth Salon, also held in Britain, Onishi, along with fellow SCC members Ella McBride and Frank Kunishige, received honors for their entries.[37] The following year, at a 1926 salon hosted by the Fort Dearborn Camera Club in Chicago, Onishi and Kyo Koike each exhibited fifty of their works, and afterward the *Chicago Evening Post Magazine of the Art World* praised the exhibition as the "best assortment of photographs by a Japanese artist that has ever been displayed in Chicago."[38]

Individual clubs and the field at large shared a symbiotic relationship, as the SCC's notoriety in competitions, exhibitions, and publications raised the popularity of pictorialism in general. When *Photo-Era* began its annual trophy competition in 1926 for the American or Canadian club whose members won the highest number of prize-awards in monthly *Photo-Era* competitions, the editors hoped the contest would stimulate interest in photography. The first year of the contest, the SCC and its Japanese pictorialists, who "said little but worked much," earned the top prize, a silver engraved cup.[39] Other strong contenders included the Fort Dearborn Camera Club, the Photographic Society of Baltimore, the Syracuse Camera Club, and the Photographic Society of Philadelphia. The victory incited a spirited competition among clubs in the United States and Canada, as the SCC vowed to repeat its triumph the following year: "To provide that the race for the Photo-Era Trophy Cup is gaining in interest and popularity among the camera clubs let me say that one club has appointed a special chairman to handle all prints for this competition. Another camera club had a lively discussion at its last club meeting in which the members went on record as deciding that it would win the trophy cup for 1926–27 against all comers."[40]

Although it would be its only win, the SCC's victory in the 1925–1926 season brought the club to even wider notice and imbued future *Photo-Era* trophy competitions with greater intensity. Until its disbanding in 1929, the SCC performed strongly in each *Photo-Era* contest, usually ranking in the top five.

Winning the *Photo-Era* trophy, participating in salons around the world, and garnering a host of other distinctions earned the SCC a prominent place in the pictorial world and the admiration of its peers. During the late 1920s, *Notan* was considered required reading for serious pictorialists in the United States and other countries and was received by libraries and camera clubs from as faraway as New York and London. The Dallas Camera Club once complimented the SCC on *Notan,* calling it "one of the most interesting club publications we receive."[41] Other photography clubs and journals were curious to learn more about the club. In 1926, for example, the editor of the magazine *Camera* requested from the SCC a comprehensive history of the organization with the nudge, "Judging from the letters we have received from the readers of *Camera* upon the appearance of the first of the Histories of the Camera Club Series, the subject has unusual interest. And no history of our making would be complete without the history of the Seattle Camera Club."[42] The club drew accolades and friends following nearly every exhibition of its work, counting among its admirers Sigismund Blumann, the editor of the San Francisco–based *Camera Craft* magazine and honorary member of the San Francisco Japanese Club. Also, in March 1929, the Fort Dearborn Camera Club of Chicago, one of its peer organizations, named the SCC one of the top ten salons in the world.[43]

A major mark of the SCC's arrival came in 1925, when it started hosting its own exhibition. It began as a national salon, and then, just in its second year, it expanded to an international annual. The exhibition experienced dramatic growth over the five years it was held, becoming one of the leading annuals in the world. At the first SCC salon, held in April 1925, 384 prints were displayed, and by the fifth in 1929, the number grew to 1,050. Over the years, the event garnered successively increasing amounts of publicity, with all the major Seattle newspapers—the *Seattle Daily Times, Post-Intelligencer, Town Crier, Star,* and the Japanese American newspapers, the *Great Northern Daily News, North American Times, Japanese-American Courier*—reporting on the 1929 exhibition.[44] Displaying one's work at the Seattle salon was a highly coveted opportunity for photographers from all over the world. For instance, for the Fourth International Exhibition in 1928, 236 photographers from 24 countries, including Argentina, Australia, Austria, Holland, Latvia, Japan, Poland, Scotland, Spain, and the USSR, submitted a total of 1,077 prints for consideration. It was one of the most selective salons of the year, and, in the end, 70 percent had to be turned away; 297 prints by 186 photographers were accepted: 106 American, 80 foreign.

For all the national and international attention it captured, the SCC always maintained a local orientation with respect to its regard for Seattle's and Puget Sound's visual beauty and desire to help turn its adopted city into a vibrant site of artistic production. We might say it was an organization that thought *and* acted locally and globally. As close observers and travelers of the local landscapes, the SCC photographers developed intimate familiarity with and strong attachments to Seattle. And because salon participation took their work far beyond the city and region's limits, the group represented Seattle to the outside world in meaningful ways. For example, Edward Dreher, the vice president of the Pictorial Photographers of America (PPA), credited the club with rising "to a commanding position and [placing] Seattle and the Northwest on the map in a manner that will command the notice of the pictorial world."[45] Often, SCC members were the only pictorial photographers representing Seattle in national and international salons. For example, at an international salon held in New York in 1925, of the eleven prints from Washington State, Seattle Japanese created nine of them.[46]

Because they were active at a time when Seattle was still a burgeoning metropolis hungry for urban distinction, the Japanese photographers of the SCC were able to play significant roles in the construction and interpretation of key local icons. In his study of New York, historian William Taylor argues that photography and cities have long been important to one another. As dense, vertically expanding phenomena, cities of the late nineteenth to early twentieth centuries were new entities, and tracing their rise underscores how urban identity is itself a historic development. Photography, moreover, was a vital part of this process of developing distinct urban identities, because as an art form, it came into its own at roughly the same time that the modern city emerged. With its documentary capacity and flexibility to capture images from different angles, it was a tailor-made medium for molding and projecting new urban sensibilities. Thus, rather than merely reproduce or depict something that is fixed and fully formed, a photographer in the early twentieth century could shape and interpret the ethos of a city.[47] Photographers chose and put to film the subjects in the landscape that they found intriguing, thereby sharing with audiences the particular objects with which to identify and in whose beauty to appreciate. Here, city-based camera clubs could also be very important, providing settings for urban residents to explore photography and to capture images of their cities.

Through their work, the Issei photographers helped create some of Seattle's and the Northwest's most recognizable iconic images and cement in their viewers' minds what made the area visually unique. It was a modern commercial metropolis and bucolic holiday getaway, combining trade, industry, and skyscrapers with nature and leisure. As discussed in the previous chapter, Seattle was viewed and sold as a city that effortlessly blended urbanity and simplicity. Images of Mount Rainier and other natural landmarks, produced in conjunction with pictures of the city's developing skyline, depicted Seattle's distinct urban-nature mix. Indeed, in this scenic appropriation, no image was as central as Mount Rainier. It was also one of Kyo Koike's favorite subjects, partly because its snowcap reminded him of Japan's Mount Fuji. He described picture-taking trips from Seattle that began early in the morning, when he departed with his 3A Kodak camera, and then meandered along one of the three major paths to the mountain, the Longmire, White River, and Carbon River trails.[48]

With the content and sheer volume of their photographs, SCC members sought not only to shape fellow Seattleites' perceptions of their city and what made it beautiful but also to enliven the local art community and to receive their due credit for doing so. In response to a 1927 *Seattle Post-Intelligencer* article lamenting the lack of a vibrant local art scene, *Notan* responded by highlighting the work of the SCC. Perplexed by the sparse interest in pictorialism in the city during the 1920s, the SCC sought to inform others about the alluring visual landscape in Seattle and Puget Sound that photographers should explore. Just outside the city were natural marvels, such as Mount Rainier, Reflection Lake, Yakima Park, Glacier Basin, Snoqualmie Falls, and Mount Baker, all of which were subjects in the work of the camera club pictorialists. Puget Sound's "wonderful timberland," flowers, snow, mountains, and lakes made the city a photographer's dream. Within the city itself, one could also find plenty of natural scenery. Koike argued that photographers had a duty to bring the city's aesthetic highlights to the world's attention:

> The city of Seattle is the beloved child of nature. You see there are many snow-capped high mountains, numerous beautiful lakes and rivers in the vicinity. They show us various forms of beauty according to the change of season all the year round. You can not overlook the beautiful shore of Puget Sound. The precipitous peaks should not be left only to the mountaineers alone. The waters, fresh and salt, are not only the fisherman's Paradise. Those scenes never refuse to enter your camera through the lens and to decorate your album. If you can find no beauty from those charming landscapes and water scenes, you are too fresh to carry your photographic apparatus.[49]

Modern subjects also abounded, which Koike highlighted in his writings. In an article that appeared in *Notan* entitled, "Introducing the City of Seattle," he described such downtown sites as Pioneer Square and the Smith Building, which he considered ideal subjects to photograph. Downtown Seattle offered pictorialists a great deal to work with and inspired such photographs as Yukio Morinaga's "Quiet-Hour Seattle," an image of Second and Columbia streets that was printed in the *Seattle Times* and displayed at a New York salon.[50] Koike's "Sunday Afternoon" showed the south entrance of the County-City Building and was awarded an honorable mention in a photo contest. Other

Seattle locations that appeared in club members' work included the Seattle Library, Colman Dock, Kinnear Park, Magnolia Bluff, Woodland Park, Ballard Locks, Sand Point, Cowen Park, and the Montlake Bridge.[51]

With their pictures of Seattle's urban and natural settings, the SCC photographers sought to display their city to a world yet unfamiliar with the visual attractions of the area. Koike and his fellow members took this mission very seriously. "Living in Seattle," he wrote, "we have the privilege, not duty, to introduce this splendid scenery to outsiders by photographic means. When you show your pretty photographic products to your friends out of town, think how deeply they will be impressed."[52] While the SCC prepared for its third international salon during the spring of 1927, *Notan* asserted its confidence that the event would help make Seattle one of the nation's centers of pictorialism. "The contributors and others whom we urged to send their products will remember the name of Seattle forever," it stated. "Yes the leading people in photographic art will never forget the name of Seattle. We will kill two birds with one stone."[53]

As discussed in Chapter 2, the bridging of the East and West was a pervasive component of the public discourse regarding growth and urbanization in Seattle by the 1920s, connoting elites' hopes that commercial, diplomatic, and cultural ties with Asia would underlie the city's prosperity and distinctive character. Also as discussed, Japanese American residents of Seattle were often invoked and directly appropriated as symbols of this trans-Pacific, transcultural bridging. This position was a role that Koike eagerly took on, as he believed he and other Japanese photographers in America could serve unique intermediary roles between the United States and Japan.[54] Addressing his fellow SCC members, he outlined their position to broker exchanges of interpretive and aesthetic outlooks between the two nations:

Now we are all Japanese living in America. You see it is clear what the members of the Seattle Camera Club should do for the advancement of photographic art. Yes, we must be the best interpreters for both nations, because we are not free of Japanese ideas, and yet at the same time we understand Western ways. We should not make our pictures aimlessly, but must try hard to combine both ideas, in other words stick to our peculiar point of view. . . . I am sure that the Japanese conception will be given a position in photographic circles some day.[55]

Local economic and cultural elites who were already seeking to bolster Seattle's ties with the "Orient" supported the club in various ways. Beginning in 1926, the Seattle Chamber of Commerce loaned its facilities for the club's international exhibitions without charge. As mentioned, in 1924, Kunishige hosted an exhibition of his work at the Seattle Commercial Club. Such organizations as the Chamber of Commerce, Commercial Club, and Japan Society, while primarily concerned with promoting United States–Japan relations in trade and other business ventures, viewed the exchange of art and culture as an extension of these relations. Thus, the organizations were also willing to lend their support in a variety of ways to the Issei artists living and working in the United States.

RACE, NATION, AND ORIENTALISM

At a time when nativist politics and racial tensions disrupted American society, yet the forces of internationalism were making the world smaller and fostering cultural contacts across social and geographic borders, in certain contexts, a person's racial "other" status could open *and* close doors. The backdrop of Pacific Rim affairs in Seattle during the 1920s may have heightened observers' and Issei pictorialists' own tendency to link their racial background with their artistry. On one level, positioning themselves as symbolic players in Pacific Rim relations and cultural exchange was a strategy that many Japanese Americans employed to overcome their domestic marginalization during the 1920s and 1930s. Young Nisei, such as James Sakamoto, especially embraced this role, which not only sought to put Japanese Americans in a geopolitically meaningful and advantageous position but also allowed members of the second generation to be leaders in the broader ethnic community. Seeing themselves as cultural interpreters, the Issei pictorialists of the SCC likewise embraced the role for Japanese Americans to be bridges between Japan and not just the United States but also the rest of the Western world. It seemed to pay off, as critics frequently commented favorably on the "Oriental" qualities in their work, and the pictorial world at large generally showed much curiosity about the SCC throughout the time it was active.

However, the frequency with which comments dwelling on their racial background appeared in appraisals of the SCC's work illustrated that the art world, although receptive to certain forms of inclusion, still held and perpetuated Orientalist views about Asian people. The Issei pictorialists of the SCC were seldom regarded as American artists; instead, they were seen as embodying an unusual amalgam of ancient "Oriental" and modern "Occidental" styles. Positive reviews of the SCC's work usually attributed the artists' achievements to their distinct Japanese sensibilities. G. W. Harding, the president of the PPA, thought the work was not specifically Japanese in aesthetic but gave the impression of "good American subjects done through Japanese eyes."[56]

One is hard pressed to find a review of Issei pictorialists in the SCC that does not indulge in some form of racial essentialism. This attention on their "Japanese-ness" was in part of the photographers' own design and intention, but it also speaks to a heightened awareness of race and culture in a field accustomed to the normative Euro-American whiteness of its participants. In any case, critics focused their comments on pinpointing and analyzing how and where Japanese sensibilities appeared in the compositions, as well as the degree to which they conveyed pure Japanese culture. One commentator went so far as to say that SCC members, despite being longtime U.S. residents, employed the "Japanese style" better than pictorialists from Japan did. According to *American Photography* magazine, the European influence on Japanese photographers in Japan was regrettable, while those in Seattle were doing a much better job at maintaining Japanese qualities in their work. Commenting on the Paris International Salon in 1926, it remarked, "And now the Japanese of Japan are taking to 'Europeanism' in art and producing hybrids that are a novelty and nothing more. What a contrast between them and the Japanese of Seattle who have discovered in the camera one of the most potent instruments for revealing beauties of Nature, which, apparently, only a native of Japan can see."[57]

Others saw the SCC as specifically merging Western and Japanese cultural styles. To these critics, the creation of Western art "through Japanese eyes" gave rise to something wholly new, an amalgamated product of the American immigrant experience. Thanks to the Issei Japanese pictorialists, stated Dreher:

> We are now witnessing a slow, gradual transformation of the Japanese conception of the art into a broader field. There seems to be an amalgamation of Japanese treatment and American composition, resulting in what may be termed a new expression of Japanese-American portrayal. . . . It is therefore quite reasonable that the working combination of Japanese perception and American standards will result in an entirely new presentation of pictorial denouement. It opens a new field. Without sacrificing either the old, traditional Japanese rule of symmetrical execution or the more diversified Anglo-American regulative principles, this new era brings forth a pleasing and colorful harmonization of two great tents in the art of Pictorial photography.[58]

In this striking expression of the melting pot ideology adapted to the art world, Dreher celebrated the photographers' work as products of immigration and intercultural influence. Regardless of the content of the commentaries and whether they were being praised or dismissed, the ways in which the Issei pictorialists represented a foreign perspective in a Western form invariably framed discussion of their work. It seemed they could not be viewed outside this box.

The SCC members closely followed critiques of their work, and, toward maintaining the club's success and profile, they were encouraged to preserve the Japanese elements, or *notan,* in their photographs. Thus, it was not just the white critics of art photography but also the Japanese photographers themselves who endeavored to bring attention to the Japanese-ness of their work.[59] Koike, for instance, cautioned club members against the wholesale imitation of Western styles and urged them to instead convey their Japanese sensibilities, as this quality was the key to their distinctive art and critical acclaim. Explaining, "My making of pictures is based on oriental ideas," he remarked further in the Polish journal *Fotograf Polski,* "We have our own individuality but we can not depart from our national tendency. I am not an exception either. Japanese value highly symbolism in their literature and art. We show less in the picture and leave it to your imagination to interpret it."[60] Koike thought every artist of Japanese ancestry had the capacity to portray Japanese "symbolism" and the "national tendency" and so encouraged his fellow Issei photographers to depict this as much they could. Whether his outlook demonstrates Koike's shrewdness of knowing his audience, a cynical pandering to viewers' Orientalist desires, or an authentic exposition of artistic strengths, the remarks above underscore the racially defined limits of the expectations to which Japanese pictorialists were subject. Although the expansive and international scope of pictorialism enabled them to enter the fold, their creativity was bound to offering aesthetic performances of their Japanese-ness. For his part, Koike seemed to find this entirely acceptable.

The conflation of race and artistry resulted in some vexing repercussions for the SCC and its members. For one, it denied Seattle Japanese photographers the possibility of being considered "American" artists. In this sense, the conflation broadened into one in which race and nationality became inextricable. Especially troubling about the critiques of the SCC pictorialists' work were the ways in which they limited the kind of success Japanese photographers could enjoy. Despite the SCC's national and international success in a field dominated by white photographers, the Japanese pictorialists were nonetheless called upon to defend themselves against critics who would not acknowledge them as American artists. Such experiences revealed the limitations of cosmopolitanism in the world of pictorial photography. It was a powerful ideal that suggested broad inclusiveness and a transcendence of narrow affiliations, but, at certain moments when Japanese reached a high degree of visibility, its superficiality was revealed. Although they did their work in the United States, most of their subjects were of Seattle and its vicinity, and the club bore the moniker "Seattle Camera Club," the members' Japanese ancestry, which marked them as foreigners, trumped all other layers of their identities.

Commentators' inability or unwillingness to separate the Japanese pictorialists' racial background from their work could have tangible consequences. Sigismund Blumann, the editor of Camera Craft Magazine, for instance, complained after one San Francisco exhibition that the Japanese American artists' work was not Japanese enough. He admitted that he offended a group of amateur Japanese photographers at that exhibit when he insisted that awards should be given to "those who showed most of the characteristic features of Japanese Art in their work."[61] Although Blumann claimed he favored individual artistic freedom, he lamented what he perceived as an imitation of Western forms and the loss of a Japanese aesthetic among the Japanese photographers. Addressing the Japanese pictorialists, he said, "You have in many ways shamed us by the aptitude with which you surpass us in our own ways and methods. . . . But a Japanese can best express his emotions in the Japanese manner. He should be proud of that and seek at every opportunity to prove to the world that he is proud of it and that the arts, customs, and manners of his land are worthy of his pride."[62]

Similarly, Ralph D. Hartman, the president of the Cleveland Photographic Society, commented on the work of SCC members after a 1926 exhibition in Cleveland. Although he thought their work was "beautiful" and "technically perfect," he complained that a Japanese aesthetic was not sufficiently pronounced in the photos:

Japanese art is unusual and unique from the American point of view, and I do not like to see a Japanese get into the habit of trying to reproduce the American art. Japanese art stands alone in its simplicity and its balance and I certainly would like to see more of it. The tendency toward American art is to be regretted and I really feel that both the Japanese and the Americans are losing something unless the Japanese are careful to avoid this tendency. Therefore, I say, let us have more of the real Japanese art.[63]

In other cases, critics simply disliked the Japanese pictorialists' work, but their dismissals sometimes expressed a disdain that went well beyond the images themselves. In 1927, following a London exhibition, an English critic named F. C. Tilney lambasted the photographs by Issei pictorialists, calling them "irritatingly ugly" and "bastard trifles," among other choice insults. The Japanese artists' "racial bent," he said, led them to create work that was "queer," and he urged "Americans" not to mimic their style. Koike responded to this attack in a German journal in which he stated that Tilney simply did not understand Japanese ideas.[64] Furthermore, Koike felt that the resentment toward the Japanese pictorialists' success and their ubiquity in international exhibitions likely fueled such racially charged criticisms.

With its focus on art appreciation, *Notan* rarely engaged in extended discussions about racial and ethnic problems, and when it did, its writers usually took a conciliatory approach. One contentious exchange in the pages of the newsletter, however, reveals some of the deeper tensions and frustrations that SCC members grappled with. The occasion was the Third International Salon of the PPA, held in New York in 1929. In July, *American Photography* magazine featured a review of the exhibition by New York photographer and critic Nicholas Haz. Of the 172 American prints featured, 33 were by Japanese, whom Haz did not regard as Americans and felt should not have been placed in the U.S. category. An American annual salon, he said, should not contain work by Japanese for 20 percent of its content: "Americans are fully able to supply enough good prints to make up an annual, showing a lot of this country, without much Japanese help."[65] It was clear in Haz's review that "American" excluded Japanese Americans. It was also apparent that some of the Japanese photographers to whom he referred were members of the SCC.

Koike replied to Haz by defending the right of Japanese to participate in American salons and to submit their work as American entries; after all, they lived and worked in the United States. Haz's complaint, Koike believed, was not entirely about photography and sprang from a deeper reservoir of racial prejudice: "We are not allowed to become American citizens by law, but we may live in America just the same. What trouble could be caused by the difference of nationality in the realm of pictorial photography, I can not understand."[66] He pointed out that Haz himself was not American-born but an immigrant from Eastern Europe[67] and suggested that the article was fueled out of spite, because Haz's own work was rejected for exhibition at that same annual: "We Japanese are also immigrants. [Haz] may be an American citizen at present, but he is not native American as we are. Is the citizenship paper worth so much in the pictorial photographic field of America? He is allowed to become an American citizen, but a Japanese cannot by law. What difference does it make to the field of American photography when both he and we live in America on equal terms?"[68]

Koike's rejoinder expressed frustration over this dilemma he and other Japanese photographers faced and the complicated path they had to negotiate as Asian immigrant photographers. Sometimes it benefited them to embrace their Japanese background and to wear it on their sleeves, but the same strategy could also produce confusion and become a license for their less-enlightened peers to try to limit the photographers' participation.

The exchange between Koike and the foreign-born Haz is revealing in exposing the tensions between nationalism and internationalism, ironically in an exchange between two immigrants in the United States. Although the European Haz had found a way to claim American-ness, the Japan-born Koike, by virtue of his Asian ancestry, was denied the same option. In any case, it became all too clear how much race had become entwined in questions regarding nationality and international participation. To Koike's latest statement, Haz wrote a rebuttal, which was also published in *Notan*. He insisted that he admired Japanese art and appreciated the contributions of the Seattle pictorialists. "The presence in America of so many splendid Japanese artists is a great boon to the United States," said Haz. "The influence they have exerted on other amateurs is very noticeable and in my opinion very welcome."[69] Aside from these compliments, he maintained that the Japanese photographers' work should be excluded from American national exhibits. To Haz, their Japanese origin, not where they worked and resided, determined their national affiliation. "I like purely national annuals more than internationals," Haz stated. "Now I happen to wish for such annuals made in for and of America." He continued, "I assure you if a naturalized Japanese would suggest that a purely national annual should be published in Japan, in which the resident American pictorialists should be kept to their true proportion, I not only would not be annoyed, but would subscribe for such a book."[70]

Haz's criterion for determining the national affiliation of the SCC and all Japanese photographers in the United States was country of ancestry, not residence. As he argued, Issei pictorialists' work belonged in Japanese nationals, not American ones, just as the work of Americans in Japan would not be appropriate for Japanese annuals. That Haz would not have subjected himself to the same standard (as he considered himself an American artist, not Hungarian) suggests that race, in addition to nativity, informed his views on how the Japanese American pictorialists should be treated. Such rigid thinking on race and nationality, often evident in critiques and commentaries of their work, was a persistent impediment to the SCC pictorialists' acceptance as American photographers. Although Koike and other Japanese photographers in the United States tried to channel racial essentialism to advance themselves in the field, they could not escape its downsides, as seen in such reviews as Haz's.

Returning to the local art scene, for a city that through the 1920s was eager to garner urban distinction and to strengthen its connections with Japan, it is curious that Seattle, especially its cultural elite, did not more fully embrace and support the SCC. It was not as though local arts patrons eschewed Asian art. In fact, by the early 1930s, with the establishment of the Seattle Art Museum and appointment of Asian art collector Richard Fuller at the helm, the city sought to distinguish its local art scene as modern with its heavy emphasis on Oriental art. Yet, according to historian Carol Zabilski, "Caucasian Seattle steadfastly ignored the earnest offers of cooperation and collaboration in the cause of photography made repeatedly by Koike and his colleagues."[71] Despite its influential admirers and handful of local supporters, the club went largely ignored by the city. Perhaps it was too much of an anomaly to white Americans. As a Seattle-based group, it was not Japanese, yet dominant attitudes at the time made it difficult for people to regard it as an American organization. Furthermore, the fact that members were famous for bringing "Japanese sensibilities" to a Western art form was a challenge for critics and observers who sought to characterize their work, which was neither truly "Oriental" nor "Occidental." The club's greatest handicap proved to be attracting non-Japanese members, evidently focused on whites only. For the most part, white photographers were unwilling to join an organization perceived as Japanese regardless of how accomplished it was. "Our Seattle Camera Club is a little over two years old and still most of the members are Japanese," noted *Notan* with some resignation. "Sometimes a few [white] Americans come to us, but they soon leave us."[72]

The SCC's experience reveals some of the contradictions that lay beneath cosmopolitanism with respect to how to deal with group difference. On the one hand, the organization and field of pictorialism at large were shining embodiments of the concept of cosmopolitanism, as it connoted the coming together of individuals of different racial and national backgrounds around a common interest. Reviews by white American and Europeans about the Japanese pictorialists' work often expressed enthusiasm and appreciation for the incorporation of Japanese conventions into a Western art form. Photographers around the world came together, albeit often by proxy, to share and to admire each other's work and to form lasting bonds with one another. Many photographers, among them Japanese pictorialists, expressed faith in this utopian vision of the art photography world. Yet even as this vision materialized in correspondences, journals, and salons, its shortcomings would be starkly revealed, as in the debate between Koike and Haz.

On the other hand, the foregrounding of ethnic and racial difference in pictorialism, a fundamental aspect of cosmopolitan formations, tended to reinforce rather than to dismantle race consciousness and perceptions of Japanese otherness. This probably contributed to local whites' unwillingness to join the organization in significant numbers. *Notan* urged white photographers to join the SCC or to form their own camera club, even offering to disband the SCC to give way to an "American" organization.[73] Voicing members' frustration, it said:

> If the American workers ask, we will disband our club and take off our hat to such organization as they may form but why do the Seattle photographers sleep so long, doing nothing? Our members have tried hard and taken chances. Now we have been able to put the name of Seattle City on the map of the world's pictorial photographic field. We are doing our duty faithfully as outsiders, but why do you hesitate to follow us and to make your name. To let us foreigners alone fight in the front line for the name of Seattle and to look on with folded arms, is it not a question of your honor? I request your honest answer at this point. What do you say, fellow photographers?[74]

The photographers faced a difficult conundrum. In effect, they were outsiders doing work on behalf of a host city and country that benefited from their efforts but continued to treat them as outsiders. This dichotomy was compounded by the fact that although the Japanese photographers hoped to attract non-Japanese to their organization and to thereby transcend racial barriers, they submitted to their own racialization. It was a situation for which there was no easy resolution and one that would contribute to the club's demise.

CONCLUSION

By 1928, only the club's fifth year in existence, *Notan* was remarking that members were not as active in exhibiting their work in salons and magazines as they had been in years past. That year, a total of 400 prints by 11 members were seen throughout the world, but this number was a drop from 1927. In early 1929, *Notan* reported that in the previous year, most members were not active, although others displayed 165 prints at more than 30 salons around the world, published 18 of their prints, and won 8 prizes: "I hope our members will awake from their long sleep and show their ability again in the pictorial photographic field of the world in the near future."[75] In October

1929, the club unceremoniously disbanded, announcing in a farewell news-letter that "nonactivities and financial difficulties of most of our members" were responsible for the group's demise. It also cited a general loss of interest in pictorial photography. The onset of the Great Depression and hard times turned some members away from photography, making it impossible for the club to continue running on member dues.

The Japanese members of the SCC never regained the international pro-file they enjoyed in the mid- to late 1920s, and the city's overall art photog-raphy scene lost its vibrancy after the club's disbanding, although by then other photographic organizations were established, such as the Seattle Pho-tographic Society in 1933, which exists to this day. Most former members disappeared from the scene, although a few stayed active in salons through the 1930s.[76] Koike remained prolific, continuing to exhibit work all over the United States and abroad as late as November 1941.[77] Also, nonmembers and younger Japanese Americans helped sustain interest in photography in the Japanese American community. Grocer-photographer Mitsutaro Fuku, who had not been an SCC member, became one of the foremost photog-raphers in Seattle during the 1930s, displaying his work in salons in the United States, Europe, and Asia, and in 1934 he became the director of the Seattle Photographic Society.[78] To encourage photography among the younger generation, the Furuya Camera Club, which formed in the late 1920s or early 1930s, sponsored children's competitions.[79] Ralph Ochi was a Franklin High School graduate who went on to become the most promi-nent Nisei photographer in Seattle. He wrote articles about photography for the *Japanese-American Courier* in the late 1930s, and established a studio in Seattle, which sponsored local amateur exhibitions.

The SCC's legacy suffered a devastating blow with the wartime intern-ment of West Coast Japanese. One of the first actions by the Justice Depart-ment after the attack on Pearl Harbor in December 1941 was to order members of "enemy alien" groups to surrender equipment that could used for spying, and cameras were on the list. About twelve hundred Japanese arrived at the Seattle police department to hand in their cameras, radios, and firearms.[80] Some of those returning cameras were elderly men who had belonged to the SCC. Among them was Koike, and a picture of him turn-ing in two of his cameras to the Seattle police accompanied a December 29 article in the *Seattle Post-Intelligencer* about the confiscation (see Figure 3.5).[81] Most of the members went to the Minidoka Relocation Center in Idaho for the duration of the war. The lesser-known photographers' work has since been lost or destroyed, but much of the work of Koike, Kunishige, Morinaga, and McBride survives, and others are slowly being recovered.[82]

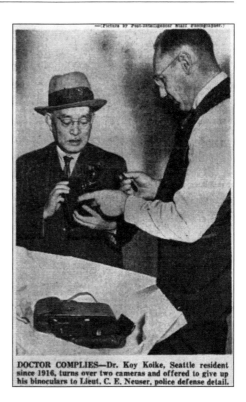

—[Picture by Post-Intelligencer Staff Photographer.]

DOCTOR COMPLIES—Dr. Koy Koike, Seattle resident since 1916, turns over two cameras and offered to give up his binoculars to Lieut. C. E. Neuser, police defense detail.

Figure 3.5. Kyo Koike turning in two of his cameras to the Seattle police. This photo originally appeared in the *Seattle Post-Intelligencer* on December 29, 1941. *(Source: Hearst Communications, Inc., Hearst Newspapers Division.)*

Pictorialism was on the decline by the 1950s, as the multiplicity of styles it encouraged caused the field to further splinter. It also had to compete with new technologies, such as television, amateur movie making, the 35mm camera, and slide screenings. With pictorialism's demise, the SCC's abrupt end, wartime camera confiscation, and Japanese incarceration, the club was largely forgotten in the histories of photography and the fine arts in Seattle. Nonetheless, it was a pioneer in Pacific Northwest art, and its historical significance cannot be denied. While the club was active, its members earned awards, enriched pictorialism, and used their work to build bridges between artists and aesthetic styles. However, the contradiction these artists embodied—as Japanese artists working in and representing the United States—impeded their full acceptance and integration into the international pictorial world and local Seattle art scene. The internationalism of pictorialism held out the possibility of equality through inclusion, but the field's reliance on national categories made for some confounding experiences for the SCC photographers. The Japanese pictorialists found they could not participate in this arena and divorce themselves from other contexts that defined their everyday lives. The field remained fixated on the nationality of Japanese artists in America, and these issues of nationality were then entwined with race.

Recreation and art were important in the lives of many Japanese Americans in Seattle by the 1920s, and in this way the story of the SCC is broadly significant. In addition to the SCC, Japanese American cultural institutions included flower-arranging clubs, sports teams, music-appreciation societies, and a theater. On the other hand, the SCC and its members possessed many singular qualities, and we might even describe the Issei photographers as quirky men who never quite fit in with the rest of the Japanese American community. Furthermore, the art photography community they were a part of was a rarefied set, characterized more by a vast geographic web sewn by photographs, newsletters, and journals than by local, face-to-face, daily contacts. The photographers' story, unique as it was, is a window to the possibilities and challenges that confronted Japanese Americans who sought to navigate their own lives between local and international concerns as Seattle transformed into a major metropolis. Yet we must acknowledge that most Japanese Americans did not get to have such experiences and consider how ordinary Japanese Americans—and other Seattleites for the matter—engaged in and experienced the multiscaled landscape of Seattle and the Pacific Rim. The following chapter shifts from the arts to examine another key institution of urban development—public education—and discusses its significance in the modernization of Seattle and inculcation of its pupils, including Japanese American students, in how to be not just "good Americans" but also good cosmopolitan residents of Seattle, "gateway to the Orient."

4

⊰⊱⊰⊱⊱

"Problems of the Pacific" in
"the Great Crucible of America"

Public Schools in the 1920s and 1930s

SEATTLE'S GEORGE WASHINGTON

In February 1924, auditions were held at Harrison Elementary School for the role of George Washington in the school's annual Presidents' Day reenactment of the famous cherry tree incident.[1] Following the tryouts, teachers and administrators selected second-grader Fred Kosaka, the seven-year-old son of a local Japanese tailor. Reaction to this news came quickly. The daily local newspaper, the *Seattle Star,* a frequent mouthpiece for the local anti-Japanese set, sent reporter Jim Marshall to cover the performance. On February 22, the paper subsequently printed, complete with a photo of Kosaka wielding his ax, an article featuring the headline, "White Children at Harrison School Ignored, While Japanese Boy Impersonates Father of Our Country" (see Figure 4.1).[2] Calling Kosaka a "vassal of the Mikado," Marshall said that members of the audience were "abashed" at the sight of a Japanese boy impersonating Washington. Also weighing in was the local chapter of the Sons of the Veterans and Women's Auxiliary, which singled out Kosaka's homeroom teacher, Miss Waite, herself a member of the Daughters of the American Revolution.[3] Suspecting that she encouraged Kosaka to audition for the role, the chapter blasted her for being "unpatriotic" and demanded that she resign from her position at the school. Another teacher at Harrison Elementary said that the decision to cast Kosaka was a mistake, adding, "I would never allow either a Japanese child or a colored child to represent Washington or Lincoln if there was a white child available, and if there was no white child available I would omit that part of the program."[4]

Seattle's "George Washington"
White Children at Harrison School Ignored, While Japanese Boy
Impersonates Father of Our Country

Figure 4.1. Fred Kosaka, second-grader at Harrison Elementary in Seattle, who was chosen to play the role of George Washington in February 1924. *(Source:* Seattle Star, *February 22, 1924.)*

Supporters of Kosaka and the school's decision answered back, and the ensuing controversy revealed that local attitudes on issues of race and American identity were fraught with disagreement. Several Japanese residents expressed anger at the *Star* and frustration over Kosaka's predicament, seeing the whole matter as symbolic of the second-generation dilemma. Nisei were encouraged by their teachers to become Americanized, but they faced attacks if they assimilated to the point of surpassing their white classmates. One Japanese resident shared his reactions with a local researcher conducting interviews about the incident:

> Japanese people try to do right and give children the best opportunity they can. They send them to public schools so they may learn the best of American life and about American heroes and try to be like them. The teachers are good and help them but what happens outside of school? If they are bad they are condemned and if they are good they are condemned. Americans are so inconsistent. This Japanese boy who acted as George Washington was trying hard to be a good American and when he did his best the *Star* condemns both him and his teacher.[5]

Most of the teachers who were asked about the incident said they had no problem with Kosaka's selection, and those who picked him said they did so because he simply gave the best audition. In a gesture that was quite bold for its time, Harrison's principal, Eugenie B. Parriseau, took a color-blind stance and insisted that Kosaka's selection had nothing to do with race, yet at the same time, she was sure to underline the racial significance of the school's action: "To me . . . a child is a child regardless of color. I have always worked on that principle and I am going to continue doing so."[6] Finally, despite impassioned calls by locals to do so, the school stood firm and refused to enact any policies barring or restricting the participation of "Orientals" in school activities.

It is not surprising that a controversy over a Japanese child playing Washington would erupt in 1924 Seattle. This year was, after all, a high-water mark for the anti-Japanese movement, during which the 1924 Johnson-Reed Act was passed. Given this backdrop of popular and political clamoring against Japanese people in America, an event as mundane as an elementary school play, something that would otherwise go unnoticed in the local media, managed to generate a brief, but intense, firestorm. By the early twentieth century, the "cherry tree incident" was a much-celebrated piece of American folklore, and its reenactment was an opportunity for ordinary people to take part in a patriotic ritual rich with historical meaning. Furthermore, the fact that this event was staged annually in schools across the country imbued it with a deep collective meaning, affirming the American-ness of its participants and their membership in the national community. In this ritual, no single participant made a stronger claim to American-ness than the student who played the role of Washington. The problem in the Seattle case was, during the mid-1920s, few groups were perceived as more foreign to American society and culture than Asians. Thus, the spectacle of a Japanese child embodying the nation's first president represented a bold challenge to the exclusion of Asian bodies from the national collectivity.

In addition to viewing this incident as one of many flare-ups of anti-Japanese prejudice during the early 1900s, we might also pause to consider the ways that it represented a contestation over American identity and the racialized boundaries of national belonging. Of equal significance to the *Seattle Star*'s rants against Kosaka was the decision that precipitated the controversy in the first place. In essence, Harrison officials went against the tide of national and much of the local sentiment and, through their action, proposed that a Japanese boy could also be a good American. A teacher at the school who supported Kosaka remarked that the controversy spoke to broader tensions in the community and highlighted "how the social forces are lined up." In her view, the incident pitted "the teachers and social workers pursuing a constructive program of education" against "other groups influenced by economic and political reasons doing their utmost to discredit the foreign groups, particularly the Orientals." Claiming the moral high ground, the teacher elaborated on the inclusive, multiracial vision of America that she and others at the school strove to bring about:

> And in the mean time what is to become of the Japanese George Washington and the other American born Japanese? If we slap them every time they emulate a noble American are we not laying the foundations for future trouble? They are residents of this country, they are legally American citizens, but spiritually we deny them citizenship; they have no desire to live in Japan, they are unfit for life in Japan under present conditions, so we are virtually making them a people without a country and in large numbers such people become a menace. I can see no light ahead except as we train more Japanese George Washingtons.[7]

In Asian American history, we tend to emphasize the nativists' victories. To be sure, as evidenced by Chinese exclusion, alien land laws, and the 1924 Immigration Act, theirs was the dominant agenda until the 1940s. However, the back-and-forth verbal rebukes prompted by Kosaka's selection underscored the uneasy and often volatile presence of conflicting ideologies about race and Americanism in Seattle. And in this case, the educators and reformers of Harrison School, wielding their vision of a multiethnic America, carried the day.

Using the Kosaka incident as a springboard for reflecting on issues of Japanese immigration, education, and Americanization in West Coast cities, this chapter examines the ways that Seattle public schools engaged the idea of the city as a cosmopolitan "gateway to the Orient" during the interwar years—specifically, how Seattle's expansion and growing position in international Pacific affairs informed their approach toward Japanese students and their broader philosophies on Americanization. As urban school districts across America coped with larger and more diverse student bodies, educators in Seattle incorporated into their Americanizing mission an internationalist, Pacific-oriented perspective. They worked to instill in their charges the civic and ideological outlook to be "good Americans" in a setting that they believed was becoming cosmopolitan due to the city's geographic location and role as a nexus of international migration, commerce, and diplomacy. Thus, Americanizing students in Seattle entailed ensuring that they understood the interconnectedness of the United States with other parts of the world, respected differences around the globe and among one another, and regarded all persons, regardless of race or cultural background, as equally entitled to being part of the civic community. With its selection of Fred Kosaka to play America's first president, Harrison School asserted that people of Japanese ancestry not only were part of the local community but also had a rightful place within the American social fabric.

An underlying concern of this chapter is to explore how the dynamics of place, in addition to national trends and discourses, have informed approaches to and philosophies about Americanization in Seattle—specifically, looking into how the city's location on the Pacific Coast, its ties with Japan, and identification as an "international" gateway factored into the work of education officials. Spatial matters are additionally important, because integrated schools, such as Bailey Gatzert Elementary and Broadway, Franklin, and Garfield high schools—the main focus of this chapter—took shape at the confluence of urbanization, migration, and residential segregation. Curiously, the concentration of many of the city's immigrants and racial minorities in a handful of the system's schools—an outcome of racial segregation in the city—led those very schools to boast that they embodied cosmopolitanism and produced students who were "citizens of the world." In addition to being useful lenses to how city institutions conceptualized and engaged matters of space and scale, such integrated schools are also fruitful sites for studying cross-racial and interethnic relations in West Coast cities.[8]

The chapter also builds on a considerable literature on Nisei and education, particularly the work of historians Eiichiro Azuma, Yoon K. Pak, and David Yoo, who have highlighted the tension between American rhetoric promising equality and success to members of the second generation and racist conditions that limited the opportunities actually available to them.[9] As much as the schools projected themselves as embodiments of an inclusive Americanism that simultaneously upheld cosmopolitan values, the persistence of Orientalist and nativist attitudes among locals resulted in numerous contradictions in the schools' social and ideological terrain. And for Japanese American students, this contradiction produced a mixed bag. The schools' interest in the Pacific Rim and their celebratory rhetoric about diversity elevated Japanese Americans to high visibility, provided them with the opportunity to interact with non-Japanese classmates in a fairly fluid environment, and availed Japanese parents and community leaders of opportunities to have their voices heard by the school district. But these inclusions and openings were limited by the racism of individuals as well as the agenda of the school district, which had its own abiding interest in affirming its efficacy as an administrator of diverse student bodies. Seattle schools might have taken bold public stances against racism and nativism, but they did not substantively challenge essentializing perceptions and condescending treatment of Japanese people.

Seattle Public Schools and Progressive-Era Reform

Toward meeting some of the social challenges stemming from the effects of industrialization, urbanization, and foreign immigration, Americans dramatically expanded public education during the late nineteenth to early twentieth centuries.[10] This expansion was just one piece of a wide range of initiatives instituted during the Progressive era, during which a general belief that society's ills could be ameliorated through the application of specialized knowledge, technology, and centralized organization guided reformers. In Seattle and many other cities, the reformers and school board members who drove education policy and shaped curricula during the Progressive era were from the ranks of the educated business and professional classes who favored broad, rather than provincial, outlooks and solutions.[11]

Population growth and the enactment and strict enforcement of truancy and child-labor laws allowed public schools to extend their reach into the lives of greater numbers of ordinary people by the turn of the twentieth century. National, and nationalist, imperatives informed much of the rationale for public-education reform during the early 1900s. The "100 Percent American" movement, which was driven by the patriotic momentum of the World War I years, was colored by a distinct antiforeigner bias and looked to schools to be the prime cultivators of national loyalty among the youth.[12] Patriotism, thus, was a key guiding principle in the movement for compulsory, standardized public education. Further, the "new immigration" of southern and eastern Europeans, Asians, and Latin Americans deepened the urgency for the public schools to expand so they could assimilate and Americanize these foreigners. From location to location, the degree of tolerance for cultural difference varied greatly, but of chief importance across all Americanization efforts in the United States was to foster an individual's *primary* allegiance to the United States.

Established in 1870, Seattle Schools' stated mission was "by example and precept to revere American institutions and the ideals of freedom and responsibility which motivated the public service of Washington and the fathers of the constitution."[13] Experiencing its most dramatic growth in the early twentieth century, the district's teacher corps expanded from 350 to 838 between 1902 and 1910.[14] Also, in the first two decades of the twentieth century, the number of schools in the district increased from twenty-one to ninety-eight to accommodate a nearly fourfold population growth.[15] Historians of Seattle usually identify superintendent Frank Cooper, who served from 1901 to 1922, as the guiding force and vision of public education during the years of expansion. Cooper's philosophy was in line with Progressive-era education reform: Schools should be involved in all aspects of a child's development.[16] He called for broadening curricula to include character development, so, in addition to reading, writing, and arithmetic, high schools during his tenure added such subjects as liberal arts, vocational training, physical education, home economics, music, and art. Swept up in the Americanization movement, Seattle Schools in 1916 adopted the core philosophies of loyalty and patriotism, implemented by civics courses, flag rituals, and instruction in "good American" personal values, such as thrift and cleanliness.

Unlike many other school districts on the West Coast, Seattle Schools never had an official policy segregating "Orientals" into separate schools. Although no definitive explanation could be found to explain this situation, Doris Pieroth suggests the district simply followed the lead of superintendent Cooper, who had early on opposed the creation of separate schools for immigrant children or students with limited English ability.[17] Although Cooper's policy did not encompass race, his position may have set a precedent with respect to other forms of segregation through the early 1900s. Nonetheless, some local support for segregation did exist, as white residents in the city made at least one—albeit unsuccessful—attempt to establish a separate Oriental school.[18] Another likely reason why Seattle did not have racially segregated schools is because residential segregation already ensured that Asians and blacks, the primary nonwhites in the city limits, would be concentrated in a handful of schools.

Whatever the reasons behind it, the absence of a policy of racial segregation was a significant fact for the district. The presence of its integrated schools allowed it, with some exterior plausibility, to claim cosmopolitan values and to tout its acceptance of all students on equal terms. Seattle historian Roger Sale also finds that graduates of these schools commonly expressed pride in having been part of diverse student bodies. Furthermore, many Seattleites at the time viewed the high school years as a time when a person's idealism was most strongly nurtured. For Seattle students during the 1920s and 1930s, the experience gave them "a strong sense that democracy was working here much more than it was in adult life."[19] With their student bodies drawn from all walks of life, cultures, and races, these integrated schools would be described as embodiments of democracy in action.

"It is a real and understandable pride," elaborates Sale, "because life in high school was on a scale that offered challenges that could be met." Yet he also contends that "the pride of graduates from the 'integrated' schools, Franklin or Garfield, or Broadway is a naïve pride, because the nonwhite minorities were there in small and undisturbing numbers."[20] Sale understands this pride in integrated schools in terms of progressive white Seattleites' general pretensions regarding racial and ethnic relations and comes to the cynical conclusion, "Also, the resulting blend of racial and ethnic minorities allowed a predominantly white, Anglo-Saxon population to feel proud of its tolerance, yet remain aware of 'the Swedes' in Ballard or 'the Italians' in Rainier Valley, or 'the colored people' and 'the Japanese' in the central area and the international district because . . . none of these minorities was close to being a majority within any given high school."[21]

To be sure, showing tolerance—or even feigning it—was not an objective shared by all. But if one condition for Seattleites to tout their tolerance was the existence of niches in the city where minorities were numerous enough to be visible but too few to threaten white dominance, then this might explain how such schools as Franklin, Broadway, and Garfield came to be regarded as proverbial centers of Seattle cosmopolitanism. For Japanese American students attending these schools, this situation would mean a host of contradictions, raising the students' hopes for inclusion and equality while reminding them of their minority position.

JAPANESE AMERICANS IN SEATTLE'S PUBLIC SCHOOLS

Although during the interwar years Japanese Americans never exceeded a fraction of Seattle's population, their concentration in a handful of schools, all located in or near the Jackson Street area, magnified their visibility. These schools were Pacific Grammar and Bailey Gatzert Elementary; Central and Washington Junior High Schools; and Garfield, Broadway, and Franklin High Schools. From the late 1920s through the early 1940s at most of these schools, between 10 and 25 percent of the student bodies was Japanese. The one exception was Bailey Gatzert, where Japanese Americans constituted the majority of the student population from its opening in 1921 until wartime evacuation in 1942. As the number of teenage Nisei in Seattle rose in the early to mid-1920s, this demographic change was reflected in a heightened presence of Japanese Americans in the high schools during these years, also indicated by their sudden visibility in yearbooks. Local Japanese Americans kept track of the Nisei presence and their progress in the public schools as matters of community interest. In 1928, the *Japanese-American Courier* reported that fifty Japanese graduated from all Seattle universities and high schools that June.[22] By 1935, at Garfield High alone, twenty-three Nisei entered the freshmen class, making up about 12 percent of their cohort, and in 1940, sixty-two Japanese American freshmen entered Broadway High.[23] In May 1936, the *Courier* boasted that 239 Nisei were scheduled to graduate from high schools in Seattle.

As mentioned, among the elementary schools, Bailey Gatzert had the highest Japanese enrollment, due largely to its location just off Nihonmachi. In 1921, the year of the school's founding, 99 percent of the 452 students enrolled were Chinese or Japanese, and through the next two decades, Japanese students made up the majority of pupils at Gatzert, up to an average of 74 percent.[24] This ethnic concentration made for an insulated, comfortable situation for the Japanese American students. Shigeko Sese Uno, who attended Gatzert during the early and mid-1920s, recalled, "I think we were very fortunate. . . . [A]t Bailey Gatzert School, I remember just a few Chinese, no black person, no Filipino. We were all Japanese. So I think we ruled the school, really. And so all of our life we never felt any discrimination."[25]

The junior high and high schools never approached the proportion of Japanese Americans that Bailey Gatzert had, but enough of them clustered in a few schools to compose a discrete group within the student bodies. Japanese American students who attended such schools as Garfield, Broadway, and Franklin remembered high school as a time when they became more self-conscious about their minority status, especially if they had attended Bailey Gatzert, where they had grown accustomed to being in the majority. Even still, their numbers were high enough that they could form distinct social groups. May Namba, who attended Garfield High during the 1930s, remembered the school as mostly white but with significant numbers of Chinese, Japanese, and blacks.[26] Sharon Tanagi Aburano was one of those Nisei who came to Broadway after having attended Bailey Gatzert and found the transition to be a very challenging one.[27] On the other hand, Louise Kashino had grown used to being the only Japanese in her classes, so for her, going to Broadway was a surprise in the opposite respect.[28] Mits Takahashi enjoyed his experience at Garfield High during the late 1930s to early 1940s, even though World War II disrupted it. He believed the school was successfully integrated and cited his many friendships with Caucasians as evidence. He also insisted that "discrimination wasn't really felt" among the Japanese Americans at the school, although he admitted that socially students would self-segregate.[29]

For most Nisei in Seattle in grades one through eight, day-to-day life consisted of attending two schools: the neighborhood public school and the main Japanese language school in the city, Kokugo Gakko. The first Japanese language schools for Nisei were established in 1902 in Seattle and San Francisco, and by 1923, there were fifty-five in California, twenty-four in Washington, twenty-two in Oregon, and forty-eight throughout Canada.[30] Before World War II, Seattle's was the largest in the United States, with an enrollment of around thirteen hundred.[31] As children, Ayako and Masaki Murakami would take daily morning treks with other neighborhood kids to Bailey Gatzert and then in the afternoon head straight to the Japanese School. Such a routine seemed to be the norm for other Japanese Americans around their age. Seiko Edamatsu, who attended Gatzert during the 1920s, remembered being one of the few Nisei who did not go to Japanese School, which left her feeling somewhat alienated: "I think mainly it was too expensive. . . . [E]veryone . . . went from Bailey Gatzert School to Japanese School, they all passed in front of our house, and I used to sit on the porch and watch them go, wishing I could go, I think, kind of, you know, to be with the rest of 'em."[32]

These schools faced a considerable amount of opposition during the anti-Japanese movement of the 1910s and early 1920s, as nativists alleged that they promoted Japanese nationalism, and reformers complained they impeded Americanization. This outcry led to several western states and Hawaii attempting, mostly unsuccessfully, to regulate these schools.[33] Contrary to the allegations that were made about Japanese language schools, historians have shown that they were neither bastions of Japanese nationalism nor impediments to Americanization. Yuji Ichioka has illustrated, for example, that the schools did not seek to resist assimilation but rather to facilitate it, especially as Japanese communities in the United States transitioned from sojourner to permanent ones around the 1910s.[34] He finds that the Japanese Association and leaders of Japanese American communities generally advocated that Americanization should be encouraged first, and Japanese education should be supplementary. Furthermore, during the school years, Nisei students spent far more hours in American schools than they did in Japanese School. Further, on the issue of indoctrination, American teachers were probably unmatched in their zeal. The gospel that they worked to spread, especially among immigrants and children of immigrants, was Americanism, taking on its greatest urgency during the interwar years.

"A Veritable Crucible"

When it came to making "good Americans," a chief mission that the Seattle Schools laid out for itself, two interrelated outlooks shaped how they approached their work. The first drew from a progressive, "melting pot" point of view that celebrated internal diversity in the schools and American society at large but still held firmly to the objective of Americanizing everyone. This attitude was consistent with the pluralist and cosmopolitan ideas of such intellectuals as Horace Kallen and Randolph Bourne who believed that people could (and should) maintain their ethnic cultural identities and develop worldly perspectives while joining and committing their primary civic loyalties to the American national community. These ideas also resonated broadly with the World War I "100 Percent American" and postwar Americanization movements that swept through the nation. In practice, however, these movements privileged Europeans and ignored nonwhite ethnic minorities. The second set of ideas overlapped with the first but was strongly influenced by considerations of place. Here, school officials also understood Seattle's cultural diversity in terms of Pacific Rim internationalism, which brought Japan and Japanese American students front and center in terms of explaining the uniqueness of Seattle's urban landscape and the challenges of Americanization facing the city's educators.

By the early 1920s, the school district was taking a sustained look at the impact of immigration and came to the realization that teachers needed to be better prepared to work with students who, upon entering the schools, did not speak English. As early as 1923, *Seattle Grade Club Magazine,* a periodical for teachers and administrators in the district, pressed employees to learn more about the "foreign elements" around them, and from that point it regularly featured articles about cultural diversity and working with immigrants and children of immigrants.[35] The magazine also frequently highlighted statistics on the origins and non-English ability of entering students to give some concreteness to the picture in Seattle. In 1928, the *Grade Club* reported that Washington School, one of the largest in the city, had a student body representing twenty-six countries and five continents; to be exact, 55 percent were eastern European Jews, 15 percent were Italian, and 3 percent were Japanese. And at Pacific School, reportedly 75 percent of those entering kindergarten that year spoke no English.[36] Eventually, schools implemented transitionary English programs for young students and special classes for parents.

The array of languages and cultures that each cohort of students in the integrated schools comprised might have represented daunting challenges for educators, but these conditions also placed Seattle on a level with the major cities of America and validated district officials' overblown rhetoric about the epic and historic significance of its work. "Upon the schools of America has fallen the major responsibility for the assimilation of this greatest human tide in history," stated Worth McClure, a district board member and later super-intendent.[37] Asserting Seattle's place amid this "greatest human tide" and the important role that fell upon its schools to transform the immigrant masses, the *Grade Club* stated, "Seattle has "her Americanization problem, and . . . the grade-school classroom is a veritable crucible."[38] The magazine admit-ted that, compared to other large cities, Seattle's foreign-born population was relatively small, but its concentration in a handful of schools gave rise to substantial teaching challenges for their employees. But also, by claiming an "Americanization problem," the district could elevate the importance of its work while also bolstering Seattle's profile as a major metropolis. Other urban school districts on the West Coast were caught up in similar demographic transformations and moved to implement curricular changes to address their diversifying populations as well as internationalization of their cities.[39]

To further heighten appreciation for the extraordinary mission being undertaken by Seattle Schools, the *Grade Club Magazine* featured "The Great Crucible of America: The Public School" as its theme in May 1932.[40] On the cover was a drawing of the exterior of Broadway High by Chinese American student Fay Chong. Chong would graduate from Broadway in 1933 and later come to public notice in the late 1930s as part of the North-west School of art. Elsewhere the magazine claimed that since September 1914, 503 students from Russia, Greece, Turkey, Italy, Spain, Austria, Bul-garia, Syria, Armenia, Siberia, Sweden, Norway, Finland, Denmark, Mexico, China, Japan, and the Philippines entered Washington School and exited as Americans with a common language and culture.[41] To demonstrate the ide-als and effectiveness of Americanization in Seattle Schools, a writer for the *Grade Club* interspersed "quotations" to reveal students' gratitude to their instructors for teaching them to love America:

> Who could doubt the intentions of the lad who said, "Ven I vas in Roosha I hadt to pray for the Tsar, but ven I godt on the sheap, I prayed for the Pressidendt of the Unidtet States." Or the appre-ciation of the illiterate Syrian youth who volunteered, "De Unidtet States is de bes' konetrie and de Seattle school is de bes' school." Or the Greek boys who volunteered and, in the doughboy's uniform, proudly returned "home" from their service on the Argonne and other battle-fronts.[42]

Seattle Schools often mixed its metaphors in claiming to be both a "melting pot" and "salad bowl," but generally it held to its professed goal of respect-ing difference and encouraging students to retain their "ancestral" cultures while becoming American, viewing these objectives as complementary, not conflicting. It was essential to "constrain" students to "respect and admire also the art, the music, the religion, the folklore of their parents, whose hardihood has brought them to the new land of opportunity. These are the rare gifts which have made them strong and which they bring to be cast into the melting pot from whence shall flow the new America, combining the strength of all her sources."[43] This "new America" would be built on diversity, not uniformity. "Those things which are true and good and beautiful in the cultures of the Old World," explained the *Grade Club*, would be the foundation of a "stronger America."[44]

"PROBLEMS OF THE PACIFIC"

As discussed above, Seattle Schools' philosophy about Americanization and immigrants was refined by geography, illustrating how issues of place prompted educators to link local and global concerns in their approach to students and design of curricula. In a variety of ways, the rhetoric of Pacific Rim internationalism and United States–Asia relations found its way into the educational discourse. In one instance, the *Grade Club* pointed out that Seattle's arrival as "The World Port! The Gateway to Alaska! Point of transshipment for millions in Oriental silks," was not only a concern for political and economic officials but also a pressing issue for educators. In 1935, Dorothy Rutherford penned an end of the year essay titled "Cosmopolitan Christmas" for the *Grade Club*. In her view, "cosmopolitan" was an apt description of a city whose internal population—not just economic affairs—had been transformed by commerce and international relations. "Cosmopolitanism," thus, was not merely an empty word that city leaders used to promote business and diplomacy but also a concept that educators believed captured the social and cultural fabric of Seattle. Furthermore, as Rutherford suggested, teachers and administrators could more effectively serve their students and the community at large if they developed an understanding of the conditions and origins of Seattle's cosmopolitanism:

> Commerce! So important as to warrant resident representatives for foreign nations. The Foreign Trade Department of the Seattle Chamber of Commerce lists thirty-one foreign consulates in our city, authorized to visa commercial documents. Just as Americans penetrate trading centers in every clime, so merchants, buyers, traders from all over the world find their way to Seattle and the Pacific Northwest. They establish homes. They are your neighbors and mine.[45]

In Seattle, the wheels of Pacific commerce were having perhaps the most concrete impact on who were "your neighbors and mine"; thus, it was important for teachers to learn about international relations along and across the Pacific Rim, especially with regard to Japan. For Japan was not just a key trading partner of the United States but also the country of origin for the largest Asian American community in the city. Obtaining knowledge about Japan and the impact of United States–Japan relations on Seattle was particularly important for teachers at such schools as Bailey Gatzert, Franklin, Broadway, and Garfield, which had large proportions of Japanese American students in their classrooms. In 1931, the *Seattle Grade Club* paid tribute to the Japanese immigrant farmers in the White River Valley, titling the issue, "In the Shadow of the Western Fujiyama."[46] Many of the articles in the issue were about Japanese immigrants who lived and worked in the Valley, emphasizing their indispensable roles in developing the economic potential of the area and mulling over whether their children would carry on this work, become professionals, or follow other trends.

Orienting public education objectives around the Pacific Rim was in line with the district's overarching vision. As historian Richard Berner explains, under superintendent Thomas Cole, who served from 1922 to 1930, educators and the school board agreed to focus the curriculum around "Community Life Studies," whose aim was to "make good citizens as well as healthy ones," and to provide students with an education relevant to local conditions and needs. This plan entailed introducing students to "the workaday world," a process to which local industries and the Chamber of Commerce contributed through arranged visits and observations as well as learning materials. Although this aspect of education was designed to turn students into productive members of the local and regional economy, the overarching aim of "Community Life Studies," Berner explains, was to "progressively [expand] their geographical and temporal frames of reference through the grades."[47]

Making Pacific relations a part of students' frame of understanding, then, was compatible with the district's philosophy. The push to promote a better understanding of Pacific affairs within the public school curriculum came from outside the district as well, and a particularly important figure in this regard was Herbert H. Gowen. Gowen, a former missionary who had worked with Chinese and Japanese migrants in Hawaii, was also the founder of St. Peter's Japanese mission in Seattle. Also acknowledged as an expert on East Asia and a proponent of United States–Japan relations, he was an active member of the Japan Society and served as the chair of the University of Washington's Oriental Studies department, which incidentally was formally established during the Alaska-Yukon-Pacific Exposition of 1909. Gowen believed such cities as Seattle could play critical roles in fostering understanding among Pacific nations but, to do so, needed their residents to be well informed on the issues. In this respect, educational institutions would play critical roles. "Here comes in the first great need, that of a trained intelligence in matters of Pacific relations," he stated. "With larger understanding of these relations will come the sympathy which eventually make[s] the civilizations of East and West complementary rather than antagonistic.[48] Contributing to the public education discourse through lectures, visits to schools, and essays for school district publications, Gowen often expressed his belief that a local citizenry informed on Pacific relations was crucial for national well-being. "No Americanism which is not at work throughout the world can in the long run be serviceable to America herself," he wrote. "A wonderful opportunity has come to us as the frontier people of the western civilization to make such a bridge of peace across the Pacific as will make that ocean worthy of its name."[49]

In terms of concrete reforms, limited and modest victories were achieved toward adapting school curricula around Pacific Rim concerns. A spirited, though ultimately unsuccessful, movement during the late 1920s through 1930s to institute Japanese-language instruction united local Japanese Americans and United States–Japan trade societies.[50] Members of the Seattle Japanese Chamber of Commerce, purporting to represent the local Japanese American community, took the case to the school board in 1933. They argued that offering Japanese language in the high schools would allow Nisei students to learn through the public education system what they were already studying at Kokugo Gakko. They then proposed that if this request for Japanese-language instruction could not be accommodated, students should be given the option of receiving credit for their work completed at the Japanese Language School. Both requests were denied.[51] The Japan Society formed a special committee to advocate implementing Japanese-language instruction in the public schools, viewing this initiative as an extension of its work in promoting United States–Japan friendship. It argued that knowledge of Japanese would benefit all students and promote good citizenship by making them better informed about the Pacific Rim. Although the movement ultimately failed to achieve its objectives during the prewar years, it did gain some key supporters along the way. These supporters included Austin E. Griffiths, a former city councilman and school board member, who put the Japanese-language issue high on his reelection platform for his board seat in 1930. Framing his support for Japanese instruction in terms of Seattle's unique geography, he told the Washington State Women's Republican

Club, "It is extremely important that we of the Pacific Coast understand our neighbor in the Orient and to this end their languages should be taught in our schools to those who wish to learn them."[52] That year, Griffiths won his bid for a second term.

Although the language courses were not adopted, the schools did incorporate Asian perspectives and attention on Pacific relations in piecemeal ways. As early as 1931, some of the high schools in the district began offering a course called "The Pacific Rim," which focused on the history of countries in this area as well as contemporary international politics.[53] Additionally, during the 1930s, Seattle Schools regularly hosted guests to speak on United States–Japan affairs from the local Japanese American community and from Japan. For instance, in 1935, Kiyoshi Uchiyama, the Japanese consul in Seattle, made his case to Franklin High students for "Oriental" language instruction in American schools, as he believed this instruction was necessary to foster a better understanding between the "Orient" and "Occident." He also defended Japan's invasion of Manchuria and insisted that this action would not endanger the friendship between the United States and Japan.[54] In 1937, students at Broadway High heard Chinese American and Japanese American students from the University of Washington debate the Sino-Japanese crisis.[55] On at least four occasions between 1920 and 1935, Franklin High hosted educators from Japan who came to learn about modern Western education and to share their own views on United States–Japan relations.[56]

Listening to these speakers discuss United States–Asia relations and other issues pertaining to international politics helped students expand their knowledge about the world outside, but the teachers' and school officials' goals went beyond just instructing students about world affairs; they also wished for their students to understand themselves in relation to the larger world. This understanding was important given Seattle's location on the Pacific Coast and its student population, which, as the district insisted, mirrored aspects of the world's diversity. As one high school teacher described, "Problems of the Pacific areas were being studied by a class comprising Japanese, Chinese, Negro, and white children. The problem was to train the pupils to discuss the race problems of the Pacific and the political problems of the Far East without hurt to the feelings or the legitimate pride of any member of the group." Thus, Pacific relations were not just a backdrop but also a key dimension of the conversation on student relations within the schools. In this class, students were told to accept each other's differences on the understanding that they were all part of one global community:

When one girl made the remark that her father was an exporter and that he "couldn't see the Japanese side at all," two columns were drawn on the board. In the one column were listed items bringing out the Japanese point of view and in the other, the Chinese point of view. The pupils were led to see that each race has made its own particular contributions to the world; that expressions like "Japs" for Japanese, "Wops" for Italians, and "Gringos" for Americans do not make for international friendliness; that trade with a nation is dependent upon the good will of its people.[57]

Other school activities reinforced students' awareness of how international relations were relevant to their own lives and relationships with one another. Clubs devoted to international affairs, such as Garfield's Open Forum Club and Franklin's World Affairs Club, stated as their goals the discussion of international problems and the promotion of friendship among the various nationalities represented in the student bodies. Additionally, oral presentations and debates, which were considered integral to Americanization and citizenship training in Seattle curricula since the turn of the twentieth century, provided students with structured settings for discussing international affairs. School debates on various contemporary issues often addressed Pacific relations, and the selection of debate topics called for knowledge of salient world events as well as sensitivity to the diverse student body. In 1924, students at Franklin High debated the U.S. role in the Philippines, as this subject was deemed an important international issue that Seattleites, as Pacific Coast residents, should be especially conversant on. Things took a controversial turn in 1926, when students and teachers considered holding a debate on whether Japanese people in the United States were entitled full citizenship rights. Although it was certainly a timely and relevant issue, administrators worried that allowing the debate to proceed would strain relationships between white and Japanese students and undermine school morale. Due to this concern, the debate for that year was called off.[58] Debating continued in 1927 with the less racially explosive but still contentious issue of abolishing interscholastic athletic competition.

Aimed at enhancing international and intercultural education in Seattle schools was a handful of arranged trips for teachers and school administrators to Japan, several of which Japanese American organizations and the Japanese government coordinated and financed. Framing these as diplomatic and educational missions, the Japanese Americans who participated in organizing the trips had several aims, which included raising American sympathy for Japan, providing teachers with first-hand knowledge of Asian history and culture, and heightening their sensitivity to their Japanese American students. At least six Seattle teachers and administrators went on such visits between the late 1920s and 1930s. These trips were also given as rewards of sorts for educators who showed particular interest in Japanese American students and the local Japanese American community. Katherine Lentz, a history teacher at Franklin, for instance, was selected to go on one of the trips, because she had studied the Seattle Japanese American community for her master's thesis, had many Japanese American pupils, and was teaching a course on the Pacific Rim.[59] Also, in 1930, when a group of Japanese parents helped finance a trip to Japan for Pacific School principal Edward Stafford, it was presented as a gesture of gratitude for his service to Nisei students. The *Japanese-American Courier* praised him for "[accepting] the Japanese children on an equal order with children of other races and [teaching] his teachers under him to show every cooperation necessary to the offspring of foreign-born parents."[60] The goodwill of such educators as Stafford, the parents believed, was crucial to the successful assimilation of Nisei and for maintaining "the existing good relations between the Japanese and American peoples."[61]

Through such efforts as lobbying for Japanese-language instruction and organizing trips to Japan for teachers, local Japanese Americans demonstrated and reinforced their strong stake in Seattle public education, and they found that they had a sympathetic audience in a handful of teachers and administrators. With the rise of the Nisei generation, described by the *Japanese-American Courier* as an "interstitial group in maintaining an intermediary station in American life," parents and Japanese American organizations took actions to prepare this cohort for its leadership of the ethnic community.[62] Parents joined PTAs and educational boards, and Japanese American newspapers diligently reported on the distinctions and honors being garnered by Nisei students. In 1936, the *Courier* boasted that twenty Seattle Nisei had been recognized as valedictorians, salutatorians, or commencement speakers.[63] It later reported that over the 1937–1938 school year at Garfield High, forty-six Japanese Americans made the honor roll, and Nisei George Okamura was elected Honor Society president.[64] Japanese Americans also celebrated such student athletes as Garfield's Harry Yamaguchi and Franklin's Roy Nagawa, Bill Yamaguchi, John Yoshida, James Sakamoto, and Mike Hirahara. Known as "barrel-chested Mike," Hirahara attained numerous distinctions while playing football for Franklin High, including serving as captain of the team and being named to the all-city team. Local Japanese American newspapers regularly noted these and other feats.

In addition to following and reporting on the progress and achievements of Nisei in the public schools, Japanese American community leaders regularly met with school officials to discuss their needs and concerns. The Japanese Chamber of Commerce and Japanese Association, for example, hosted dinners and forums for this purpose.[65] At one luncheon in 1929, hosted by the Associated Businessmen's Club and held at the Maneki Café in Nihonmachi, Dr. Caspar Sharples, a prominent Seattle physician and member of the school board, spoke to a group of Japanese Americans to tout the positive work that the district was accomplishing in Americanizing students and teaching the "children of the varied racial groups [to] conform to American institutions and ideals."[66] He also praised Japanese parents for "never [making] a howl about wanting this and wanting that, but [showing] a quiet and close cooperation with the school board in attaining whatever is possible for the betterment of the schools to which their children go and for the betterment of their young ones' education."[67] Such contacts between Seattle Japanese Americans and education officials became more extensive into the mid-1930s as the Nisei population in the schools grew. One setting in which they regularly came together was a weekly public forum sponsored by the Board of School Directors and U.S. Office of Education where citizens could discuss important issues and stimulate cultural and recreational interests. At the inaugural meeting in 1937, held at Bailey Gatzert, Principal Ada Mahon presided, and University of Washington professor Howard Martin facilitated the discussion. Japanese American participants included prominent members of the ethnic community, such as James Sakamoto, Reverend Murano, and Masaru Akahori, the managing editor of the *Great Northern Daily News*.[68]

On Campus

The efforts to bring into the classroom an appreciation of internationalism and an understanding of the connections between global migration, Pacific Rim commerce, and local conditions seemed to find some resonance with students. For example, writings by students in their school newspapers and yearbooks indicated that the concept of "cosmopolitanism" had a positive ring and was meaningful for explaining their own surroundings. Thus, at one time or another during the 1920s and 1930s, the students of Franklin, Garfield, and Broadway all proclaimed theirs to be Seattle's most "cosmopolitan" school. In making this claim, they expressed pride in their student bodies' diversity and posited that the pluralism of their schools was a microcosm of the world, paralleling the discourse in the city at large.

To illustrate an example, in 1920, the students of Franklin High anointed their institution Seattle's most "cosmopolitan" school. As indicated in the following passage from their newspaper, the *Tolo,* they understood this concept, which they believed was evident in their own classrooms, as a condition growing out of the forces of international migration: "Here at Franklin besides the students from China, Japan, the Philippines, et cetera, there are those from all parts of North America. In a very short time, however, these new students gradually begin to forget their Southern accent, their New England 'superiority' or their Alaskan mannerisms, and become more like the rest of us, way out here in 'faraway' Seattle."[69]

Their description of Seattle as an American city where of people varied ethnic backgrounds became "like the rest of us" and as a "faraway" locale where students "from China, Japan, the Philippines, et cetera" converged reflected a broader perception that in West Coast cities such as Seattle, identifying with America and the Pacific went hand in hand. In 1927, Franklin's annual yearbook featured the "Pacific Rim" as its theme. The inside cover, moreover, bore an inscription that strongly echoed boosters' descriptions of the city: "Beyond the blue Pacific lies the Orient, land of flowery charm and courtesy. Wise with the learning of the ages, she has reached her glowing zenith." Following the tradition of identifying each class with a different theme, the seniors represented the "Orient"; the juniors, South America; the sophomores, the South Sea islands; and the freshmen, Alaska. The senior class's naming itself the "Orient" is suggestive of the privileged place that Asia held in students' perception of the Pacific.

Garfield High was another school whose students touted its cosmopolitan characteristics. In May 1926, its newspaper, the *Messenger,* reprinted a letter from Tracy Strong of the Young Men's Christian Association (YMCA), who had visited the school earlier that year. Impressed with what he observed, Strong had high praise for the school as an exemplar of the American melting pot, and his letter, in turn, was a source of pride for the students:

> I have come to see more clearly than ever some of the great opportunities before the boys of Seattle, not only for developing individually into the best possible citizens, but also to demonstrate how the children of various nationalities can be welded together in one group. The world needs to learn that lesson today. I believe that Garfield, as much as any school in the city, is at work on such a problem, but I hope that they will be able to demonstrate even a greater truth than how children of different nations can become Americans, namely how they can become Americans and still maintain some of the older nations from which they have sprung.[70]

In their own writings, students would also elaborate on why they thought Garfield was Seattle's most cosmopolitan high school. In 1933, a student explained in the pages of the *Messenger* that this status stemmed from Garfield's embodying the principles of equal opportunity and interracial understanding. "It matters little of our faith, race, or color," wrote the student. "Our success in life depends upon that which we are able to give to the world." [71] As to where this equal opportunity flourished most, the writer cited the school's sports teams as "models of inter-racial as well as athletic teamwork." Similarly, in 1938, Garfield's yearbook, the *Arrow,* made racial harmony its theme, and it was dedicated to the "student body of Garfield, whose friendliness stimulates interracial understanding." The annual's foreword read:

Daily, through the portals of Garfield, enter and go representatives of scores of races. Within the four walls, they learn the principles of self and community government. Here, perhaps for the first time, they become aware of their mutual interests, their common destiny. Here, they learn the rudiments of brotherly love and the respect for the institutions and culture of the other races. This *Arrow* strives to enkindle the spark of heart-felt love for a brother man and to make stronger the hand clasp across the sea.[72]

It continued:

There is a thriving community, comprised of many races which are bound together by the staunchness of the Bulldog tradition. Here, at this veritable crossroad of international by-ways, a competent, tolerant faculty and a friendly, cosmopolitan student body work together in perfect coordination to produce the unbeatable combination— the Garfield personnel.[73]

Newspapers outside the schools likewise contributed to the construction of Seattle schools as "cosmopolitan" utopias. In 1939, the *Seattle Times* profiled Broadway High School, describing it as "educational melting pot" with students representing the Philippines, Canada, Finland, Nicaragua, Italy, Norway, Japan, Ireland, England, the Netherlands, Denmark, and China, among other nations. "Mingling daily at Broadway High School in Seattle are students of more than twenty-five nationalities," it stated.[74] To illustrate the array of races and ethnicities that flowed through the halls of Broadway, the article included pictures of students captioned with their names and nationalities.

Characterizing an entire city or school as cosmopolitan required demonstrating, or at least professing a commitment to, racial and ethnic inclusiveness. Along these lines, minority students were regularly elevated to heightened forms of attention in student publications and school activities. Japanese American students, who were accomplished in their own right but might not have otherwise garnered schoolwide notice, occasionally found themselves the subjects of great interest. Students celebrated such individuals as Ralph Ochi of Franklin High, who created the school's first photo club in 1923 and later went on to become one of Seattle's foremost Nisei photographers. In 1931, an article in the *Tolo* lauded Kenjiro Yamada with the headline, "Kenjiro Yamada Shows Students Just What One Boy Accomplishes." The piece detailed the many responsibilities he juggled—working in a card room and a rooming house, delivering newspapers—and on top of it all, he always finished his homework. In 1936, Nisei Bill Yamaguchi, mentioned earlier as one of Franklin's athletic standouts, was the subject of praise in the *Tolo*. In admiration of his work ethic and multiple talents, his peers held him up as a role model for other students. Among Yamaguchi's accomplishments that the *Tolo* highlighted were membership in the school's French Club, World Affairs Club, and Improvement Committee and holding office as president of the Service Club.[75]

Such tributes to Japanese American students at predominantly white schools demonstrated how in self-described "cosmopolitan" places, minorities could enjoy significant degrees of visibility. Not only would Nisei be profiled in student publications; on occasion, they also wrote for and edited them. Others rose to prominent leadership roles in clubs, attained schoolwide academic honors, and made varsity in athletics. However, these examples did not change the fact that, for most Nisei students, the high school years were marked by internal segregation and an incomplete acceptance by their white peers. Because the schools exalted internationalism and pluralism, acts of blatant racial hostility by students were rare and could not be publicly condoned. Sharon Tanagi Aburano said that the "melting pot theory we grew up under" had a positive impact on student relations: "The student body got along very well."[76] However, Broadway student Ruby Inouye recalled that, despite its integrated student body, white students were clearly the "heroes" of the school. And although Mits Takahashi fondly remembered his years at Garfield, he acknowledged, "socially . . . the different groups did not get together."[77] Yae Aihara described the thoroughness with which students segregated themselves: "We stayed together. . . . [W]e didn't associate with the other students at all, white students. It was kind of understood. You couldn't hold office, it was understood. We couldn't go to the prom because it was held in a country club. . . . [I]t was a way of life. The whites were the dominant people."[78] May Namba took a similarly nonchalant view toward racial segregation within the schools, acknowledging its pervasiveness yet insisting it never bothered her, because "that's the way it was."[79]

STUDENT-TEACHER RELATIONS

Although Nisei elicited the occasional but notable acknowledgement by their white peers, teachers showed a keener interest in the Japanese students whom they encountered in their classrooms. Teacher-student relations are an overlooked but significant dimension of interracial relations in urban public schools during the early twentieth century, as nearly all teachers employed by school districts were white. In recounting his years as a student at Bailey Gatzert, Victor Ikeda said all his teachers were white. Furthermore, he recalled that these teachers, most of whom were female, seemed unusually dedicated to their work. "One of the things that we noticed quite a bit is when we went to school, most of the teachers were single, so that they didn't have this dual responsibility of the school and taking care of the family," he said. "So they spent lots and lots of energy and time with the kids in school."[80] Doris Pieroth explains that many of the teachers during the interwar years were single migrants who had arrived unaccompanied from the East and Midwest. With school district resources stretched during the 1920s and 1930s, they might have also faced pressure to stay unmarried and to devote most of their energies to their work and students. The teachers who worked closely with Asian students often brought a missionary zeal to the task of transforming their charges into "good Americans." Their views were no doubt colored by pervasive assumptions of Orient-Occident difference, which convinced them that their Japanese students, some of whom did not speak English when they entered school, were in greatest need of their attention. There was also a self-serving element to this; when Japanese pupils expressed gratitude to their teachers and exhibited signs of becoming Americanized, the instructors and school administrators could, in turn, congratulate themselves for their effectiveness.

At least part of the teachers' interests in their Japanese students stemmed from a general curiosity about how Asians in the United States coped with the East-West cultural divide and assimilated to American life. Subsequently, some of them wrote about their work with Japanese pupils so their experiences and insights could be of larger social value. In 1924, Franklin High history teacher Katherine Lentz wrote an essay titled "My Contact with Orientals" for the *Survey of Race Relations,* a research project led by University

of Chicago sociologist Robert E. Park. Lentz said that working with Japanese and Chinese students had been a positive experience. Describing a typical class of twenty-five to thirty-five students, which would have at least two
or three Asians, she said that the Asian students were usually diligent and
ambitious.[81] Belying some of the recollections of Japanese Americans' own
experiences in high school (as noted above), Lentz insisted that they were
not maladjusted or socially isolated amid the predominantly white student
body. "Japanese boys who were prominent in athletics mingled with white
boys," she said. "One Japanese boy who was a star player in football received
the approbation of his mates quite as freely, it seemed to me, as did the
white star players."[82] Ruth Bailey, another teacher at Franklin, concurred
with Lentz's assessment, saying, "Socially the Oriental pupil gets on nicely
with the white children," and "They attend school parties and I have seen
white boys dance with Oriental girls and vice versa."[83] In terms of academ-
ics, Bailey observed that Japanese students "hold their own" intellectually
against their white counterparts.

More direct evidence of the Americanization of Japanese students was
sought through the writings of the pupils themselves, and district employees
periodically circulated among themselves essays conveying Nisei gratitude to
the schools, purportedly representing the fruits of teachers' labor. In 1938,
the *Seattle's Principals Exchange* printed essay excerpts from a senior composition class at Broadway High, and two of the four excerpts were written by Nisei. "It wasn't getting good grades that counted the most," wrote
Shizuko Tanaka, "but . . . the development of our character and citizenship
through the years." In January 1941, Ada Mahon, of Bailey Gatzert, presented to the school board a letter she had received from George Ishikaura,
a former Gatzert student who had since moved to Japan. Ishikaura sent a
letter to Mahon in which he thanked her for being an inspirational teacher
and reflected on the education he had received. The school board, naturally,
was gratified to learn of this note and expressed much pleasure at hearing
of Ishikaura's "eagerness to be a good American and that his loyalty to the
United States had never wavered."[84] Meant to shed light on the progress
of Japanese and other Asian students as well as to blunt the nativist argu-
ment that they could not assimilate to American life, such stories tell us
more about the aspirations of teachers and administrators than they give us
a clear sense of Nisei attitudes and experiences. They elicited self-congratula-
tion and validated the liberal vision of the school district. Moreover, despite
school officials' insistence that Japanese students were becoming Americanized and that the social distance between them and their white classmates
was closing, the underlying curiosity and fascination about "Orientals" from

which their observations and writings sprang merely reinforced perceptions of Japanese people's "otherness" and foreignness.

A handful of teachers during the interwar period distinguished themselves through their service among and interest in Japanese students. Katherine Lentz and Ruth Bailey of Franklin High School were among these. As teachers whose careers were shaped by the dynamics of place as well as race, gender, and class, their experiences and outlooks would likely have been much different had they worked at schools in outlying neighborhoods populated by middle- and upper-class whites. The career of Ada Mahon, the principal of Bailey Gatzert Elementary from 1921 to 1945, perhaps best exemplified the ways in which dominant Orientalist perceptions, concerns about race relations between Japanese and whites, and Pacific Rim internationalism all came to bear on the work of Seattle educators having extensive interaction with Japanese students. Mahon's background was similar to those of many other women teachers in Seattle Schools during the early 1900s. She was a migrant, having grown up in New Brunswick, Canada, and she came west to Seattle in 1888. Mahon became an influential figure in the school district, owing to her long service and outspoken support for her Japanese American students.[85] Viewing herself as an "ambassador of goodwill" between the Japanese American community and Bailey Gatzert—a title endorsed by many Japanese Americans—Mahon's professional identity would defined by her work with Seattle's Japanese.[86]

Many Nisei who had attended Bailey Gatzert remembered Mahon as a devoted teacher who faithfully served not just her Japanese American students but also the entire Seattle Japanese American community. Sociologist S. Frank Miyamoto, who had actually attended Bailey Gatzert during the late 1910s when it was known as Main Street School, said Mahon was strict but revered and loved by students and parents alike: "[She] was demanding . . . that they perform at a high level, as much as they could."[87] Sharon Tanagi Aburano recollected that Mahon took very seriously her duty to Americanize the Japanese students who made up the majority of the population at Gatzert: "She really was like a social worker . . . trying to indoctrinate us into being a 'good American (citizen)' and what it meant, the democratic principles (explained)."[88] As part of these efforts, Mahon created the Good Americans Citizens Club at Gatzert, in which students learned to perform patriotism by way of such acts as flag rituals and marches to the music of John Sousa.[89] Mahon's work in Americanizing students went beyond drills, as other students described how she taught them how to drink soup properly (i.e., the "American way") and instructed girls on Western feminine hygiene.[90]

Students and parents showed great appreciation and regard for Mahon and the combination of firmness and open-mindedness that she brought to her work with Japanese pupils. George Yoshida remarked that she was unusual compared to other teachers in that her approach to Americanization did not entail making Japanese students feel embarrassed of their ancestry and customs. "I think she really enjoyed providing, not formal Americanization lessons but to teach us what we are, American citizens," he said. "And I didn't resent that at all. She didn't say, 'You're not Japanese.' But she encouraged us to speak English."[91] Her efforts to learn about Japanese culture and history as well as her interest in the day-to-day lives of her students further enhanced her standing among local Japanese Americans. While serving as principal of Gatzert, Mahon took Japanese language and history classes at the University of Washington as a way to bolster her understanding of her students and, thus, be more effective in her job. She also reportedly visited the homes of each of her students in the course of her tenure as principal.[92] Mahon's good standing among Seattle Japanese Americans also drew benefits for Bailey Gatzert; for instance, in 1921, a group of Japanese American parents of Mahon's students presented her with a check in the amount of $1,078.70 for the purchase of a moving picture machine and pictures for the classroom walls. The school board responded with a note expressing its appreciation to "these Japanese people" for the gift and their "loyalty" to the school.[93] Mahon also benefited personally, as she was one of the handful of Seattle teachers sent by the Japanese Association on educational tours of Asia. She went on at least three of these trips between 1928 and 1931.

These "educational missions" afforded white American educators the adventure of international travel and the opportunity to become cosmopolitans in their own right, but they also bonded them to serving the Seattle Japanese community. Mahon would be reminded during her visits to Japan that these tours were intended to reaffirm her commitment to her work with Japanese Americans in Seattle. During a reception in Japan in 1931, newspaper publisher Hikoichi Motoyama, of the *Osaka Mainichi,* thanked Mahon for her "inestimable service rendered to the educational cause of Japanese children on the other side of the Pacific."[94] While on another visit, the Tokyo Teachers Association honored Mahon with a banquet, during which former Broadway High student Jiuji G. Kasai urged her to continue serving the Japanese of Seattle. "As a graduate of Broadway High School," he said, "I owe a debt of gratitude to the people of Seattle and the teachers whose noble influence I have so deeply felt. Seattle, the queen city of the Pacific Northwest, with her beautiful hills, Queen Anne, Capitol Beacon, great harbor, splendid homes, and above all with the wonderful people full of initiative and pride of 'Seattle Spirit,' have given me a great inspiration."[95]

Raising the oft-invoked status of the Nisei as "bridges of understanding" between the United States and Japan, Kasai elaborated on his view that such American educators as Mahon had critical roles to play in grooming the second generation for this exalted duty:

> Japan . . . appreciates the services America has rendered in her the last fifty years. So will you teach the Japanese born in your country, who under the constitution of the United States are citizens of the United States, the highest virtues of your people and at the same time the noblest examples of their ancestors, so that they may become the true and loyal citizens of the United States to carry on their shoulders the banners of freedom, justice and humanity. Thus may they become the bridge that spans the Pacific Ocean to be the great highway for peace and international friendship.[96]

Throughout her tenure as principal of Bailey Gatzert, Mahon seems to have greatly impressed students and parents, and, for her part, she continually reaffirmed her commitment to Japanese Americans in Seattle. Furthermore, her concern and knowledge about local Japanese American affairs went beyond her classroom responsibilities, as she took steps to stay informed about major community developments and used the occasions to cement her relationships with important people and organizations. For example, in March 1935, after the election of new officers to the Japanese Chamber of Commerce and Japanese Association, Mahon wrote letters to the organizations in which she congratulated the winners and thanked the groups for their support and cooperation in her duties at Bailey Gatzert. "It is my hope," she wrote, "that the relationship between the Association and the Bailey Gatzert School will continue to be as helpful and cordial as it has been in the past. If at any time there is any way in which the school can serve the Association or render greater service to the community we shall be most happy to hear from you."[97]

Such teachers and administrators as Mahon performed important groundwork that enabled Seattle educational institutions to back up the claim that they were helping to bridge the East and West. The courses she took in Japanese language and history, her trips to Japan, and the Japanese guest speakers she invited fulfilled this function while making Bailey Gatzert a welcoming place for Japanese American students. As the *Japanese-American Courier* wrote about her in 1928, "It is infinite, incapable of measurement, what has been and are to be the fruits of her years of counsel and impressions upon the then plastic minds of her pupils, who now, on different sides of the earth are living examples of her teaching; interpreters of the West to the East and the East to the West."[98]

The conditions in the area south of Yesler, with its concentration of minority residents and presence of integrated schools with high Japanese enrollments, shaped the careers of such educators as Ada Mahon. According to district officials and publications, in Seattle, effectively serving immigrants and children of immigrants called for the development among educators of a worldly outlook as well as a commitment to spreading Americanism. Furthermore, through their relationships with such teachers as Mahon, Japanese parents and ethnic leaders sought to ensure that the vision, goals, and methods of Americanization in the schools were informed by district employees' ties to the local Japanese American community and their travels to Japan. In this regard, Mahon appeared cognizant and grateful. Describing a 1931 trip to Japan, she said, "My trip O'Dreams was a thing of joy that nothing can take from me." She marveled at the country, which to her was a "fairy land" composed of "dainty miniature islands" and was charmed by the "innocent" and "winsome" Japanese children she encountered.[99]

In Seattle during the early 1900s, school district leaders and employees seemed to work from the principle that education informed by a worldly outlook was preferable to a provincial one, a view compatible with the urban image that Seattleites were cultivating at the time. But if a capacity to understand local problems through a global mindset promoted harmonious social relations in diverse settings (as school officials were wont to claim), this vision went unrealized in the arena of race relations in the schools. For as much as the schools claimed that they embodied the melting-pot ideal and described themselves in relation to the Pacific Rim, conditions on the ground often told a different story. Franklin High teacher Ruth Bailey, for instance, said that her Asian students got along well with white students but then qualified her statements when she got to the topic of dating and marriage. "I doubt if the social mixing goes farther than the school environment," she conjectured. "The day may come when white boys will fall in love with [Japanese girls] but that is a long way off."[100]

A JAPANESE AMERICAN VALEDICTORIAN

In her statement in the previous paragraph, Ruth Bailey may have been speaking from her disappointment that many challenges still lay ahead with respect to improving student race relations. To her credit, she devoted considerable time and energy to encouraging her Japanese students and instilling in them the belief that they were, or could be, Americans along with the rest of their classmates. Furthermore, the lengths to which she and other teachers went to educate themselves about Japan and to reach out to local Japanese Americans were admirable. Where teachers and administrators showed less concern, and, thus, where their claims to cosmopolitanism fell short, was in identifying and addressing racism within the schools. This failure reflected not only the shortsightedness of school officials but also the tenacity of racial prejudice as an explicit and underlying force in daily life. The remarks of students about internal social segregation discussed earlier certainly underscored this issue. The Fred Kosaka incident that opens the chapter revealed disagreement between people inside and outside the school, although it told us little about student relations. Another event, also from 1924 and reported in the *Seattle Star,* but occurring three months later at a high school, does give us a glimpse into troubling aspects of student relations that bubbled just beneath the surface.

In May, about a month before graduation at Franklin High School, teachers and administrators selected as the senior class valedictorian Tadao Kimura, the American-born son of working-class Japanese immigrants. This news was not received well by some of his classmates. According to a teacher at Franklin, a group of white American students complained, saying Kimura "has never done anything for the school, i.e. he has never taken part in school activities. . . . There were many other students . . . who might easily have been valedictorian if they had done nothing but study. Without going into activities for the sole purpose of pleasure they had gone into them from a sense of loyalty to the school, which Tadao had ignored."[101] Things took a disturbing turn when, a few days before the ceremony, another teacher heard rumors of a plan by a group of senior boys to assault Kimura to keep him from arriving at the ceremony to deliver his valedictory address. Although the plan did not materialize, the rumor succeeded in stirring up much tension leading up to the commencement.

This controversy extended beyond the school, however. Once the *Seattle Star* learned of Kimura's selection, it spun it into a sensational "Yellow Peril" tale and condemned the school system's misguided philosophy, which had enabled this latest threat to take form: "On the evening of June 11 parents and friends of 211 seniors from Franklin high school will meet for the commencement exercises. Those exercises are typically an American institution. To them come proud mothers, smiling fathers. Winsome Americans and sturdy American boys in white graduation frocks and unaccustomed 'best suits,' live through what is to many of them, the greatest event of their lives."[102]

But this "greatest event of their lives," this "typically American institution" would be polluted or, worse, hijacked, because, "When these hundreds of Americans gather . . . they will have the experience of listening to Tadao Kimura, 17 year old subject of the Mikado." Kimura's valedictory title signaled that "Japan is determined to make western America a Japanese colony; every Japanese is determined, by hook or crook, to put this program over. And to put it over, American institutions, American progress, American facilities are used to the limit."[103] To blame for allowing such an appalling situation in which "the young Oriental" would "tell American mothers, fathers, boys and girls about 'the Power of Education'" was the school, which had not just allowed but also encouraged this travesty to occur. Eager to show "visible proof of the power of American education, grafted upon the morality, ideals and civilization of Japan," the teachers and other school officials, the *Star* alleged, had "educated one of them [Japanese] to a point of excellence above that attained by 210 other students, nearly all white Americans." This was the great failing of "our liberal American way."[104]

Coming to Kimura's defense were Franklin High administrators and members of the local Japanese American community. In an editorial that appeared in the *Great Northern Daily News,* a writer responded to the attack on Kimura, remarking, "I think the article . . . is one of the worst insults that paper has given to Japanese people. This Kimura is a citizen of the United States by birth; he has lived here all his life and has been a loyal American. He has studied hard instead of wasting his time and now because he reaps the reward for his many hours of labor *The Star* insults him and thereby insults all persons of Japanese connections."[105] Yaye Sakura, another Seattle Japanese resident, called out the *Star* for its hypocrisy. Why attack Kimura for achievements he had been inculcated to strive for, not by the empire of Japan but by the Seattle school system? "He is a full-fledged American citizen in soul and body," Sakura wrote. "You educate hundreds of American citizens of Jap parentage and insult them as you do."[106]

Although schools officials might have been prompted by a sincere affinity for Kimura and an impulse of color-blind fairness toward all students in their actions before and after the public fallout, their responses to the attacks seemed largely aimed at damage control to preserve Franklin High's reputation as an open, enlightened cultural melting pot. One strategy was to turn the issue into a debate about journalism and the *Seattle Star*'s role. When "a mere child, a boy of seventeen years, is made the subject of a wanton attack by the public press," remarked one teacher in an editorial that appeared in Franklin's newspaper, the *Tolo,* "high school students might wonder whether the profession of journalism is an honorable one after all."[107]

Although the debacle revealed the existence of racial tensions among the students at Franklin, teachers continued to insist that the incident was an aberration provoked by outside parties and that it did not reflect the otherwise "broad-minded" student body. One teacher said that the controversy had largely blown over by the time commencement rolled around, helped by Kimura's dignified demeanor throughout the ordeal as well as the open-minded disposition of most of Franklin's students: "This night, just hearing his voice you could not have told that he was anything but American. He spoke so earnestly that he deeply impressed his audience and he received a very prolonged applause. If there was any hissing it was drowned out in the applause and I was so glad. I think the students realized that anything they did to make the situation unpleasant would be a reflection upon the school."[108]

If it seems disingenuous for the teachers to claim that racial tension was not an issue at Franklin, some of Kimura's actions during the controversy indicated that, from a Nisei point of view, the climate of student relations was far from tranquil. Upon learning he had been named his class valedictorian, Kimura reacted not with elation but distress. According to one of his teachers, he wanted to turn down the title, "because he was afraid it might cause unfavorable comment due to his race."[109] Kimura also requested that his photograph not be taken and featured along with other Seattle high school commencement speakers in the *Seattle Star* and agreed to be the valedictorian and have his image featured only at the urging of his teachers (see Figure 4.2). He was persuaded that, because "there had been so much anti-Japanese propaganda lately," he could, through making a dignified impression, help "vindicate the character and worth of the Japanese people in America."[110]

In some ways, the teachers and administrators of Franklin High should be commended for selecting Kimura to be valedictorian and then standing behind him in the face of the uproar. The mid-1920s were troubled times with respect to anti-Japanese sentiment and politics—President Calvin Coolidge signed the 1924 Johnson-Reed Act just eleven days after the *Seattle Star* article was published—so they were surely aware of the potential fallout from elevating a Japanese student to such a coveted position. Elsewhere, Japanese American students who had reached the top of their class were denied the valedictorian title. For instance, Kay Matsuoka, a student at Narbonne High in southern California during the early to mid-1930s, earned the highest grade point average in her class but was told that she could not be the valedictorian at her school's graduation, because "they had never had an Oriental valedictorian."[111] The Kimura episode illustrated the mixed bag that racialized visibility offered Nisei students in Seattle. The construction of Seattle schools as cosmopolitan spaces called for white teachers, administrators, and some students

Will Mr. Coolidge Listen?
Proud Americans to Hear Japanese Boy Deliver Valedictory at Franklin Hi School

Figure 4.2. Franklin High School senior Tadao Kimura *(bottom left)*. This photo appeared in the *Seattle Star*, along with an inflammatory article, after Kimura was selected as the valedictorian for his graduating class in 1924.
(Source: Seattle Star, May 15, 1924.)

to place accomplished and distinguished Nisei under an intensified spotlight. In turn, however, this attention probably heightened Japanese American students' vulnerability to resentment and attacks, exposing the persistence of racism and Orientalism in settings where they were purportedly accepted.

The Shortcomings of Cosmopolitanism

Especially ironic about the Tadao Kimura incident was that just four years earlier, the students of Franklin had claimed that their school was Seattle's most "cosmopolitan." In perusing the pages of Franklin's yearbooks during the 1920s and 1930s, we might agree, for it appears to have been one of the most racially and ethnically diverse schools in the city. The same could be said of Broadway High and Garfield High. But if we look closely at students' writings and consider the memories that Nisei students had of their high school days, it is evident that racial boundaries were not erased or even blurred but rather reworked in the integrated schools of Seattle. As Namba of Garfield shared, "I remember graduation, we weren't allowed to go to the prom, because they went to a club that we, Japanese were [not] allowed. And so I remember forming our own dance . . . and doing our own thing."[112] Rather than look back on this memory with anger or shame, she says such treatment "didn't affect me, or it was acceptable, because that's the way it was." This set of observations, in which students voluntarily segregated themselves, certain activities were understood as off limits to nonwhites, and that this situation was "just the way it was," was remarkably common across Nisei recollections of the high school years.[113]

Illustrations of white students' simultaneous admiration and Orientalization of their Japanese peers can be found in articles from school newspapers about Nisei student athletes. Sports were regularly touted as a rare truly race-blind arena in which individual ability and sportsmanship transcended group prejudices and allegiances. But when white students wrote about their Japanese American teammates, their praise was usually underlined by a wonderment at and amusement over what they perceived as a distinctly "Japanese way" of playing. For instance, in 1933, a white student writing for Franklin High's *Tolo* praised "the Japanese method of playing Western sports." In particular, he found their sportsmanship impeccable and worthy of comment: "The teams line up and take a pledge of 'amateurism and good sportsmanship.' . . . No one ever criticizes the umpire."[114] In 1937, Garfield High School's newspaper, the *Messenger*, spotlighted Japanese student athletes for an article about the Japanese-American Courier League. The writer speculated that the "Sons of the Samurai" who tried out for school teams must have been getting extra practice somewhere.[115]

Along similar yet more obvious lines, in Franklin High School's 1924 yearbook, Nora Waldron authored the "Senior Prophecies," a feature of most annuals in which a member of the senior class would make predictions about where his or her classmates' lives would lead after graduation. Among Waldron's prophecies were that Francis Wilson would become the "Poet of the Age," and Whitson Woodard would go on to be an "accomplished mouth-organist." She also made predictions about many of her Japanese American classmates but envisioned all their futures in Japan for no apparent reason other than it being their country of ancestry. Tadao Kimura, Waldron wrote, would become the mayor of Tokyo, and classmates Yoshito Fuju, James Shinkai, Tokuo Kondo, Oliver Noji, Aituro Suzuki, Ochi, and Seiichi Washizuki would serve as his councilmen.[116] A few years later in 1931, Franklin students staged a performance of the popular British musical *The Geisha*. This choice was perhaps intended to showcase the students' cosmopolitan, Pacific Rim–oriented outlook, but it also exemplified their affinity for Orientalist cultural productions. The *Tolo* promised that *The Geisha* would be one of the greatest performances ever put on at the school.[117] Even though the musical about the clash of East and West cultures was set in Japan, most of the principal characters were European. Moreover, of the cast of more than one hundred, white students held all the lead roles. The most prominent Japanese American involved in the production was Rose Hamada, a junior who had the behind-the-scenes job of obtaining costumes and finding a Japanese dance teacher. Too often, being cosmopolitan at Franklin and other high schools amounted to little more than white students talking about their Japanese peers and engaging in Orientalist performance.

It is hard to say exactly where Japanese American students fit into the wider landscape of student life in the high schools during the 1920s and 1930s. Some individual Japanese Americans seemed to have cracked the racial barrier by attaining distinction among all their peers and becoming close friends with white students. On the other hand, looking at broader social patterns among the students reveals the persistence of ethnic and racial prejudices and affiliations. Extolling cosmopolitanism, furthermore, seemed to deepen, rather than efface, the perception of differences separating racial and ethnic groups while prescribing minority students to limited "ethnic" roles. The participation of Asian American students in schoolwide affairs usually took place in the guise of internationalism. In perusing the student clubs at Garfield, Franklin, and Broadway, the vast majority consisted exclusively of white students, with the occasional Asian face sprinkled in here and there. The only clubs where significant numbers of Asian American students were found were Asian themed. For instance, in 1933, Japanese students at Franklin organized a group called Amerasia, and in 1935, Chinese students at Garfield established a group called the Cathay Club. The stated aims of these two groups were to strengthen friendships among students and to provide forums for talking about international affairs. For their members, these clubs were important social spaces where a nascent Asian American identity took shape and expression.[118] However, when it came to engaging their white classmates, Asian Americans' roles were largely limited to representing the "Oriental" perspective. For example, in 1936, Franklin High School students staged an annual circus in which Japanese students took part in an internationally themed sideshow by serving rice cakes and refreshments and performing songs about Japan.[119] Also common were pageant-style cultural presentations held in assembly settings for entire student bodies, such as a 1939 spectacle by the Japanese Club at Franklin called "A Visit to Tokyo."[120]

CONCLUSION

In trying to untangle the sanguine rhetoric of cosmopolitanism from the daily realities of life and race relations in the schools, it is also important to be mindful of the changing currents of United States–Asia relations, as the "Pacific Rim" was always a crucial backdrop for understandings of cosmopolitanism in Seattle. With growing tensions in United States–Japan relations, especially during the 1930s, some Japanese American students—even within the insulated environs of the schools—sensed that their standing and, along with it, their claims to American identity were vulnerable. In 1937, the *Great Northern Daily News* reprinted an essay by a Nisei student at Franklin High, whose name was omitted at her request. Departing from the optimistic sketches that other Nisei wrote for their teachers and that found their way into district publications, the student detailed some of the difficulties she faced as an American of Japanese ancestry in light of the troubles in the Pacific. "I was strictly pro-Japanese," she wrote, "yet I am supposed to be an American." Although Nisei were encouraged to believe that in Seattle it was possible to have pride in their Japanese heritage and to be "good Americans," in reality they found negotiating these two expectations to be perilous and untenable, especially by the 1930s in light of rising geopolitical tensions in the Pacific world: "I feel that no matter what happens, I will be looked down upon to some extent. In reflecting upon the Jewish or Negro race, I realize that I am much better off with a powerful nation, though only of ancestry, behind me." The student asserted that she did not want "real protection," because she wished to remain in the United States and enjoy full citizenship. She ended the essay with the statement "Where our future lies, only God knows."[121]

Events would take a grim turn with Japan's attack on Pearl Harbor. While still in shock over this news, Japanese Americans and liberal whites hoped, perhaps naively, that the spirit of tolerance, worldly engagement, and inclusiveness that the schools had long been promoting would prevail over the ugliness of anti-Japanese racial scapegoating. On December 8, 1941, the day after the attack, the *Seattle Post-Intelligencer* printed an article with the headline "What's War to Friends?" Featuring a photograph of a racially mixed group of smiling, well-dressed teenagers, the article said that the students of Broadway High School, with their long history of interracial friendship and international understanding, were standing firm in their loyalties to one another in spite of recent events. The story was also picked up by the *Great Northern Daily News,* which printed the same photo on its front page and stated, "Despite the war between the United States and Japan there is still a stronger bond between the white Americans and their loyal Japanese American friends."[122] Within the schools, teachers and administrators sought to allay students' worries and to assure them that existing friendships and goodwill would overcome the racial hysteria. Arthur Sears, the principal of Washington School, called an assembly the day after the attack to impress upon students the need for tolerance and open-mindedness in these circumstances. Following the assembly, Nisei students in an English class at the school were asked to write essays about it, and one student remarked, "This morning Mr. Sears [gave] us a good talk. 'When we were friend[s], we love[d] each other, but suddenly we hate each other. . . . This is [the] same [at] school or between two nations. In school we were playing together, but some thing is not good, or the thing they don't like. And started to hate. War broke out in the same way.'"[123]

As the faith in friendship and understanding to overcome the antipathies of the coming war gave way to a more sobering reality in which the Pacific world would be split apart and "cosmopolitan Seattle" destroyed, no inspirational rhetoric could assuage the realization of imminent mass removal. With Japanese evacuation from Seattle under way in early 1942, Garfield's *Messenger* printed a poignant commentary about the larger meanings of this turn of events for the school: "Garfield has always drawn strength from a cosmopolitan student body. Her great football teams, her famed track squads, her aggressiveness—these are the results of a dynamic school spirit which in its pursuit of a greater Garfield, has overlooked racial prejudices and recognized us all only as Garfieldites—not as black, or white, or brown, or yellow men, but as classmates and comrades."[124]

According to the *Messenger,* the loss of Japanese American students symbolized much more than a shrunken student body or numerous empty desks, although those aspects of removal were certainly jarring, nowhere more so than at Bailey Gatzert Elementary (see Figure 4.3). As the article continued, the removal of Garfield's Japanese Americans, some 225 by its estimation, would have broad and profound ramifications, as it would "affect not only the evacuees themselves, but also the communities which they must leave. Garfield will suffer. No school can lose 225 loyal, capable students and not be the worse for it. Even as these students are reluctant to abandon their homes and friendships, so does it sadden Garfield to see so many who have represented her so well, go."[125]

During the interwar years, Seattle Schools disseminated a vision and ethos that gave students a framework for understanding the connections between Americanism, their local surroundings, and their relationship to the larger world, which was substantially predicated on an outlook that placed a high value on international friendship and peace in the Pacific world. Although this endeavor was fraught with contradictions, it does speak to how educators sought to cultivate a modern, informed citizenry strong in its loyalty as Americans but also aware of the world outside and embracing its

Figure 4.3. Students at the Bailey Gatzert School singing in front of statues of George Washington and Abraham Lincoln sometime in early to mid-1941. The school was populated mostly by students of Japanese descent. *(Source:* Seattle Post-Intelligencer *Collection, Museum of History and Industry.)*

diversity. A combination of factors, chiefly the schools' propensity to treat racial and cultural differences in a manner that was more fetishizing than thoughtful and teachers' and administrators' eagerness to measure their own successes, led the city's educators to fall short in terms of rooting out racial tensions and divisions in student relations. None experienced the contradictions of these conditions more fully than Seattle's Nisei.

In other aspects of daily life, more remote from the purview of white peers and authorities, Japanese Americans participated in a variety of activities that not only lent additional meanings to ethnic identity and community belonging but also clarified how their relationship with local space and identity was strongly informed by their awareness of and engagement with larger spaces, be they regional, transborder, or trans-Pacific. The next chapter turns to sports, a popular pastime in prewar Japanese America, which strengthened local ethnic solidarity while also facilitating encounters across ethnic, racial, and spatial boundaries. As the chapter illustrates, sports also became an effective medium through which Japanese Americans could articulate cosmopolitanism in their own terms, with respect to social relations as well as space.

5

⊃╫╠⊂

"That Splendid Medium of Free Play"

Japanese American Sports during the Interwar Years

One evening in March 1934, George Okada, the president of the Seattle Taiyo Athletic Club, gave an address during the Courier Broadcast on radio station KXA. Looking to boost the club's membership and to impress upon listeners the importance of physical fitness, he extolled the many personal and professional benefits that accrued from engaging in play and exercise: "The art of physical development is the one form of amusement, which is not only invigorating, but beneficial to mind and body alike. One cannot be a good athlete, in any branch of sport, without being in perfect physical condition, keenly alive mentally, cheerful of spirit, and of high moral character. It is obvious that such training prepares a man to better fulfill whatever career he may undertake."[1]

At the time, such rhetoric touting athletic play as a nurturer of good physical and moral qualities resonated broadly in American culture. It echoed the sentiments of legendary baseball promoter Albert G. Spalding, who wrote in a book published in 1911 that "the emotional and moral as well as the physical side of a man's nature are brought into play by Base Ball. . . . And there is nothing better calculated than Base Ball to give a growing boy self-poise and self-reliance, confidence, inoffensive and entirely proper aggressiveness, general manliness."[2] Belying the universal register of such statements, Spalding's cause was unmistakably commercial and nationalistic. The title of his book from which the above quotation comes is *America's National Game,* and in it, Spalding further intoned, "Base Ball elevates and . . . fits the American character."[3] Bringing a patriotic purpose to his endeavor, Spalding channeled the baseball's popularity to sell sporting goods and to promote an ideal of the United States as a nation of athletic, confident, and *manly* citizens.

Okada tapped into this view of sports as morally and physically fortifying, but for different ends. He sought to convey a more tailored message of personal improvement and ethnic solidarity to his fellow Japanese Americans in Seattle. In the course of his remarks, however, he shifted gears and widened his scope, although not to pay allegiance to any particular nation or national cause as Spalding had. Instead, looking to the global arena where United States–Asia affairs were fraught with tensions over Japan's recent actions in China, Okada suggested that sports could contribute to a "real good understanding between America and Japan."[4] Indeed, during the 1930s, goodwill trips to Japan by American professional athletes drew the notice of observers who saw in these trips reason to feel optimistically about the prospects for continued United States–Japan friendship. For example, in 1939, a writer for the *Japanese-American Courier* elaborated: "I always said participation in any clean sport does more towards creating understanding and strong friendship than anything else. If these politicians and so-called statesmen spent less time arguing for more guns and battleships, and put in more effort towards advancement of the international sports competitions, perhaps we wouldn't have to worry so much about wars and misunderstandings."[5]

During the prewar decades, sports filled the time of thousands of Japanese Americans in Seattle, whether by playing or watching, and ruminations about the larger social and political meanings of athletics preoccupied leading Japanese American opinion makers who would air their thoughts in the ethnic press and occasionally on the airwaves. Sports elicited impassioned commentary from such community figures as George Okada, who saw in them a path toward myriad improvements in Japanese American life, whether they pertained to personal development, interracial understanding, or better relations between the United States and Japan. In reality, athletics in the early-twentieth-century United States—from urban playgrounds to professional leagues—were highly segregated, and, in the context of internationalism, such sports as baseball were subject to the nationalistic claim that they were unmistakably *American* pastimes. Yet, as evidenced in the second part of Okada's remarks, something about sports—perhaps their color-blindness in theory—sustained the hope that a universal humanity, made concrete by common interests and shared passions, could overcome the divisions that ordinarily separated people. This belief offered some consolation to observers who wished that the United States and Japan could remain friendly despite the troubles in the Pacific as well as to racial and ethnic minorities in America who saw athletic participation as a democratic route to personal advancement, community uplift, cultural assimilation, and mainstream acceptance.

Departing from the existing literature about Japanese Americans and athletics, which tends to examine the significance of sports somewhat narrowly in terms of local ethnic identity and solidarity, this chapter widens the focus to consider how athletics were a flexible terrain on which Seattle's Japanese Americans confronted and negotiated racial, ethnic, spatial, and geographic boundaries. It examines the meanings and material aspects of sports, exploring what Japanese Americans expressed about them as well as some of the varied experiences and social encounters that athletic participation made possible. A significant amount of the competition that Seattle Japanese American athletes faced came from Japanese in the countryside, other parts of the American West, Canada, and even Japan. Attention to these translocal dimensions of sports illuminates the salience of place and scale in Seattle Japanese Americans' conceptualization and articulation of their dualistic identities as Japanese and American. As a common symbol for international relations and one of few activities that offered Japanese Americans the chance to travel outside the city, sports helped map their increasingly expansive outlook on and engagement with the world. Sports were also a location in which an early pan-Asian consciousness was cultivated, as competitions involving local Filipinos and Chinese played out against the backdrop of Pacific Rim politics.

Japanese Americans turned to sports to express their ideals and hopes with respect to local and international concerns. Throughout the 1920s and 1930s, leaders from the ethnic community, such as George Okada, invoked sports to reflect upon the prospects for continued peace in the Pacific, to call for friendship between the United States and Japan, and to voice their desires for interracial understanding in their own communities. Because, as stated above, in theory anyone could play and physical ability—not racial or ethnic background—determined the outcomes, sports could be a productive space in which to discursively challenge a white-only vision of Americanism and to pose an egalitarian, cosmopolitan Americanism as an alternative. Although achieving this ideal in the real world was a separate matter, and racial segregation in American sports largely went unchallenged until after World War II, Japanese Americans and other minorities in Seattle did have one play space in the city that embodied and emboldened their hopes for a more inclusive America. At Collins Park, the playground closest to most of the city's nonwhites and ethnic minority residents, a veritable multi-hued mosaic of young Seattleites emerged by the late 1920s. Hailed as the city's most "cosmopolitan" park, the people who used its facilities and worked there regarded Collins with pride and described it as an exemplar of an enlightened, open, and globally conscious Americanism that drew strength from internationalism and diversity.

The literature on sports, ethnicity, and race relations in American history is rich and highlights an important set of questions.[6] Whether examining the significance of American sports in ethnic communities or the struggles of minority athletes in white-dominated athletic environments, such scholars as Peter Levine, Gail Nomura, Samuel Regalado, Adrian Burgos, and Kathleen Yep have demonstrated how racialized minorities have sought belonging and worked to break racial barriers through athletic participation. Careful not to overromanticize their subjects, they show how success in this arena—through building their own organizations or distinguishing themselves in mixed settings—while significant in its own right, had little or no impact on challenging discrimination in the broader society. This chapter likewise refutes simplistic characterizations of the relationship between sports and society, particularly the notion that adopting "American" sports somehow set minorities on a direct path to assimilation and mainstream belonging. As the chapter shows, sports *could* be nationalizing and confer a sense of American-ness among Seattle's Japanese, but in unexpected ways.

Sports and Recreation in Seattle and America

In the context of modernization and crisis in the late nineteenth to early twentieth centuries, sports emerged as a popular pastime and became a common form of recreation among ordinary people in the United States. At this time, Americans confronted a new era as the pace of industrialization and urbanization accelerated, work lives became more regimented, and foreign immigration diversified a predominantly Anglo Christian population. Pronouncements that the "frontier" was closing and laments about "overcivilization" sent people searching to capture and to preserve aspects of a bucolic, premodern world that they feared was slipping away. In this context, members of the growing middle class turned to outdoor recreation and physical play as an antidote to the physical and psychological strains of living in a modernizing, fast-paced world. A generation of experts imbued with the Progressive era's faith in science and expertise touted the benefits of structured play for children's physical and moral development. Among the leaders of the recreation movement spreading this "gospel of play" were middle-class reformers and specialists working in such organizations as the YMCA, YWCA, and American Playground Association.[7] The construction of hundreds of resorts in the East and Midwest during the late 1800s enabled well-heeled families to partake in the emerging recreation culture in peaceful, natural settings away from the overcrowded cities.

The need for parks that provided people with settings to play or to sit in quiet contemplation became especially pressing in rapidly growing cities toward the turn of the twentieth century, including those in the American West. Proponents of the construction of spaces for recreational and athletic uses argued that structured, supervised play was a wholesome alternative to the dangerous vices that lurked in urban settings. In terms of recreational options, Seattleites were blessed by geography. The surrounding lakes and mountains made the Puget Sound area a haven for skiing, hiking, mountain climbing, and boating. As discussed earlier, boosters worked hard to promote Seattle as a unique city that offered nature and urbanity and, hence, the best of both worlds. Furthermore, urban planners sought to shape the city's development around showcasing these qualities. In 1884, Seattle's first public park was built and three years later, a Board of Park Commissioners was established to oversee the development of a citywide park system. Progress was slow going, but in 1903, the board hired the Olmsted Brothers firm to design the park system. One of the board's objectives was to place every resident within walking distance to a park so that all Seattleites could avail themselves of scenic, bucolic spaces for quiet meditation or vigorous competitive games.[8]

The national recreation movement coincided with an unprecedented wave of foreign immigration that transformed the American population, particularly in the cities. Concerned about the effects of urban life and the challenges facing new immigrants, Progressive reformers looked to sports and structured play to help facilitate newcomers' acculturation and to promote good values and habits. Advocates working within such groups as the Playground Association of America and YMCA took the lead in arguing for the universal benefits of sports. Because the ability to play required only physical aptitude and comprehension of a set of rules, sports appeared to be a unique arena in which otherwise insurmountable cultural barriers were brought down and understanding across social boundaries prevailed. Furthermore, to many native-born white Americans, the spectacle of foreigners from Greece, Poland, or Russia—people seen as barely removed from their premodern old-world existences—participating in such sports as baseball or basketball was an encouraging sign of the triumph of American values in the hearts and minds of immigrants. Although images of immigrants taking to American sports could be powerful symbols of the transformative power of the national culture, the realities of segregation and nativism meant that, more often than not, minorities played sports with and against members of their own racial and ethnic groups. That many athletic associations in the United States during the late nineteenth and early twentieth centuries were organized along ethnic or religious lines further reinforced group boundaries and solidarities rather than effacing or challenging them.[9]

Among Seattle's Japanese, sports could be Americanizing and confirming of ethnic leaders' and institutions' authority. As early as the turn of the twentieth century, the significance of sports as an institution was abundantly clear in this community. Coverage and commentary filled a quarter of to half the content of Japanese American newspapers, and by the 1930s, the Seattle Japanese American community had one of the largest organized athletic leagues in the city, the Japanese-American Courier League. In the decades leading to World War II, thousands of Issei and Nisei, boys and girls, men and women, took part in organized sports through schools, athletic clubs, and leagues and competed in a variety of sports, including baseball, softball, basketball, football, bowling, skiing, track, and tennis.[10] In her work on Japanese baseball in Washington's Yakima Valley, Gail Nomura argues that sports strengthened ethnic identity and solidarity among the Japanese Americans in that community, because most of the time they played against other Japanese teams. Community leaders endorsed sports for the youth as a wholesome alternative to activities they disapproved of, such as drinking alcohol and gambling. Because they were sensitive about public perceptions of their co-ethnics and accusations of their unassimilability, they extolled athletics for fostering a "clean" image and allowing Japanese people to demonstrate their capacity to become "American" and, thus, to counter the claims of naysayers.[11]

For those who participated in them, sports brought structure into the lives of Japanese Americans, especially young Nisei, and a way to feel connected to the ethnic community. S. Frank Miyamoto attributed the popularity of sports to the organizational propensity and skill of Seattle Japanese Americans. "The sports activities in the Japanese community were very much better organized than in my white society," he recalled. "In the Japanese community, it was typical that if you played football or played baseball or basketball, very rapidly you would get drawn into some kind of team organization."[12] With the presence of such a well-developed structure, sports became a foray into a rich social life for many Japanese Americans. As Toshio Ito noted, "In the older days I think the sporting, sports events, and participating in that was one of the major social outlets for the *Niseis,* because so many of the other mainstream activities were closed to the Japanese at that time."[13]

For Japanese in America otherwise accustomed to being viewed and treated as outsiders, being part of the sports world, whether as spectators, commentators, or participants, could reinforce a sense of belonging and empowerment. Talented athletes on all-Japanese teams or in mixed settings attained distinction, at times hero status, among their fellow Japanese Americans. Their accomplishments not only brought them admiration but also represented symbolic triumphs over racism. Organized sports also contributed much to the broader social scene in Nihonmachi, as teams and clubs relied on regular dances and mixers to raise funds, and community-wide events would be held to celebrate major victories or to mark the start and conclusion of a given season. Japanese Americans also drew symbolic meanings from athletic competition with respect to their hopes for advancement in American society. Ethnic leaders and writers sought to inspire ordinary Japanese Americans by insisting—much as Progressive whites did—on the potential for sports to bring different people together in a color-blind spirit, thus fostering understanding and equality. Such rhetoric, lofty as it was, could nonetheless be a source of consolation that fueled Japanese Americans' hopes for overcoming the cultural and structural barriers that they faced in their daily lives as racial minorities.

Baseball and Ethnic Authority

Toward understanding the emergence and key features of the sports culture in Seattle's Japanese American community, we must begin with the creation of Issei baseball clubs around the turn of the twentieth century. As early as the 1910s, a common sight in Nihonmachi on any given Sunday afternoon was the scene of young Japanese men battling it out on the local diamond before cheering spectators. The earliest athletic organizations for Japanese in the city were devoted to baseball, the first being the Seattle Nippons club, which was formed in 1906. The Nippons were composed primarily of working-class Issei men employed in the city and its vicinity as cannery employees, janitors, domestics, and other low-wage workers. For them, playing baseball was a welcome diversion and much-needed physical and psychological outlet from the drudgery of their work lives.[14] By 1911, three Issei baseball teams had been formed in Seattle: the Mikado, the Seattle Nippons, and the Asahi. Into the 1920s, with the rise of the Nisei and as the first generation grew older and less inclined to spend their spare time at the diamond, baseball became more identified with the second generation. For a time, the Japanese Language School provided the only structured outlet for Nisei baseball, and in 1911, it formed the Cherries, the first Nisei baseball team in the city. The Seattle Japanese American sports infrastructure grew substantially in 1924 with the establishment of the Nippon Athletic Club (NAC), whose creation was intended to defuse tensions between the Asahi and the Mikado but also to meet players' and fans' desires to have a sports club for the community and not just a few individual teams. Shortly after the NAC's formation, the Taiyo Athletic Club was established, and the two clubs commenced a spirited rivalry that lasted until the outbreak of World War II.

The available evidence suggests that Japanese American baseball fans were very passionate about the sport and supporting their favorite teams, so much so that on occasion, rivalries became all-consuming and threatened to divide the community. One way that fans showed their loyalty to teams was through boycotts of businesses run by the supporters of rival teams. Several times, these boycotts reached such a level of rancorousness that community leaders had to step in and call for calm and an end to the pettiness. Other problems stemming from overzealous sports fans included betting on teams and fighting at games.[15] As mentioned above, the formation of the NAC aimed to heal community factionalism caused by the Asahi-Mikado rivalry, but the creation of the Taiyo Athletic Club two years later wound up simply replacing an old rivalry with a new one. At the height of the NAC-Taiyo squabbles, a group of Taiyo fans organized a boycott of stores run by NAC supporters. As they did during the Asahi-Mikado rivalry days, community leaders and local journalists were drawn in. "The present N.A.C.-Taiyo feud is a thorn in the side of the Japanese community for real harmony and progress," a columnist wrote in the *Japanese-American Courier* in 1928. "Small as this keen, embittered rivalry is considered by many of the business men of the Japanese center, it bids well to crop into an inflammatory malady that may take years to remedy." The writer then beseeched fans to summon their "intelligent" and "commendable qualities" to overcome this "ill" before it got too out of hand.[16]

Individuals who became respected and influential figures in the Seattle Japanese American community were instrumental in establishing baseball's popularity. Perhaps more than anyone else, Frank Fukuda, affectionately known as the "Father of Japanese Baseball in the Pacific Northwest," dedicated himself to building a baseball tradition among Seattle Japanese. In 1917, he founded the Asahi Club, located at Tenth and Washington, and managed the team for eleven years, during what locals later referred to as Seattle Japanese baseball's "glory days."[17] A fixture in Nihonmachi by the 1910s, Fukuda's admirers viewed him as something of an ethnic miracle worker who, through his tireless championing of baseball, helped transform the community's boys into strong, disciplined men. Although females participated in organized sports throughout the early 1900s, Fukuda's singular interest in baseball and the development of young men reflected and shaped his highly gendered view of sports. He reportedly complained once in 1935 that "Sunday picnics and girls" represented the biggest threats to sustained community engagement with the sport.[18]

During his time in Seattle, Fukuda's presence in the community was pervasive. In an article honoring his work and legacy, the *Japanese-American Courier* recounted how Sunday mornings in Nihonmachi frequently found him "making the rounds" from house to house, rousing neighborhood boys to come out and play ball and convincing their parents to consent. "He early taught the lads through baseball," stated the *Courier*, "the advantages of team work, of quick thinking and of the never-say-die spirit." Mindful of all aspects of his players' development, Fukuda also held weekly meetings on Fridays where he "developed in them the art of public speaking, which they gained unconsciously when they stood up in their gatherings to tell their comrades of their ideas."[19] Although parents and fans sometimes found his enthusiasm to be a bit overbearing, they "hate[d] to admit the good that Fukuda accomplished in this city but to him much of the credit should be given for the benefits that their sons received through his training."[20]

A turning point in the history of Japanese American sports in Seattle was the formation of the Japanese-American Courier League in 1928, which brought an extensive organizational apparatus to Japanese American baseball as well as other sports.[21] The league was the brainchild of newspaper publisher and sports enthusiast James Sakamoto. A former Franklin High School football star and professional boxer blinded due to an injury sustained in a boxing match, Sakamoto had ambitious hopes for the league. He envisioned it as one large independent sports league for all the Japanese athletic teams in the Puget Sound area.[22] He also hoped it would help unite Japanese Americans and lift them above the petty club rivalries of earlier years. As an organization primarily for the Nisei, the Courier League reflected a broader demographic shift in the Japanese American community as well as Sakamoto's view that sports could play key roles in Nisei acculturation and the generation's mission to serve as "bridges of understanding" between the United States and Japan, a phrase he often used in his writings.[23]

From 1928 to 1941, the Courier League was the heart and soul of Japanese baseball in Seattle. Initially, it was made up of ten teams, but within three years it grew to fourteen. At its height in the late 1930s, thirty-two teams representing four classes—AA, A, B, C—made up the Courier League. As the number of athletes taking part in the league grew, so did the number of fans attending the games. Additionally, although Seattle was the league's headquarters, it included teams from other cities and outlying rural towns, such as Kent, Tacoma, Fife, and Auburn.[24] The teams were typically formed around churches, neighborhoods, and already existing athletic clubs. The Taiyo and NAC eventually joined the Courier League in the early 1930s after initially refusing to do so.

In describing the social significance of baseball in Japanese American history, Gail Nomura and Samuel Regalado have argued that the sport's popularity from the bottom-up as well as community leaders' endorsement of it strengthened ethnic bonds and identity. A somewhat surprising aspect of baseball was that, unlike other forms of "American" culture, such as certain types of music or dating practices, baseball did not appear to cause generational friction. Issei leaders and parents did not worry that Nisei were becoming less Japanese or that the older generation's authority was being undermined. Instead, when it came to baseball, the Issei, in fact, often claimed *they* were more devoted to the sport. Because many first-generation immigrants had been introduced to it in Japan, baseball represented generational continuity rather than discontinuity. In 1928, the *Great Northern Daily News* waxed nostalgic about the "old days" of Japanese baseball in Seattle and chided the Nisei for lacking the dedication of their predecessors to the game:

> The Taiyo and NAC do not take their baseball as seriously as the old-timers. The players of years ago ate baseball, slept baseball and talked baseball continually. The present day youngsters may be better ball players but they do not possess that faithful spirit. The ball players of years ago would never think of staying down town shooting pool until eleven or twelve o'clock on Saturday night; they would shudder at even the thoughts of such unholy things.[25]

BASEBALL AND JAPANESE NETWORKS ACROSS SPACE

The group ties and sense of ethnic camaraderie among Japanese Americans cemented by a shared passion for baseball went beyond the geographic limits of Seattle, as games also linked Japanese communities throughout the Northwest, along the West Coast, and on both sides of the Pacific.[26] The Courier League covered the entire Northwest and included teams from throughout Washington State and Oregon. It also organized and sponsored traveling all-star teams to play against their co-ethnics in California and British Columbia on a regular basis, further extending the league's geographic networks.[27] Because few other activities offered ordinary young Japanese Americans the opportunity to travel to the countryside and across state or international lines, participating in sports leagues brought adventure into their lives while also expanding their horizons on the world outside Seattle and Nihonmachi.

Although Western sports as Americanizing forces, facilitators of interracial understanding, or solidifiers of ethnic solidarity are familiar topics in broader discussions of the social significance of athletics in the United States, comparatively little consideration has been given to the factors of space and place. This oversight is curious, because, with respect to the concrete dimensions of sports, such issues as play space, location, and travel are paramount and unavoidable and, thus, mediate the social and ideological meanings that players and observers draw from athletic competition. In the city, participating in sports informed and deepened people's engagement with urban space. When they allowed for travel or the chance to interact with visitors from far away, sports illuminated and reinforced Japanese Americans' subjectivities as urban, northwestern, and American, thus clarifying the significance of geography and place in the formulation of identity.

In terms of forging a regional outlook, Japanese Americans in Seattle were part of an enduring and dynamic Pacific Northwest baseball culture as early as the 1920s. Japanese American players from the cities and rural communities of Washington, Oregon, and British Columbia traversed the region each season from April to August in a quest to achieve distinction as the Northwest's best. Annual events, such as the Fourth of July tournament, the Labor Day international series, and the crowning of the Courier League champions, solidified this regional sporting culture by bringing to it a sense of tradition. Moreover, elaborate banquets and socials that were held whenever visiting teams came to Seattle allowed athletes and others to form new friendships that would in turn help sustain long-distance contacts between otherwise disparate Japanese American communities. In some ways, intraregional play fostered an ethnic consciousness that transcended the local community, but it could also heighten Seattle Japanese Americans' identities as urbanites, particularly when they faced competitors from outlying rural areas. For instance, sports fans in Seattle admired and paid homage to the Wapato Nippons of central Washington, as this team was respected for its talented players and for dominating the Mount Adams League in Yakima County. The characterization of the Wapato Nippons as "rip-roaring, sun-burned, lean-muscled luminaries," however, was one indication of how Seattle Japanese Americans viewed their rural counterparts.[28] Additionally, rivalries that emerged from intraregional play strengthened

Seattle fans' and athletes' identification with their city, which could either heighten the thrill of victory or intensify the agony of defeat. For instance, when the 1935 season came to an end and teams from White River, Fife, and Portland had taken nearly all the top titles, the *Japanese-American Courier* lamented, "Painfully, the Seattle Japanese community wrote finis to the 1935 baseball season," adding that the season had been "the most disastrous year in local diamond history." The only consolation for "local rooters" was a team from Green Lake's victory over the Wapato Nippons in the annual Northwest tournament sponsored by the Seattle Japanese Association.[29]

Coastwide play also took place but to a more limited degree. Although Seattleites showed interest in the prospect of a regular baseball series between teams from the Pacific Northwest and California, a robust intercoastal tradition never materialized before World War II. In 1921, the Seattle Asahis battled their brethren in the "Southland" of Central California, and, despite the community excitement this event generated, it would be the only such meeting for more than a decade, in part due to the considerable logistical and financial costs involved. When a Northwest-California "clash" resumed in 1937, thanks to the fund-raising and organizational savvy of local sports booster G. K. Nakamura, the *Great Northern Daily News* hailed him as the "Man of the Year."[30] Following this trip, which was hyped as "the greatest mass baseball movement ever staged in the Northwest," local chatter quickly emerged about the possibility of an annual all-star Japanese Northwest-California matchup that would be billed the "Lil' Tokyo World Series."[31] The so-called Lil' Tokyo World Series never came to pass; Nakamura's death in 1938 left a void in the local Japanese American baseball booster community, and subsequent games against Californians would be sporadic and irregular. Nonetheless, interest in intercoastal play remained strong. During a Northwest baseball squad's 1938 trip to the San Francisco Bay Area, the visiting athletes were struck to find how eager California clubs were to play against them. "Word of Northwest hospitality must be circulating rapidly," said the *Japanese-American Courier,* "for the San Jose Asahi baseball club was pretty hot about coming north for a series. They hope the make the trip next spring."[32]

The Japanese baseball networks also crossed the Pacific. During the heyday of widely publicized college and professional American baseball players' world tours in the 1920s and 1930s, other lower-profile tours were also taking place: those of Japanese baseball teams to the United States and Japanese American teams to Japan. According to Riyochi Shibazaki, a "Seattle-Japan baseball connection" dates back to 1905, when Waseda University's baseball team visited the United States to play against American college teams.[33] The event also had a deep impact on local Japanese Americans, who felt great pride as they witnessed this exchange of hospitality between people from their country of origin and their adopted homeland. To show support, the Japanese Club of Seattle presented money and gifts to members of Waseda's team when they came to Seattle to play against the University of Washington. Inspired by such visits and eager to maintain ties with the homeland, Issei club managers organized trips to Japan for their players. The Mikados were the first to make such a visit in 1914, and then again in 1921 and 1922. During the 1920s, Frank Fukuda took the teams he managed to Japan several times for what he called "educational tours," and the boys' and girls' divisions of the Taiyo Athletic Club went on similar visits at least five times during the 1930s.

Eventually, as the number and ability of Seattle's Japanese squads grew and improved by the late 1920s, they started to host and even to play against teams directly from Japan. The visiting Japanese ranged from middle-school teams to professionals, and their visits usually included elaborate banquets and social events as well as the games themselves. In 1928, the Kwansei Gakugin, a team of Japanese secondary-school students, came to Seattle to play against a Courier League team.[34] Although the Kwansei Gakugin beat the Japanese Americans handily, the Courier players were commended for "[making] it interesting and . . . [showing] their gameness." The game reportedly drew the largest crowd of the season and included "quite a number of Americans."[35] Other highlights of Japan-Seattle baseball included a visit in 1929 by Keio University's team to compete against the NAC and Taiyos and a 1939 meeting between an all-star Courier League team and the Tokio Giants.[36]

AMERICANISM THROUGH INTERNATIONALISM

These baseball tours that had Japanese and Japanese Americans crossing the Pacific is an aspect of the internationalization of the sport, a topic that privileges as its central narrative the export of baseball from the United States to other countries as a function of the rise of American global hegemony. As the sport was introduced abroad by missionaries, diplomats, sporting-goods manufacturers, and professional athletes, it became simultaneously an international phenomenon and the "great American pastime."[37] A belief in the efficacy of baseball as a diplomatic tool reached to the very top, as presidents Franklin D. Roosevelt and Warren Harding, for instance, endorsed its use to promote international friendship and to export American influence abroad. Tours of professional players beginning in the late 1800s did much to cement the link between baseball and Americanism in the global popular consciousness. They reached their height in popularity and scope in the 1930s, when such icons as Babe Ruth and Lou Gehrig were on the scene. Like other American excursions abroad, the tours tapped into missionary and capitalist impulses. Albert Spalding led several and described them as endeavors to spread American values and to demonstrate ideal masculinity, although he also acknowledged during an 1888 tour that he was motivated by the prospect of expanding sales of his sporting goods.[38]

Understanding the export of baseball from the United States to other parts of the world in terms of cultural and economic imperialism is persuasive and useful in some ways, but the emphasis on American power as the sole frame of analysis can obscure the perspectives of the recipients and how they shaped the meanings of baseball to suit their own ideological purposes. In the case of Japan, baseball may have started out as an American pastime, but it eventually became Japan's national sport. Many Japanese immigrants to Seattle were, thus, familiar with it long before they arrived in North America. As much as such Americans as Spalding insisted that baseball reflected American values, Japanese devotees argued that it was compatible with *their* national character, especially the qualities of loyalty, honor, and courage.[39] Additionally, a distinct Japanese style of playing baseball was said to have evolved, in which pitching, speed, and bunting were emphasized over American baseball's trademarks of "heavy hitting" and home runs.[40] Sports historian Robert Sinclair argues, "Not only did baseball enhance any sense of national identity among the Japanese people, but the country's excellence in playing the summer game, particularly against American opposition, helped redefine Japan's international image."[41]

The Seattle-Japan baseball connection that linked Seattle Japanese Americans to their brethren in the home country reflected the growing popularity of the sport around the world, but this connection should not be understood merely as functions of international diplomacy or rising American global influence. A close examination of these meetings and the discussions around them disputes the simplistic notion that playing baseball made Japanese immigrants and their children less Japanese and more American, or less "ethnic" and more "mainstream," and, thus, calls for a more complicated analysis of the meanings of the phenomenon. If baseball was culturally Americanizing for Seattle's Japanese, it appeared to be so in ways that also affirmed their ethnic identities and allegiances.

To take one example, in American society by the early twentieth century, the Fourth of July holiday had become widely associated with sporting events, and immigrant communities came to share in this tradition. Among

Seattle Japanese Americans, the "Northwest's biggest sporting event" was the annual Fourth of July baseball tournament, which began in 1931 and was sponsored by the junior and senior Japanese Chambers of Commerce and the Japanese Association of North America.[42] By 1935, this tournament included some 250 athletes and 16 teams from all over the Northwest. But it was not a carbon copy of white, middle-America Fourth of July celebrations, only with Japanese bodies. The 1935 tournament, for instance, included a *bon odori* in which three hundred Japanese "dressed in gay colored kimonos" performed outdoors on Maynard Avenue and then the following day at the Toyo Club. Also, as part of the festivities, the JACL invited all local and visiting Nisei to a dance at the Faurot ballroom, where Rosemary Oshio performed a tap dance, Clarence Arai conducted a flag ceremony, and former congressman Ralph Horr gave a "short talk on Americanism."[43] This event, thus, exemplified the multifaceted nature of Japanese American identity and practices during the early twentieth century. Celebrating the holiday in itself signaled assimilation as it involved observing an American holiday, but the substance of the celebration was Japanese *and* American. Furthermore, carried out as an explicitly Pacific Northwest tradition, it also placed a new regional identity at the fore.

BECOMING AMERICAN, AGAINST THE CANADIANS

The Fourth of July tournament was an important community event, bringing together teams from Seattle and the Northwest to determine who was the best in the league, while fans and families came out to enjoy the summer weather, to watch the games, and to take part in other activities during the full, festive weekend. The popularity of this tournament led to the organization of another baseball series, also held over a major American holiday weekend. The Labor Day International Series, which began informally in 1928 and became an official annual affair in 1936, further sheds light on the complex and unexpected ways that Japanese in the United States understood and performed their American identities. The team that was named the AA champion of the Courier League at the end of a season earned the right to play in this series, and the opponent was always the Vancouver Asahis from British Columbia, Canada. The Labor Day International Series was to be the climactic end to each baseball season, bestowing upon the winner the unofficial title of champion of Northwest Japanese baseball. Over the years, such Courier teams as the Fife Nippons, the Seattle Western Giants, and the Auburn Nine faced the Asahis in dramatic, widely attended contests at Sick Stadium and other larger venues reserved for the occasion.

If baseball had an Americanizing effect on Seattle's Japanese, it was most evident when they played against Japanese Canadians, during the Labor Day tournament as well as other occasions over the regular season. When Japanese Americans played against white Americans, these games were typically discussed in terms of carrying out friendship on behalf of Japan or the "Japanese people." When they traveled to Japan or hosted teams from Japan, these encounters would be framed as meetings of fellow countrymen or educational opportunities to learn more about Japanese culture. However, when they played against Japanese Canadians, they were not meeting authorities on Japanese culture or learning a different way of playing baseball, nor were they encountering a group of racial or cultural "others." The most significant imagined difference in these gatherings was the *national* one, and the games became contests between Americans and Canadians. Furthermore, on these occasions, the heated rivalries between Japanese American teams scattered throughout the Northwest would take a backseat to a unified and collective determination to beat the Canadians.

As mentioned above, the perennial Canadian team to beat was the mighty Asahi club from Vancouver. This semiprofessional team was formed in 1914, and between 1919 and 1940, it won five league championships, making it one of the biggest draws in its league and earning the support of Japanese and white fans.[44] That they proved so adept at a Western sport and frequently beat their "hakujin" ("white") competitors generated pride among the Japanese in Vancouver, although, as discussed above, they did not necessarily regard baseball as something they had adopted from whites. Their "sportsmanlike attitude, the skill and fervor the Asahis displayed in their game," earned these "nimble Nipponese" the respect of their non-Japanese competitors.[45] Because the Asahis were usually the only Japanese team in the leagues to which they belonged, they rarely faced Japanese competition unless it came from outside the area, most notably from just south of the border in Washington State. After making its first trip to Seattle in 1919, the club's border-crossing excursions became more regular the following decade. Because of the Asahis' formidable reputation and the large crowds that their games consistently drew, teams from all around the Puget Sound area would eagerly seek to schedule series against them. And although the 150-mile trip between Seattle and Vancouver was much shorter than the journeys to Oregon or California, the added hurdle of having to clear Customs at the border elevated the drama around these series, dubbed international "clashes" and "invasions."[46]

Although Seattle-Vancouver baseball generated excitement by focusing attention on the international boundary, it also strengthened ties between the Japanese communities in the respective cities. For the Vancouver athletes, these games were often their only opportunities to cross the international border and to travel along the West Coast. They would furthermore receive the royal treatment from their Seattle hosts, with banquets and picnics thrown in their honor. Their trips to new towns also afforded experiences off the beaten path: the chance to make new friends and even to partake in otherwise taboo activities, such as seeing a burlesque show.[47] Also, the movement, or, to be more precise, circulation, of athletes between teams in Vancouver and Seattle helped carve out a well-worn route between the two cities. Tom Niichi Matoba was one of these athletes, playing for the original 1914 Vancouver Asahis and later joining the Seattle Asahis, only to rejoin the Vancouver team in time for a tour of Japan. Other Vancouver Asahis played on a part-time basis for Seattle teams on weekends. From 1928 to 1934, Asahi Mickey Maikawa would travel across the border every weekend to play for the Seattle Taiyos. One of his reasons for keeping such a travel schedule was that he wished to see his friends in Washington. Shortstop Roy Yamamura was known as one of the most popular Asahi players during the 1920s and 1930s and had also been the only Japanese on the Fraser Café Senior A Team and Arrows. He and Asahi catcher Reggie Yasui were invited to play every weekend for the Seattle Nippons.

The Labor Day International Series got off to a rousing start in 1928, when the Asahis came to Seattle and in dramatic fashion beat the NAC in what was described as "the best Japanese baseball game played on record in the Northwest."[48] From there, the series became one of the most anticipated and widely attended annual events in Seattle's Japanese community and even attracted its share of white spectators.[49] Part of what intensified community interest, in addition to the series being billed as "international clashes," was the significant time lag—which could be more than a month—between the first game and the subsequent doubleheader. This delay gave sportswriters and fans time to analyze the matchups, to make predictions, and to build anticipation. As far as the games themselves, the Seattle-area teams usually came up short. In the series' thirteen-year run, the Vancouver Asahis won eight times, winning consecutive titles between 1937 and 1941. Most of the time, the Courier teams could not overcome the superior pitching of such Asahis as "Lanky Lag" Nishihara and the batting prowess of such players as "flashy" Reg Yasui.[50]

After the Asahis won its fifth straight title in the International Series in 1941, Budd Fukei, a sports writer for the *Japanese-American Courier,* bemoaned the embarrassment that the International Series had become to Seattle's Japanese. He sought to rally them, as Americans, to regroup and to reverse their losing record to the Canadians:

Regardless of weather, crowd or publicity, it has been the accepted custom of this town to allow the Class AA champions to absorb a beating from the Vancouver Asahis for the Northwest diamond championship each year. The fans are getting mighty tired of the old act. . . . This thing—the Canadian brothers whipping our pals season in and season out without so much as a thank you—has gone far enough. We Americans must not stand idly by and watch our friends be beaten to helpless hunks of cheese.[51]

Fukei believed that for Seattle-area teams to prevail over the Asahis, the rules needed to be changed. Instead of having the Courier AA champions take on the Canadians, he proposed that the winners of the Fourth of July tournament play against them. The standing rule, argued Fukei, had resulted in a losing record and created the impression that "Americans produce only puny ball clubs."[52]

Fukei's exasperation and the International Series more generally exemplified how the dynamics of "becoming American" did not always play out in expected ways. As tempting as it might be to characterize the Seattle Japanese American baseball scene as evidence of this ethnic community's incorporation into the rituals of Americana, such a position ignores a number of factors. By itself, baseball did not foster an intimate identification with or allegiance to American culture among Japanese Americans, because, more often than not, it brought them into contact with other Japanese— in the United States, Canada, and Japan. For Seattle's Japanese Americans, proximity to the United States–Canada border proved to be the most palpable reminder of their American-ness. And in looking at the big picture of the baseball networks, the physical mobility the sport afforded Japanese American athletes brought into focus the salience of place in how the players understood and articulated their identities. When they played against Japanese from Vancouver, they referred to themselves as Americans; when they traveled to California, they identified more with the Northwest, and when they played against rural neighbors, they felt more urban.

THE MEANINGS OF INTRAMINORITY ENCOUNTERS IN SPORTS

In addition to facilitating encounters and forging bonds among geographically dispersed Japanese peoples, sports afforded numerous opportunities for social interaction across ethnic lines. This interaction was particularly common among children. Longtime Seattle resident Shigeru Osawa remembered playing sandlot baseball at a diamond on Fifth and Main as a child around the turn of the twentieth century. He recalled playing catch with Chinese and Japanese friends on the way to and from school and occasionally challenging the Jewish and Italian children who lived nearby on Tenth Avenue.[53] On organized Japanese American teams, some of the notable players were actually non-Japanese. In the early days of the Mikados, for instance, an American Indian pitcher, known only by the nickname "Chief Cadreau," threw several winning games for the team.[54] Finally, on occasion, Japanese American baseball teams would compete against non-Japanese minority teams. In April 1930, the Seattle NAC opened its preseason with a game against the Royal Colored Giants, a local black team. The well-trained NAC "[mixed] hits with squeeze plays" and "proved too much for the colored boys," winning by a score of 9–0.[55] Eight years later, however, the Taiyos would fare worse against the same team, losing to the Colored Giants in a game in which the "powerful colored boys toyed with Taiyo, and made Taiyo look helpless indeed by stealing home twice in one morning."[56]

Looking at other sports, the picture becomes even more diverse. A sampling of sports pages in the ethnic press from the 1920s and 1930s reveals a wide spectrum of athletic involvement in terms of age and skill level, venues, leagues, and the sports themselves. Although they have received less attention from scholars, such sports as basketball, bowling, wrestling, golf, football, boxing, and tennis were also part of the Japanese American sporting culture during the early 1900s. In 1928, one of the major basketball victories of the year was the Japanese Girls' triumph over the AME Church Girls, an African American team. Perhaps more than any other sport, boxing placed Japanese American athletes in multiethnic settings. Mixed bills at Seattle's Crystal Pool, with "Nordic, Negro, Filipino and Japanese" boxers drew large crowds.[57] Hal Hoshino, the most revered Japanese American boxer of the early 1900s, drew much of his fame from his victories over non-Japanese challengers. One of his most celebrated wins was over Filipino American Young Nationalista II from Watsonville, California, in 1938.[58]

In Asian American history, the subject of interethnic relations during the early twentieth century is often approached through the themes of American racism and economic competition. In other words, on the one hand, members of different ethnic groups might find common cause in resisting discrimination by the white majority. On the other hand, interethnic understanding and cooperation could be thwarted by an overriding interest in the pursuit of group advantage. In Asian American history, considerable barriers have impeded broad and sustained interethnic cooperation and pan-Asianism. In his study of Japanese-Chinese-Filipino relations in the rural Sacramento Valley before World War II, historian Eiichiro Azuma illustrates how interethnic conflict among these groups manifested within and in response to a restrictive political economy in which a minority's best hope for group leverage was to undermine another minority, a "divide-and conquer" strategy that ultimately benefited white landowners.[59] Arguing that interethnic conflict between Japanese immigrants and other Asian groups was "fundamentally a product of their quest for survival," Azuma shows how Japanese joined in the popular uproar against Chinese immigrants, hoping to deflect racial animosity that might otherwise be directed toward them.[60] This strategy went both ways; after Japan's 1931 invasion of Manchuria, Chinese in San Francisco and New York organized boycotts of Japanese-owned businesses to express their outrage against the attack on their home country and to show their agreement with the U.S. government's condemnation of the action.[61] This "group survival" strategy, mediated by conditions at home and abroad, posed considerable hurdles to the emergence of an Asian American consciousness and recognition of a common set of interests.

Interethnic encounters in the sporting arena between Japanese, Filipinos, and Chinese compelled participants and observers to reflect upon, to clarify, and at times to reconceptualize the boundaries between these communities. Occasionally, they gave rise and expression to an "Oriental" consciousness. An intense but spirited bowling rivalry between Seattle Japanese and Filipinos during the 1930s was one such instance. It reached a crescendo in the middle of the decade and for a time dominated the front page of the *Great Northern Daily News,* which recounted such nail-biters as Takeo Yoshijima and Spike Nakamoto facing off against Filipinos Ciso Guzman and Bill Seladang. Japanese aggression in Asia did not seem to have much of an impact on Japanese-Filipino relations in America until its invasion of the Philippines in 1941; the relationship between these communities could, however, be strained by economic and social conditions in the United States. This tension stemmed from class disparities, especially in agriculture, where Japanese farmers often employed Filipino laborers, and in salmon canning, where they vied for group advantages in wages and working conditions.[62] Further, a series of sensationalized headlines about Filipino-Japanese courtships resulting in disaster were another source of strain.[63] These intergroup tensions were more intense in rural communities, but differences along ethnic and class lines likewise separated urban Japanese and Filipinos. Spatially, however, they very much occupied the same world.

In the bowling rivalry between Japanese and Filipinos, described as an "international bowling feud," the power dynamics were reversed, as the Filipino bowlers tended to dominate.[64] The rivalry reached its climax in late 1934 after Japanese bowlers had lost a series of matches against a team called the Filipino Barber Shop Four. Determined to end the losing streak, Japanese American bowler Kaz Tamura vowed in late October to stop shaving until a Japanese team beat the Filipino Barbers. Each week in November would build up to Sunday matches at Larman's Recreation Center on Maynard, where the Japanese would do their best to unseat the Filipinos. Before a November 11 match, the *Great Northern Daily News* speculated that, with persistence and luck, the Japanese might prevail: "The Filipino Barber Shop team is itching to scalp the Japanese All-Stars. The Luzon boys are looked upon to take the series on the basis of past performances, but the Nipponese, who have the knack of turning in inspired bowling, may play over their heads to upset the dope."[65]

A packed house of Japanese and Filipino men, women, and children at Larman's witnessed the much-anticipated match between the Barber Shop Four and Japanese All-Stars. Playing for the All-Stars were the big guns: Hiko Setsuda, Taiji Takayashi, Spike Nakamoto, and "Dr. Nomura, the bowling dentist." Kaz Tamura was, unfortunately, out of town that day. Despite the hype and anticipation, the Japanese team lost by a score of 1,661–1,422. The following Sunday, a different Japanese team, the Alley Cats, played against the Barber Shop Four in a match promised to be the "top-notch sporting event" of the weekend. This time, Tamura was there, reportedly looking like a "Bolshevik bombthrower."[66] Another full house watched the Japanese team go down in defeat against the Barbers in a three-game match, and this outcome repeated the following weekend.[67] Frustrated in their team efforts, Japanese had some measure of success in individual matches against Filipinos. Clarence Arai, the "second generation lawyer and unofficial Mayor of Main Street," became so determined to beat a Filipino at bowling that, according to his wife, he would sneak away from home on occasion to get in some extra practice.[68] When he broke a score of 200 and beat Filipino V. Agot, the all-time record holder at Larman, Arai was hailed as a local hero in Seattle's Japanese community.

The bowling contests between Japanese and Filipinos give us a glimpse into a remarkably energetic and diverse social scene in Jackson Street, a neighborhood that, when not neglected by white Seattle, was derided as the city's "Skid Road." They also represent an aspect of the lively sports culture in Japanese Seattle, in which a bowling match would make front-page news and become a community-rallying event. The rivalry between Japanese and Filipino bowlers additionally sheds light on how such everyday situations were occasions in which to work out and to articulate the meanings of race and ethnicity. In the context of the bowling matches, Japanese and Filipinos aligned with their ethnonational affiliations, reaffirming their identities as

Japanese and *Filipinos*. But for Japanese Americans, these matches were also opportunities to express an emerging Asian American outlook, as defeating a Filipino bowler or team conferred two kinds of gratification—overcoming stronger competitors in the "Manila boys" and claiming victory as the best "Orientals." Winning in an intraethnic setting entitled one to claim only being the best among other Japanese, but beating competitors from a different Asian community made the victory seem more consequential. And acknowledging that a win secured "Oriental" supremacy was tacit affirmation of a nascent pan-Asian consciousness.

Athletic competition involving Japanese and Chinese Americans in Seattle similarly highlighted the points above while also illustrating the conceptual navigations of scale that Japanese Americans, especially sports writers, engaged in to explain the significance of the encounters. Historian Chris Friday has shown how, during the 1930s, Japanese Americans and Chinese Americans routinely drew upon international events to understand and to articulate their local, concrete realities and goals. Although Sino-Japanese relations offered useful parallels and a set of meanings to help delineate interethnic boundaries in Seattle, events in Asia were physically and imaginatively remote enough that they did not preclude Japanese Americans' and Chinese Americans' recognition of their common status as "Orientals" in American society.[69] Furthermore, as Japan ratcheted up its aggressions in China during the 1930s, this denied the possibility of friendship between the two nations, but the buffer of the Pacific Ocean allowed Japanese and Chinese in North America to respond to changing circumstances and to maintain their interethnic relationships by distancing themselves from Asia, whereas in other contexts they might have drawn it close. Such moves also illustrated how Chinese American and Japanese Americans existed in what Friday calls the "contradictory but innovative grey area between an imagined culture of the 'homeland' and their vision of America."[70]

As compelling a backdrop as events in Asia were for Chinese American and Japanese American athletic encounters, other more immediate conditions mediated the relationship between these communities. In Seattle, they lived in the same neighborhoods, often attended the same schools, patronized each other's businesses, and formed lasting friendships with each other. Sports created an additional set of bonds that drew upon and defied the metaphors of Sino-Japanese relations. Inklings of this could be seen in the pages of the *Japanese-American Courier* and *Great Northern Daily News*, where readers learned about the athletic feats of fellow Japanese as well as Chinese athletes, such as local Art Louie, the center for the Chinese Students team and Garfield High School, and Buck Lai, the "wonder boy" third baseman from Hawaii.[71] Lai had played for the semiprofessional Eastern League in Bridgeport, Connecticut, and his signing by the New York Giants in 1928 was the subject of a "Sports Scope" column in the *Courier*.[72] The University of Washington student and budding journalist Bill Hosokawa, who had a sports column in the *Courier*, supplied much of the information about Chinese American athletes for the paper. A Seattle native and a 1933 graduate of Garfield High School, Hosokawa, who would go on to have a long career with the *Denver Post* after World War II, grew up amid the multiethnic social landscape and sports scene in the city, from which he developed admiration for and friendships with the "colorful Celestials from Canton, King Street, and way points."[73]

Over the decades, all-Chinese teams competed in a variety of sports in the Japanese-American Courier League, but they made their greatest impact in basketball.[74] In the late 1920s, with the inauguration of the Courier Basketball League, Chinese teams were among the first to join, and by the start of the 1935 season, four Chinese teams, including Young China, the Chinese Students, and the Lotus Troys, applied for entry into the league.[75] Before the Courier formed a basketball league, Chinese American teams were limited to playing in citywide leagues in which they achieved notable success. During the 1929 City League season, for instance, the China Club put together a seven-game winning streak and led the Class B South Division.[76] As part of the Courier League, which it joined, also in 1929, the China Club was a dominant force, leading its coach, Stanley Louie, to once boast that his team's record entitled it to the "mythical Oriental Basketball Championship of the Pacific Northwest."[77]

By 1937, the Courier Basketball League had grown to forty teams and about four hundred players, with the Chinese-Japanese clashes being the major highlights of each season.[78] The fact that the Chinese American teams were known to be very strong further fueled the rivalry, and the games, framed as contests to determine the superior "Oriental" team, subsequently drew keen interest among local fans.[79] By late 1940, the Japanese American teams, which still composed the majority of the Courier League squads, were simply no match for the handful of Chinese teams that dominated at nearly every level from AA to C.[80] Although this situation certainly frustrated the Japanese American players and coaches, they also reveled in the added excitement and heightened athleticism that the Chinese brought to the Courier League. Clarence Arai, who managed the Japanese Hi-Stars, praised the Chinese Athletic Club team for its "splendid showing in the Class 'B' City League and . . . clean record against any organized Oriental basketball team in the Northwest for the past four years." Despite his team's difficulties against the Chinese Athletic Club, he asserted, "We feel that it is a great honor to meet the Chinese boys even in victory or defeat."[81] Arai's remarks navigated between the strategies of asserting ethnic boundaries and acknowledging a shared status as "Orientals," showing that although affinities between Chinese and Japanese existed and were strengthened by these encounters, a proactive pan-Asian solidarity under which ethnic particularities were subsumed was still a ways off.

Chinese-Japanese athletic meets outside Seattle and the Northwest also generated much interest among Japanese American sports writers and further added to the narrative of interethnic friendship. In 1931, for instance, the *Japanese-American Courier* reported on the commencement of an annual Japanese-Chinese All-Star football game in San Francisco's Kezar Stadium. According to the paper, it "originated several years back when a group of Japanese and Chinese youths decided that the Americanization process necessitated a regular football game."[82] Perhaps to underline that objective, non-Asian coaches were brought on, with Frank Wilton, a former Stanford football player, leading the Japanese team, and "Smoke" Francis, who had played for the University of California, coaching the Chinese team. Despite the organizers' emphasis on Americanization, the game saw players falling back on their ethnic affiliations, again demonstrating the constant negotiation between ethnic particularism and common ground that characterized Chinese-Japanese relations during this period: "The quarterbacks call signals in their native languages which make it difficult for the opposition to know what they will do. Special precautions are taken not to permit Chinese students in Japanese Language schools and vice versa."[83] In 1936, the Chinese Students team of Seattle went to California to face off against several Bay Area Japanese American squads. Covering the story, Chinese American Seattleite Eddie Luke remarked, "In recent years, there have been few athletic relations between Chinese and Japanese in the Bay Region. . . . Perhaps the Student-Y [YMCA] example will bring about a resumption of athletic competition between the two communities."[84]

Although Seattle's conditions and geographical location were far removed from East Asia, commentators nonetheless looked to the Far East as a reference point for discussing Chinese-Japanese sporting competitions. In January 1935, for instance, when the China Club defeated the Japanese Black Hawks by a score of 21–14 at the Garfield High gym, the *Japanese-American Courier* invoked Sino-Japanese relations, remarking that the game renewed "basketball hostilities" between the two groups.[85] Mainstream Seattle newspapers also employed such analogies. In 1941, as tensions in the international arena mounted, the *Seattle Post-Intelligencer* ran a story about

Garfield High School's basketball squad, which included Chinese and Japanese teammates Phil Mar Hung, Bill Yamaguchi, and Al Mar. Although these students played on the same team, the newspaper nonetheless likened Garfield basketball to the Sino-Japanese War in Asia, saying, "With the Japanese and Chinese at each others' throats in the Orient, there's also an 'all-out' fight being staged right in the high school basketball league."[86]

In addition to bringing drama and excitement to the basketball court and generating material for sports writers, athletic meetings between Japanese Americans and Chinese Americans in Seattle facilitated the formation of important relationships between these ethnic communities. The story of Chinese American Eddie Luke, mentioned above, stands out as an example. In 1936, Luke was asked to guest author the *Japanese-American Courier*'s "Hangovers" sports column. By that time, he was well known to Japanese American sports fans, having distinguished himself in the Japanese-American Courier League playing baseball for the Chinese Students team during the mid-1930s. He helped lead the Chinese Students to a top division berth and in 1937 won the Courier League's Kay Okimoto most inspirational player award.[87] Substituting for his friend Bill Hosokawa, Luke wrote several "Hangovers" columns and devoted his guest authorship to bringing Japanese American readers' attention to the local Chinese American sports scene in Seattle, particularly the exploits of the Chinese Students basketball squad. Luke's service as a guest author in the *Courier* was in itself significant and unprecedented, as the newspaper was narrowly focused and targeted throughout its run. Luke's columns also shed light on how he, as a Chinese American, related to Japanese Americans he encountered through athletic participation. He recalled a 1934 Courier League road trip to rural Wapato in which "the highlight of that trip was eating a full Japanese meal next to Art Kikuchi's mother without her discovering that I was a son of Cathay. Thank you so much for the meal, Mrs. Kikuchi."[88] Crossing ethnic boundaries to access the social and culinary world of Japanese Americans, Luke's experience was mediated by the fact that he looked like his hosts, indicated by "Mrs. Kikuchi" not realizing he was a "son of Cathay." As this example and others from the sporting scene illustrate, Chinese-Japanese relations in Seattle were informed by the simultaneous recognition of their differences, signaled by references to food, language, and geography, and their similarities, by way of physical features, use of the term "Oriental," and, on occasion, food. In June 1937, Luke left Seattle for California to pursue a career in acting, and the *Courier* bid him farewell with a tribute: "Perhaps more than any other person, Eddie has been responsible for the friendly relations which exist today in Seattle between the rice-eating descendants of Cathay and Yamato."[89] In connecting Luke's contributions to Chinese-Japanese relations writ large, the author imagined interethnic relations playing out along multiple, connected scales. On the broadest level, the "descendants of Cathay and Yamato" surely had their differences, especially at the time the tribute was published, but zooming in, what remained in the picture, and presumably what mattered most, were the "friendly relations . . . in Seattle."

Depending on the occasion and objective, Seattle's Japanese Americans would pivot back and forth between emphasizing the international arena and privileging local friendships as they sought to understand and define their relationships with Chinese Americans. As shown above, framing sporting matches in terms of Sino-Japanese relations brought an air of international consequence to otherwise mundane events, and commentators would note that the athletes' lives in America and their shared experiences as "Orientals" fostered a pan-Asian consciousness that transcended their differences. This transcendence was bolstered by the fact that, by the 1930s, more and more Chinese and Japanese meeting on the playfields were born in the United States. Before a girls' softball game between Chinese and Japanese teams, the *Japanese-American Courier* remarked, "China and Japan may be at war; some meddling crackpots may be trying their darndest to make the Chinese and Japanese in America fight a little war of their own over here, but the second generation Chinese and Japanese girls don't seem to let those things dampen their friendship."[90]

Here, the *Japanese-American Courier* drew on the Far East, as it was a common point of reference, but it did so primarily to distance Seattle Japanese Americans from that part of the world and to insist on the primacy of local conditions and relationships. Doing so also allowed the writer to insist that interethnic friendship prevailed despite the troubles between Japan and China. Before the 1937 basketball season began, the *Courier* expressed its hope that Chinese teams would return "and have a good time with us again. It is unfortunate that there should be such trouble in the Orient, but I believe that is not going to spoil the friendship that has grown up between the Japanese and the Chinese second generation of this city."[91]

SALVATION THROUGH SPORTS

It is commonly asserted that sports are a neutral and neutralizing terrain where the preconceptions and prejudices that individuals often bring to their day-to-day interactions with others take a backseat to the color-blind rules of the game. And with the growing internationalization of sporting culture from about the turn of the twentieth century onward—signified, for example, by the revival of the Olympic Games in 1896—the idea that athletic competition was a level playing field, so to speak, bolstered among some people, nonwhite and white, the belief that racial minorities could achieve social transformation and salvation through this medium. As discussed earlier, Progressive-era reformers touted a "gospel of play" to promote the health and general well-being of growing children; we could also say that in racialized communities, a "gospel of sports" held that an individual could, through superior athletic performance, transcend otherwise impenetrable racial barriers and win over his entire nation (it usually was a figurative "he"). The *Northwest Enterprise,* one of Seattle's black newspapers, invoked this gospel in exalting the performance of African American athletes at the 1936 Olympics, with especially high praise for the sprinter Jesse Owens. "The accomplishment of these athletes," stated the *Enterprise,* "will do much toward building up a greater respect for and more kindly feeling toward the Negro race, for in the end, fair and just treatment must be accorded a people who are consistently loyal, fair, and just to their country and its cause."[92]

Japanese Americans voiced similar hopes about the power of athletic competition to bring about racial understanding and reconciliation. In this regard, among individual athletes, no Japanese American seemed to inspire more hopes than the aforementioned boxer Hal Hoshino. A featherweight from Pendleton, Oregon, Hoshino fought nationally during the late 1930s and was a hero to many of his co-ethnics. He certainly became a local celebrity in Seattle after he moved there in 1935 to train with manager Lonnie Austin. In 1937, Hoshino began fighting professionally and won the Seattle Golden Gloves title.[93] After he defeated two white opponents in 1938, the *Japanese-American Courier* declared that this win was also a victory for racial progress and, thus, something all Japanese in America could share in: "If Hal Hoshino had knocked out those two white boys in any other place except the boxing ring, the 'indignant' whites would have mobbed the 'Jap' who insulted the white people. But . . . he used his punches in the ring and at once, the white people acclaimed him as the champion to represent the whole Northwest in the featherweight division."[94]

The passage above illustrates the tremendous symbolic importance that Japanese American sports writers saw in a victory by one of their co-ethnics over a white opponent. Hoshino's accomplishments would not have generated such pride had they not been achieved in mixed-race settings. Furthermore, making them even more profound was the fact that the anti-Japanese movement of the 1910s and 1920s still resided in the recent memories of many Japanese Americans. The writer above seemed particularly gratified that Hoshino prevailed over white competitors in the inherently violent, hypermasculine sport of boxing. In racialized communities in the United States, this attitude was not uncommon. Historian Linda España-Maram, for instance, has illustrated similar dynamics among Filipino American boxing fans in Los Angeles who viewed co-ethnic boxers' wins against whites as symbolic victories for all Filipinos in America.[95] In Seattle, Japanese Americans were aware that their African American neighbors likewise attributed much significance to the triumphs of their boxing heroes, indicated, for instance, when the *Great Northern Daily News* said that Hoshino was to Japanese Americans what Joe Louis was to "the colored colony on Jackson Street."[96]

One of the distinctive features of the Japanese American gospel of sports was its strong internationalist outlook and advancement of a vision of a "global community" in the sporting world. Such people as Hoshino, as U.S.-born, English-speaking athletes who could make persuasive claims to American identity, bolstered ethnic pride and embodied many Japanese Americans' hopes for challenging the negative views of them and achieving belonging. But Japanese Americans' perceived options in regard to gaining respect and acceptance in American society was, as previous chapters show, linked to domestic and international conditions. Japan's standing with the United States was a major factor shaping the treatment of Japanese in America. Thus, discussions about the relationship between sports and inter-racial understanding would turn on visiting athletes from Japan as much as homegrown "all-American" heroes, such as Hal Hoshino. According to Riyoichi Shibazaki, this interlinking of local and international understandings was one of the reasons why the 1905 Waseda University baseball tour was so significant to Japanese in America.[97] Hopeful that such tours, in which visitors demonstrated their physical prowess, good sportsmanship, and love of the game, would elevate the standing of the people of Japan in white Americans' eyes, Seattle Japanese Americans believed that such an image makeover would also lead to improved treatment of Japanese in the United States.

Japanese Americans concerned about conditions in their own communities, their status in the United States, and the state of United States–Japan affairs could turn to sports to articulate their hopes. As shown at the beginning of the chapter, with respect to Pacific relations, Japanese American sports writers said that encounters between the United States and Japan in the sporting arena could do much toward fostering the goodwill and friendship crucial to maintaining a peaceful, harmonious Pacific world. Ruminating on exchanges between college teams, which by the 1920s were taking place on a regular basis, a 1928 editorial in the *Japanese-American Courier* said the following:

> In the creation of goodwill and mutual respect nothing has ever suc-
> ceeded to a greater extent than athletics. Facile diplomatists with
> their silvery tongued orations and superficial announcements of idle
> declarations of friendship have at all times fallen short and failed of
> achieving the object. . . . Athletics have often given expression to
> a spirit of good sportsmanship through actual demonstrations. To
> the ordinary sport fan nothing strikes a more respectful and sympa-
> thetic chord than demonstrations that bespeak of sportsmanly con-
> duct and action. Where diplomacy failed clean sportsmanship has
> succeeded.[98]

Even though in the games between American and Japanese teams, the latter usually lost, they reportedly always made a "very good impression on the American public."[99] After Meiji University's baseball team made a 1929 visit to Seattle, Frank Sugiyama wrote in his "Sports Scope" column that the event proved that sports were a more effective means of facilitating international peace than formal meetings between heads of state. He wrote that Meiji's visit "will probably create greater lasting amity than anything that the statesmen of the two countries could do in the same time. . . . Periodic visits to and from Japan of college athletic groups is a much wiser method of promoting international friendship than treaties or pacts."[100] Japanese in Seattle looking for more direct evidence sought the perspectives of people in Japan. In 1933, the *Japanese-American Courier* reprinted remarks from an article that appeared in the *Japan Times* on the subject of sports and United States–Japan relations. Author Haruo Yonemoto said that the advance of sports, such as baseball, swimming, tennis, and boxing, in Japan attested to the positive influence of American culture on the country and furthered "the cause of friendship and amity between the two powers on the Pacific."[101] The following year, the *Great Northern Daily News* reprinted the remarks of Prince Iyesato Tokugawa, made during a luncheon in Tokyo hosted by the America-Japan Society to honor a team of American major league stars, including Babe Ruth and Connie Mack. Stating, "It is no longer possible for you Americans to claim baseball as a national game for America alone," the prince pressed the goal of international amity: "Between two great peoples really able to understand and enjoy baseball there are no national differences which cannot be solved in a spirit of sportsmanship."[102]

For Seattle's Japanese Americans, the concerns of international and interracial understanding were linked. The hopes they placed on sportsmanship and play, thus, went beyond United States–Japan diplomacy; as racialized minorities in America, they also looked to sports to foster improved race relations. In the summer of 1939, following a softball game between the visiting Togo All-Stars from Japan and the white East Madison YMCA team, in which the All-Stars lost 6–2, a writer for the *Japanese-American Courier* insisted that the game's significance was not in who won or lost but that "Americans" (presumably referring to white Americans) were able to witness firsthand the good sportsmanship of Japanese people. The writer hoped the fond feelings generated at this meeting would, in turn, positively affect how white Seattleites viewed their Japanese neighbors. "That All-Star gang did more than just play a softball game. I'm willing to bet my last nickel that some of the Americans who watched the game went home feeling might friendly towards the Japanese," stated the writer. "Some of these first-generation who are howling so much about 'Japanese-American friendship' ought to look into this sport angle of creating good-will."[103]

In a column titled "Democracy in Action" that appeared in the *Japanese-American Courier,* Nisei writer James Shinkai built on the idea that sports were effective vehicles for building and strengthening relationships across ethnic, national, and other boundaries but focused his remarks more explicitly on domestic race relations. Looking for local examples, he singled out Seattle high school athletes, such as Dick Itami, the captain of Cleveland High's football team; Homer Harris, the black all-city football player from Garfield; and Roy Nakagawa, the all-city guard from Franklin. To Shinkai, such an assemblage of accomplished minority athletes demonstrated that sports were the "most democratic institution in America" and furthermore the one field "where they do not care whether your ancestors came over on the Mayflower or in the steerage of the Miike Maru."[104] In what was likely a deliberate reference to the Japanese ship that made the first regular steamship run between Japan and Seattle in 1896, Shinkai placed Japan and Japanese people squarely into the saga of immigrant America, which usually revolved around trans-Atlantic migration and such icons as Ellis Island, Plymouth Rock, and the *Mayflower*. In 1932, a writer for the *Courier* elaborated on the connections between sportsmanship, interracial understanding, and Japanese belonging in Seattle, observing, "Many American fans attend the games played by Japanese baseball teams" and "are surprised at their speed, their clever headwork and their good sportsmanship."[105] Instead of describing the most recent visit of a team from Japan to the United States, however, the article looked into the history of Japanese American baseball and discussed, for example, the Selleck Yamatos, a rural Washington team from the 1910s. According to the piece, during the summer of 1915, a group of white American mill workers went to see them play out of "idle curiosity and were amazed to see the Yamatos with Mizutani, Bert Kochi and Sano as the backbone of the team set back a visiting team from Seattle." It also described a team from Eatonville, which included players "M. Kawazoo and Sakura and Kondo" and became known as the "Yellow Peril of the Mountain Road."[106]

Also notable were columns that ruminated on how sports freed individuals from otherwise deeply entrenched preconceptions that strained daily social interactions and enabled them to see people in a new light without the blinders of racial prejudice. Playing sports gave young Japanese in Seattle a glimpse at a utopian world in which race had no bearing on outcomes. As a sports writer for the *Japanese-American Courier* reflected:

> One thing I like about this sport circle is that no one is left out of it just because his face is not white. People may talk about "Boycott the Jap," "lynch the niggers," "drive out the Filipinos" . . . but, let one "Jap" "Nigger" or "P.I." excel in any branch of the sport and he is at once accepted by the white people. Nobody says "He can't fight in this ring because he is a 'Nigger,'" nor do they say "You can't play on this football team because you're a Jap."[107]

Although such passages as the one above trade heavily in a naïve sort of idealism, it is perhaps beside the point to explore whether social equality or world peace actually resulted from international or interethnic athletic competition. This discussion would probably be naïve in an altogether different way. Instead, we ought to focus on how writings such as those quoted above highlight the idealistic hopes that Japanese Americans, along with other minorities, held to transcend the racialized barriers that limited their life prospects and fortunes in America. As a popular pastime that was also an amenable vessel for communicating a variety of ideas, hopes, and dreams, sports mattered to Japanese Americans in deeply complex and meaningful ways.

COLLINS PARK

As discussed earlier in the chapter, participation in athletics enabled Japanese Americans to cross social and geographic boundaries, and these encounters, in turn, clarified their local identities and positions in terms of international metaphors and trans-Pacific and transborder relationships. Playing and watching sports also called for an explicit awareness of and engagement with space, and if a single location in Seattle existed where the interracial, spatial, and ideological dimensions of sports converged for Japanese Americans, it was at Collins Park. With respect to issues of space, this chapter has focused on how Japanese Americans crossed, transcended, and redefined it, but playing sports, of course, also requires a direct engagement with certain kinds of urban spaces. One cannot play baseball without a diamond, basketball without a court, or football without a field. This spatial engagement is a crucial part of the story of Japanese American sports in Seattle, because a specific locale within the city—Collins Park—became a prime object of the community's cosmopolitan imaginary and its claims to local belonging. Collins's history exemplifies the ways that ordinary people inscribed cosmopolitanism onto physical space and also typifies the interplay of real and imagined space in the construction of community in Jackson Street.

Located on Washington and Sixteenth, Collins Park was several blocks east of Jackson Street's center; nevertheless, it was the main park that Jackson Street residents used. Consisting of a playfield and field house, Collins by the 1920s was well known as the city park with the most diverse users. It became a social center for many, and for children it provided a safe alternative to spending their time out on the streets. Collins also offered after-school programs with singing, free play, handcrafts, parties, and athletics. The field house schedule for the week of September 27, 1929, gives an idea of a typical week at Collins and its multiracial crowd: Monday, three Japanese teams; Tuesday, the Twenty-third Avenue team and Bankers team; Wednesday, the Black Manufacturers Union Pacific; Thursday, three Chinese teams; Friday, the Washington Bakeries and City Light. The Italian Society was on the waiting list.[108] In 1931, a park employee who worked with children there observed, "No spot in the city holds more imaginary tragedies more truly interesting incidents or more courses for joy . . . than the plot of ground and its frequenters, located at 16th and Washington." It was, in her opinion, the embodiment of the American melting pot, a meeting ground for the people of the world: "All nationalities, faces and creeds meet as individuals on a common level here through that splendid medium known as free play or recreation of some type."[109]

Seattle's Japanese Americans had a long history with Collins Park, going back to the first decade of the 1900s. Because it was the closest city park to Nihonmachi, it was one of the few nearby open spaces where Japanese American youths could play sports. This attachment to the park led Japanese American residents to organize a signature drive to protest the firing of a well-liked park employee. In 1911, about one hundred members of the community and a few non-Japanese submitted a petition to the Seattle Park Board protesting the dismissal of Harry Anderson, a playground supervisor.[110] In the letter, they praised Anderson's service, especially his fair treatment of Japanese people:

> Although there have been occasional misunderstandings between the Japanese and the American patrons of the playground, these were always settled with perfect satisfaction and good feeling to the parties involved . . . all through the unprejudiced efforts of Mr. Anderson. . . . There seems little reason why he should be supplanted by another who may be unknown to us and whose fitness to the position is yet uncertain. We ask this not from our own individual opinion, but from and in accordance with the sentiment of Japanese residents of Seattle.[111]

Over the decades, Japanese Americans in the city continued to use and claim Collins, although as their numbers grew, calls came to build a park closer to the center of the ethnic community. An editorial in the *Japanese-American Courier* argued that the park's location was inconvenient, that it was too far away, and so pressed the Japanese Association to look into the matter.[112]

Although the racial and ethnic mix of people found at Collins was inspiring to some, for others, it could engender problems. Despite all the feel-good sentiment pervading most descriptions of Collins, it was, nonetheless, a site that different groups of people would make claims over, only to have their claims contested by members of other groups. Nor did the utopian descriptions of the park mean that the minorities who used Collins were always treated with the equanimity to match the rhetoric. For example, a Japanese high school student who had immigrated to Seattle in 1919 wrote about an experience he had there. "My two friends were playing tenis [*sic*] at the Colins [*sic*] Field," he said. "A Jewish boy was passing by . . . and . . . said to one of my friends that we could not play there, for that court was for only those who could be naturalized, or Americans. I know that Jewish boy, for he was one of my classmates at school and graduated from our school first honor student."[113]

Collins employees helped construct the park's image as a cosmopolitan space within Seattle. Many of the first workers at the park had been recruited from the YMCA, and, over the years, the organization would provide much of the vision and direction for programs at Collins. Park workers often commented on the striking diversity of children who played there and enrolled in its recreation and education programs. In 1930, Alice M. Lopp, an employee who held the title of "play leader," remarked:

> The children who attend the field house are . . . very appreciative of all that is done for them and are very responsive to the field house activities. Although there is a minimum amount of quarrelsomeness among the children, most of them are learning the rules of good sportsmanship. They get along with each other admirably well for such a cosmopolitan group which includes Spanish and Turkish Jews, Japanese, Negroes and representatives of many other nationalities. It is a group which is different from any in any other parts of the city.[114]

Other employees who worked with the multiracial and multiethnic groups of youths at Collins similarly appreciated the park's uniqueness, which grew out of its heterogeneity. Their impressions conveyed curiosity and pride in Collins's distinctiveness compared to the other field houses in Seattle. Employee Nobuko Yamaguchi stated in 1930, "I was surprised at the many nationalities represented on the playfield. Japanese, Chinese, Negro, Italian, and different sects of Jews as well as the white people. I don't say Americans because they are all Americans regardless of race. . . . The district is so cosmopolitan and so crowded that many types of environment is [sic] shown."[115]

At Collins, the belief that recreation and play were wholesome and salubrious combined with images of people coming together across racial and ethnic lines. One employee there remarked that in sports competitions, or "that splendid medium known as free play," children of all "nationalities, races and creeds" met as individuals on an equal level.[116] In this sense, Collins took on a symbolic importance on top of its practical uses among those who played and worked there.

Around 1920, the city started a basketball league in which Collins's teams attracted attention for their diverse crews and skillful playing. Field houses in Seattle organized several teams of various levels to compete in interdistrict tournaments. Over the years, thousands of young Seattleites took part, and, at one point, 120 teams from 10 recreation centers encompassing junior, junior-giant, intermediate, senior, and senior-giant levels competed. A league for women athletes ages eighteen and older was formed, and each field house had three women's teams, playing at A, B, and C levels. At Collins, the basketball squads included black, Jewish, Chinese, Japanese, and Filipino players, many of whom were recruited from nearby Garfield,

Franklin, and Broadway High Schools. In 1936, sixty-eight Japanese played for Collins teams.[117] They were once described as the "cosmopolitan Collins casaba crew" and a United Nations basketball team.[118] Teams from Collins, which included such players as the Okamotos, Al Mar, and Al Wong, dominated much of inter–field house basketball in the 1930s and 1940s. They were especially successful in the annual Northwest basketball tournament, which had begun in 1930 and was sponsored by the *Seattle Post-Intelligencer,* the Park Board, and the Seattle Inter-League Council.

After World War II, Collins remained a formidable force in local basketball, and descriptions of its multiethnic teams continued to draw parallels to the international arena. In 1946 and 1947, it won interleague council titles and advanced to the Northwest AAU Basketball Championships. Widely celebrated for his success, Gene Boyd, the coach at Collins, was also noted for working with "the melting pot of youngsters at Collins Fieldhouse in the Central Area from 1938 to 1951. There were Chinese, Negroes, Japanese, Filipinos, Greeks, Jews—you name it and Gene could produce one, and all held him in high esteem."[119] Boyd came to Collins after coaching in the Green Lake district, because, as he explained, he wished to help youths of lesser means and opportunities by not just coaching them in athletics but also in teaching them to be better citizens. As before the war, the multiethnic makeup of its teams remained one of Collins's most striking characteristics, something commentators could not resist remarking on. "Collins Fieldhouse looks like a juvenile edition of the United Nations," said Phil Taylor of the *Seattle Times,* "but in this case one world means a friendly basketball game, not a subject for debate."[120]

CONCLUSION

It is perhaps fitting that before the wartime removal of Japanese from the city, one of the last organized events that Seattle Japanese Americans held took place at Collins Fieldhouse. In January 1942, the city Park Board agreed to allow the JACL's Emergency Defense Council to hold a Red Cross Relief Fund dance there. Seeking to show their loyalty to the United States and support for the war against Japan, many of the city's Japanese Americans, led by the JACL, threw their lot with the country that would eventually oversee their removal and incarceration. Shortly after the fundraiser, James Sakamoto wrote a letter to Ben Evans thanking him for the use of the field house and for the Park Board's support of the Japanese community during this uncertain time.[121] Once the site of a dynamic multiethnic play community and the symbol of cosmopolitan dreams, with the war, Collins

Park would be transformed into a bastion of U.S. nationalism from which the people of Japanese ancestry who had been so integral to its distinct character would soon be expelled.

Also with the U.S. entry into World War II, the celebration of sports as a pastime that brought together peoples and nations in a spirit of friendship, at least where Japanese and Japan were concerned, abruptly dissolved. In an atmosphere of belligerent nationalism, Americans reclaimed baseball as their sport and repudiated any claims that Japan had made over it. According to sports historian Richard Crepeau, "The fact that the attack on the United States came from Japan was especially galling to many connected with the national pastime."[122] Building on the anti-Japanese baseball propaganda, the popular magazine the *Sporting News* derided Japanese baseball players as second-rate hitters who "lacked the genuine fortitude that made baseball America's national pastime."[123] No longer regarded as a medium for fostering international friendship, baseball was redefined during the war as the exclusive domain of the United States. This attitude was an especially jarring change of circumstances for Japanese Americans for whom baseball and other Western sports had been part of the fabric of their identities and routines for decades. Although they continued to form teams and to play sports in the internment camps, athletic participation took on much different meanings in the context of wartime incarceration. Whereas the activity was once an avenue that opened up Japanese Americans' social and geographic horizons and highlighted their relationships to space in ways that validated their claims to local belonging, during the war, in a breathtaking turnaround, playing sports became chiefly a way to endure social isolation and physical confinement.

6

The Eve of War

The United States formally entered World War II following an attack on Hawaii's Pearl Harbor by the empire of Japan on December 7, 1941, an event that would leave Japanese Americans on the West Coast vulnerable to rabid calls for revenge and, consequently, an excruciating crisis of identity. This situation was a dramatic turnaround for this population as well as the entire city of Seattle. Before this war, excepting for a brief disruption during World War I, conditions were favorable for the flowering of a local cosmopolitanism rooted in the belief that the city's location, ambitions, relationships with Pacific Rim nations, and enlightened population poised it to become the U.S. "gateway to the Orient." As Seattle matured over the decades, the city imagined itself on two maps; as part of the United States, it sat at the edge of the western "frontier," which simultaneously vaunted and marginalized its reputation. Yet it also commanded a central position in the Pacific world. Appropriated as symbols of the city's cosmopolitan credentials, Japanese Americans sought local and national belonging on this basis while also forging their own identities and associations that reflected their fluid perceptions of place and scale. But this would all change with the outbreak of the war. The Pacific Rim internationalism that combined Americanism and cosmopolitanism was no longer tenable as soon as the United States declared war on Japan. And as the Pacific world to which Seattle had long hitched its future was ripped asunder, the exigencies of wartime patriotism also swept away the conception of the city as a "gateway to the Orient."

During the war itself, Seattle, along with other industrial cities, underwent unprecedented prosperity and immense trauma. Industrial mobilization brought unforeseen growth in terms of demographic and economic expansion, but accompanying these welcome changes was tremendous social upheaval. The minority-concentrated neighborhood of Jackson Street experienced the wartime changes on an intensified scale. With the ongoing conflict between China and Japan and then Japan's invasion of the Philippines, relations among the Chinese, Filipino, and Japanese residents of Jackson Street became quite strained. The creation of wartime jobs triggered a wave of in-migration, which included many blacks seeking housing in already-crowded Jackson Street. And then, of course, the effects of uprooting about nine thousand Japanese Americans were felt most profoundly in this neighborhood, where for more than four decades, they had been an integral part of daily life.

By examining life in Japanese American in Seattle during the years leading up to the U.S. entry into the international conflict of World War II, this chapter discusses how the specter of war affected the tone and material conditions of daily life. Much of the time, in response to the changing circumstances, Japanese Americans went on the defensive and asserted to themselves and to others that their primary concerns and loyalties were local. Other developments challenged them to reorient their civil rights agendas around an interracial strategy that included cooperation with local African Americans. Indeed, as international events exposed the racism of German Nazism, and local developments revealed the interconnected fates of Jackson Street's minorities in their own struggles against racial discrimination, the possibilities of an antiracist Americanism emerged. But the U.S. entry into the war and subsequent evacuation of Japanese Americans from the city would cut short any progress on this end. Aligning itself with the jingoistic patriotism that consumed the rest of the country, Seattle reversed its earlier pattern of cultivating cooperative business and diplomatic relations with Japan. Instead of touting itself as an international gateway city, it would become one of the fastest growing and most vital centers of the defense industry. And instead of welcoming Japanese commissioners and commemorating the anniversaries of United States–Japan treaties of amity and commerce, Seattleites would channel their energies and resources into the defense industry, including the construction of planes and warships that would be used against its former friends, now the Japanese enemy.

A discussion of the changes in Seattle during this time brings into focus what was lost, culturally and materially, with the uprooting of Japanese Americans and drastic reconfiguration of Pacific relationships. One consequence was that cosmopolitanism was untenable as a discourse, as it was now out of sync with local conditions and global imperatives. As Eiichiro Azuma has observed, "When geopolitics provided no alternative or need, naked nationalism took hold at the cost of persecuting anything heterodox or subversive, that is 'international,' in the language of war."[1] Japanese Americans whose claims to belonging had relied significantly on the construction of Seattle as a cosmopolitan city had to reenvision and to rearticulate their positionalities, in local and global terms. Compelled to distance themselves from Japan and Pacific affairs and to detach their understandings of Americanism from the values of worldly openness and engagement, Japanese Americans moved toward embracing an Americanism that was more explicitly oriented around local conditions and their minority neighbors. This attitude was not the same kind of hyperpatriotic, accommodationist Americanism that such organizations as the JACL would be identified with. Rather, it was an Americanism that pursued the ideal of racial equality while challenging dominant U.S. social and legal practices. Although the onset of war proved a detriment to Seattle Japanese Americans' ability to achieve meaningful and concrete ends with this ideological outlook, as we shall see in the epilogue, the seed of a multiracial activist tradition that would flower in the postwar years was planted during this period.

The Storm Gathers

Throughout the early twentieth century, United States–Japan relations had been precarious, carefully forged between a rivalry for influence in the Pacific and a shared interest in peace and commercial prosperity. By the end of the 1930s, however, the balance increasingly tipped toward mutual distrust and then all-out war.[2] A key turning point was Japan's invasion of Manchuria in 1931 and subsequent creation of the Manchukuo puppet regime, actions that violated its earlier pledge to the United States and other Western nations to respect China's territorial sovereignty in the Open Door agreement. The United States expressed its displeasure with Japan but otherwise did not respond with concerted action, for the invasion occurred when Americans were in the thick of the Great Depression and preoccupied with domestic economic recovery.[3] By 1937, the stakes were ratcheted up with Japan's attack on Shanghai, Nanking, and Northern Shanghai. By 1940, with Japan's continued refusal to withdraw from China and its aggressions in other parts of Asia, the United States formally abrogated its commercial treaty with Japan and enacted a series of trade embargoes aimed at undermining the nation's ability to wage further military aggression. In July 1941, the United States went a step further, freezing all Japanese assets in the country. By November, a Pacific war seemed inevitable.[4]

Years before these steps were taken, branches of the federal government had been quietly preparing for the possibility of a military conflict with Japan and the other the Axis powers. Worried about the potential presence of a fifth column and Japanese designs on American territory, the Federal Bureau of Investigation (FBI) and the Office of Naval Intelligence (ONI) had been collecting data on mainland Japanese residents since 1932. Individuals with direct ties to the Japanese government or associated with organizations that promoted political or commercial relations between the United States and Japan were singled out.[5] In 1940, in an attempt to crack down on potential subversives and to ease the work of monitoring Japanese, Germans, and Italians, the U.S. Congress passed the Alien Registration Act, also known as the Smith Act. It authorized the collection of background information on nearly five million aliens living within U.S. borders, required resident aliens to report changes of address within five days of a move, and decreed that all aliens temporarily in the United States were to report every three months.[6] By 1941, the FBI had files on more than two thousand Japanese residents, placed in one of three categories of suspicion: A, B, or C.[7]

How did the mounting tensions and growing distrust between the United States and Japan and Axis aggression in Asia affect life for Asian Americans? As shown in the previous chapter, invoking the Sino-Japanese conflict animated Chinese-Japanese sports in Seattle with a sense of high-stakes drama. But the repercussions of Asian affairs for Seattle's Japanese Americans could also be more serious, putting community leaders on guard. Before Japan's invasion of Manchuria, Japanese leaders and white educators had been working to cultivate an informed local understanding of Pacific Rim relations, but after 1931, they found themselves increasingly on the defensive and called upon to explain Japan's seemingly aggressive course in Asia. In 1936, for instance, Broadway High School hosted a series of talks on foreign affairs led by University of Washington Professor of Oriental Studies Robert Pollard. The topics addressed included Japanese demands on North China and Chinese attitudes toward Japan.[8] In late 1937, the *Great Northern Daily News* observed that the news coming out of Asia was increasingly painting Japan in a negative light and signaled a possible reversal of American sympathies with the nation, all of which underlined a need for Japanese Americans to more vigorously explain Japan's side of the conflict to their neighbors.[9] In addition to supporting and participating in public forums, Japanese Americans continued to work the topic of foreign affairs into their debates and oratorical contests. In 1938, the Japanese Association sponsored an oratorical contest, held at Nippon Kan Hall. At this event, Broadway High School senior Takashi Matsui defeated four opponents with a speech in which he laid out why China was not ready for independence. His oratory was so acclaimed by his co-ethnics, for content and style, that he gave a repeat performance over the airwaves on a local radio station.[10]

Of course, Japanese Americans were not of one mind on the meaning of the events in Asia, but the public and semipublic responses of some of the most visible among them, such as those described above, did not do much to ease simmering antagonisms held by their Asian American neighbors whose homelands were under threat by Japan's actions. Indeed, the repercussions of international circumstances on local conditions soon materialized in ways that proved unfavorable and inconvenient for many Japanese Americans. In Seattle and elsewhere, groups denouncing Japan's invasion of China called for and organized boycotts of Japanese goods and Japanese-owned businesses.[11] For Koreans and Chinese in America in particular, participating in anti-Japanese campaigns proved to be a powerful way to forge ethnic solidarity while contributing to the struggles of their homelands from afar.[12] In her memoir about growing up in Seattle before World War II, Monica Sone portrayed the precarious tenor of daily life in the mid-1930s for Japanese Americans, which she attributed to the international turn of events. "As the nations went, so went their people," she reflected.[13] She remembered being especially jarred by the increasingly vicious images of Japanese people, such as cartoons that depicted Japanese with "enormous, moon-shaped spectacles," "beady, myopic eyes," and mustaches "perched arrogantly over massive, square, buck teeth."[14] Sone also recalled a chilling effect on interethnic relations as a result of the escalating problems in Asia and described neighbors suddenly treating Japanese people with disdain: "I felt their resentment in a hundred ways—the way a saleswoman in a large department store never saw me waiting at the counter. After ten minutes, I had to walk quietly away as if nothing happened. A passenger sitting across the aisle in a streetcar would stare at me coldly."[15]

As Sone remembered, it was her Chinese neighbors who exhibited the greatest antipathy toward Japanese Americans. She recollected one incident from the 1930s in which a group of Chinese American employees of Japanese-owned businesses quit their jobs in protest of Japan's actions in China. As a result of such episodes, Sone became much more self-conscious and tense in encounters that she had before approached with a carefree case: "I dreaded going through Chinatown. The Chinese shopkeepers, gossiping and sunning themselves in front of their stores, invariably stopped their chatter to give me pointed, icicled glares."[16]

The inflaming of local passions by events abroad concerned Japanese American leaders and journalists who feared interethnic conflict might get out of hand and endanger not just the economic well-being of Japanese Americans but also their physical safety. In 1939, the *Great Northern Daily News* reported on a "brawl" on Jackson Street between Japanese and Chinese that illustrated these worries. It began when Fred Nimi, a Japanese driver who worked for the Chinese-owned China Cab Company, responded to a call to pick up three Chinese men from a nearby rooming house. After Nimi arrived, the Chinese men ascertained that he was Japanese and refused to ride with him. They went to the China Cab Company office and assaulted the owner, Harry Marr, after accusing him of being unpatriotic for employing a Japanese.[17] The *Great Northern* also noted and expressed alarm at what appeared to be a rise in physical fighting between Chinese and Japanese American youths, in and outside school. One incident, which occurred in 1940, nearly a year and a half before the bombing of Pearl Harbor, involved two Chinese Americans who allegedly stole a Japanese boy's bicycle. The situation escalated when another Japanese, Yutaka Habu, the son of local florists, entered the fray and tried to get the bicycle back from the assailants, leading to a violent altercation in an alley between Weller and King streets near Maynard and Seventh. Casting its sympathies with the Japanese Americans, the *Great Northern* praised Habu as a "hero of the Sino-Japanese struggle."[18] Such incidents, in which the troubles in East Asia played out in the streets of the Jackson Street neighborhood, created an unsettling atmosphere and showed that distance alone might not be sufficient to keep Sino-Japanese problems from infecting relationships and daily life in Seattle.

By the late 1930s, events in Asia and growing tensions between the United States and Japan made analogies and links between local conditions in Seattle and the Pacific Rim increasingly problematic. To Japanese American leaders in Seattle and elsewhere, the pressure of public opinion and recent events signaled a need now for sharper lines between the perspectives of Japanese in America and the actions of Japan. For example, reporting on an attack by a Chinese boy on a Nisei girl in San Francisco, the *Great Northern Daily News* expressed regret that the Sino-Japanese crisis might have contributed to the assault. "Young minds are easily disturbed and influenced," the paper lamented, "and so an unfortunate incident, arising from the unfortunate incident in the Far East, occurred in San Francisco Wednesday afternoon."[19] The paper quoted the assaulted girl's mother, who blamed the whole affair on "the local Chinese elders who influence little Chinese hearts to act that way in another country and among other people who have no control over things occurring thousands of miles away."[20] Regarding this and other incidents, the *Great Northern* urged readers to resist looking to the Far East as a model for local relations and suggested instead that the common bond of Americanism and desire for local peace should define Chinese-Japanese relations in the United States. For instance, regarding the China Cab altercation described earlier, the *Great Northern* stated, "Harry Marr and his drivers are all American citizens and have no interest in the Sino-Japanese trouble in Asia, 4000 miles away."[21] It was certainly a practical move on the paper's part to turn away from the Pacific and to insist upon a vast separation—geographic and otherwise—between events in Asia and concerns at home. It was also a reversal of a decades-long pattern of Seattle's Japanese Americans forging links with Japan and interpreting their surroundings and circumstances in terms of Pacific Rim relations.

Through depictions of friendship between Chinese Americans and Japanese Americans, the *Great Northern Daily News* sought to counter the growing perception and fear that the war in Asia was threatening to seriously unsettle the local community. A 1938 article titled "Odd Friendship to Occidentals" highlighted the close bond, described as an "international friendship," between local Chinese and Japanese women to illustrate how individuals were rising above the politics of the Far East for a greater cause. "China and Japan are now engaged in war—bitter as wars always are and there will be scars for years to come," stated the *Great Northern,* "but does that necessarily imply that all Japanese and Chinese over here must be enemies?"[22] The story, which reflected a desire to tamp down on further interethnic misunderstanding arising from the international crisis, also illustrated the maneuvers of imagined geography that Japanese Americans engaged in to reposition themselves in light of recent events. As it was less and less tenable and useful to imagine Seattle as part of the wider Pacific world, they turned to insisting that living in Seattle, especially for the second generation, nurtured instead a loyalty to the United States only: "Marshaled under the banner of loyalty to the land of their birth, second generation Japanese and Chinese of Seattle and vicinity are disregarding reports of hostilities, charges and counter-charges and misunderstanding in the Far East and are meeting their mutual problems in the United States in a spirit of cooperation and friendship."[23] The *Great Northern* also looked outside Seattle for examples of interethnic unity prevailing over international tension. Just two months before the attack on Pearl Harbor, it reported that Chinese and Japanese pastors in San Diego—Kei T. Wong of the Chinese Mission and Seizo Abe of the Japanese Congregation—traded pulpits as a demonstration of solidarity and a testament to "the racial tolerance encouraged in this country."[24]

As events made clear, internationalism and cosmopolitanism were becoming untenable as frames for talking about Seattle, much less strategies through which to seek local belonging. With respect to intra-Asian relations, circumstances by the late 1930s compelled Japanese Americans to increasingly foreground the concerns of U.S. citizenship and antiracism—rather than Sino-Japanese politics—in their relations with Chinese Americans. These years also marked the beginning of a new, albeit interrupted, chapter in Japanese-black relations in Seattle. Until the years leading up to the war, these two communities significantly overlapped, socially and physically, but were not a part of each other's affairs and concerns in a substantive and sustained manner. Things would begin to change as local and international circumstances brought Japanese Americans and blacks into closer view of and contact with one another, giving rise to a nascent intraminority solidarity that underlined their shared status and aspirations in U.S. society.

Throughout the early 1900s, Japan's rise caught the notice of many Americans, including African American intellectuals. By the mid-1930s, the subject was a regular topic of discussion in the Seattle black press. In particular, commentators would hash out what Japan's ascendance might eventually mean for all the world's nonwhite races.[25] In 1934, the *Northwest Enterprise* reported on a symposium in New York hosted by an organization called the Inter-racial Forum. At this event, Japanese and Chinese speakers disagreed on the question of whether Japan was a "friend of the darker races."[26] The *Enterprise* noted the remarks of Dunje Omura, a Japanese speaker and graduate student in the United States, who said that Japan was "laying the foundation for the rest of the darker races to get similar respect."[27] Seeking other sources to gauge Japan's perception of nonwhite peoples, in February 1935, the paper quoted a recently published Japanese Ministry of War pamphlet, which shed a different point of view, stating, "the existence of 12,000,000 black men in the United States is an eternal cancer." It furthermore advised that one way to defeat a belligerent state was to weaken it internally by pitting the races in the country against each another.[28] On the whole however, the *Enterprise* seemed guardedly optimistic about Japan's rise. In a front-page story appearing in January 1935, it lauded the formation of a chapter of the Pacific Movement Inc. in Philadelphia, an organization started in St. Louis by African Americans whose objective was "the wiping out of the status which abridges liberties of colored races." Because the Philadelphia chapter was to be led by a Japanese doctor, this connection raised hopes that Japan and its people might be counted on as allies of blacks in America.[29]

Much was changing in the dynamics of daily life in Seattle's Jackson Street by the late 1930s. Within its communities of color, individuals were mulling over and confronting what recent events in the Pacific might mean for them. Chinese Americans responded with some hostility toward Japan and their Japanese American neighbors. African Americans were debating the pros and cons of Japanese expansionism and whether it would have any significance for their hopes for racial liberation. Mounting distrust between the United States and Japan and later economic sanctions were rupturing the Pacific world, an imagined geography that Japanese Americans and Seattle boosters had earnestly and hopefully occupied for several decades. For Japanese Americans on the eve of war, conditions seemed to be approaching either a breaking point or a breakthrough. Interethnic tensions and anti-Japanese feelings still existed, but opportunities for cross-ethnic understanding and alliances also emerged. Pacific Rim politics had gone irrevocably off course, necessitating deep reflection on and a reformulation of how Japanese Americans fit into local society and the wider national landscape. Two events occurring just months before the United States' entry into the war illustrate how some of this played out, both of which also entailed a critical rethinking of Japanese-black relations.

THE SEATTLE HOTEL CONTROVERSY

The city's black population grew only slightly, from approximately thirty-three hundred to thirty-eight hundred, between 1930 and 1940, but by the beginning of the 1940s, signs of a new chapter in African American Seattle were emerging. As elsewhere, Seattle began mobilizing its industries for war about two years before the United States actually entered the conflict in 1941, which prompted a new influx of internal migrants, including African Americans, eager to seize new job opportunities.[30] Obtaining adequate housing had always been a pressing issue facing African American residents of the city, and this problem was exacerbated as the growing demand created by population growth outstripped the supply. Due to long-standing patterns of segregation throughout Seattle, Jackson Street, where the physical conditions were less than ideal, was one of the only neighborhoods where blacks could live. And because of the configuration of the local economy, many sought housing in Japanese-owned residential hotels.

For the most part, new arrivals were able to obtain temporary and permanent accommodations without incident, but by the summer of 1941, the still-looming threat of war, an overstretched housing supply, social misunderstandings, and a good deal of bureaucratic confusion led to a public relations crisis between the Japanese American and African American communities. In response to more than a dozen complaints by blacks who had been denied service in Japanese-owned hotels in the city, the Seattle Industrial Labor Union (SILU), a branch of the Congress of Industrial Organizations (CIO), investigated the matter for possible racial discrimination. In the fifteen cases reported to the SILU, the would-be patrons tried to obtain rooms using vouchers issued by the King County Welfare Department. Although the vouchers represented valid forms of payment, they were still turned away. Seeking recourse, the voucher holders turned to the SILU for help.

The SILU, the *Northwest Enterprise,* and the NAACP had certainly dealt with racial discrimination cases before, but the issue before them was whether to handle these cases just as they would incidents of white-owned businesses discriminating against black patrons. Although still admonishing the Japanese hotel owners and calling on the Japanese Hotel and Rooming House Association to rectify the situation, A. E. Harding, the SILU's executive secretary, couched his protest in terms of an intraminority crusade against racism. Japanese business owners probably behaved in a racially discriminatory manner, Harding noted, but beyond merely condemning them, he urged them to remember that they too were common targets of racism:

> There are thousands of Orientals in CIO Unions in Seattle, many of whom are Japanese. We are proud to have these men in our organizations, and we have gone to the defense of our Oriental brothers time and time again when various elements have attempted to discriminate against them. . . . We feel, therefore, that we have every right to request that you show the same courtesy to the Negro people that we in the CIO accord all races, Whites, Orientals, and Negroes alike.[31]

The CIO was one of the only labor unions that explicitly disavowed racism, and in this case, as in others, it worked to overcome the divide-and-conquer mentality that had prevented the formation of a broad, interracial coalition in so many other contexts. Although this situation had strong class dimension, as it began with a conflict between owners and customers, the SILU approached the issue as a race-relations matter, seeking to unite blacks and Japanese around a shared commitment to racial equality.

The *Northwest Enterprise* followed a similar strategy and harshly criticized the Japanese hotel owners for their hypocrisy in denying accommodations to African Americans. As racial minorities themselves, they bore responsibility for treating all other nonwhites equitably, it suggested. The paper also pointed out that Japanese Americans' actions amounted to a violation of constitutional principles. "This act is a flagrant breach of the State Constitution," the *Enterprise* stated. "It would seem that the Japanese a minority group the same as the Negro would think twice before helping foster a condition which will eventually be a bar to them in the full enjoyment of all the rights of an American citizen."[32]

Toward addressing these cases of housing discrimination and eventually improving intraminority understanding, the SILU, the *Northwest Enterprise,* and the NAACP, in effect, created a public relations problem for the Japanese American business community. By shining a light on the incidents and urging the business owners to think first about their common struggle against racism with other minorities, they challenged all of Seattle's Japanese Americans to rethink their relationships with their African American neighbors and how to best work toward acceptance and inclusion in America. In the way of a response, the *Great Northern Daily News* agreed that Japanese hotel owners were wrong in rejecting the black customers and acknowledged that such behavior was particularly troubling in light of their own racial minority status. "These things do not look right when you look at the Japanese in the light as a minority group, always complaining about its pressed American citizenship rights," said the *Great Northern*. "They stink like a bad odor of prejudice."[33] The message emerging from this encounter for blacks and Japanese alike seemed to be that rights alone would not ensure justice and that members of minority groups, particularly because of their shared status, must be sensitive and respectful to one another. For if they could not treat each other with the dignity that they sought for themselves, their demands for racial equality would always be hollow.

Although this was likely not the first misunderstanding between Japanese business owners and black patrons, it certainly was one of the most public incidents that culminated in voices from the black and Japanese communities calling on Seattle Japanese Americans to engage in some soul-searching about how they ought to approach their neighbors and continue in their own struggle for equality in America. As hopes for the restoration of friendship between the United States and Japan and a peaceful Pacific world diminished, at least some Japanese Americans began to turn to local and domestic matters to guide their strategies for achieving belonging and inclusion. Such incidents as the hotel controversy pushed them in this direction, and, before the summer of 1941 came to a close, another episode would once again link Japanese and blacks in Seattle, but this time to fight together.

No Blacks or Japanese Allowed:
The Colman Pool Incident

It is not clear whether any decisive changes in the policies or practices of Japanese hotel owners came about as a result of the public censuring they received due to the hotel discrimination incidents, but the issue of racial justice remained at the forefront of local affairs for many of Seattle's minorities as the summer of 1941 proceeded. Beginning on July 4, 1941, local passions flared up again, although this time not over policies at a hotel but instead at a swimming pool. On this day, the city opened a new pool at Colman Park, which immediately became a popular attraction for residents seeking relief from the summer heat. Within days, however, pool operators became concerned about overcrowding, and reports surfaced that on at least two occasions, on July 6 and 21, employees had blocked access to Japanese and African American boys and girls.

This time, black and Japanese leaders were quick to join forces to take action against the city. The NAACP and the Urban League, which investigated the incidents, found evidence that some of the Park Board members had quipped that blacks were a venereal disease threat as justification for their exclusion from the pool.[34] In an attempt to deal public shame and pressure onto the Park Board, the *Northwest Enterprise* printed the members' names and called for their resignations.[35] James Sakamoto contacted Park Department Supervisor Ben Evans on behalf of two Nisei youths and intimated possible legal action to pursue their grievance. "The two boys," Sakamoto stated in his letter to Evans, "say they are willing to file affidavits stating the exact circumstances that reflected on their natural sense of pride and self-respect."[36]

That this controversy erupted against the backdrop of fascist atrocities in Europe made the practices at the Colman pool especially egregious, and this irony was not lost on the protesters who argued that this treatment of blacks and Japanese was not only racist but also un-American. For instance, Hugh DeLacy, president of the left-leaning Washington Commonwealth Federation, suggested that the Park Board's actions amounted to behavior becoming of Nazis. Not only was the exclusion of blacks and Japanese from the pool reprehensible in light of the ongoing war, he charged, but it was also a flagrant breach of the equal protection guarantee of the Fourteenth Amendment of the U.S. Constitution. Other protestors similarly invoked the Constitution, the war in Europe, and the un-Americanness of domestic racism to argue their case. In an editorial criticizing the Park Board, the *Northwest Enterprise* insisted that although "Negroes, Chinese, and Japanese" in

Seattle, peoples routinely marginalized in the larger society, were all "good American citizens," the members of the Park Board, purportedly advocates of wholesome values and fairness, were the ones behaving in an un-American fashion, "because no good American will deny to another the equal protection of the laws."[37]

In addition to fending off an onslaught of written complaints regarding the pool incidents, the Park Board faced a delegation of Japanese Americans and African Americans at a meeting held on July 24. Among those present were Clarence Arai, who had earlier sought a state assembly seat with the support of the African American community, Seattle NAACP President John E. Prim, Mrs. J. P. Robertson, B. E. Squires, and Bernard Reiter, and some of the youths who were excluded from the pool. Members of these two minority communities appeared not to merely protest their poor treatment; having endured persecution and responding with forbearance and resistance, they sought to demonstrate that it was *they* who embodied the true spirit of Americanism. At a time when racial and patriotic passions were running high, this strategy was a provocative one. Blacks and Japanese challenged the city at large, arguing that if it had been true to the Progressive and inclusive ideals it touted in other contexts, such incidents would have been immediately rectified. Reiter, an attorney for the Seattle Urban League, pointed out that denying minorities' access to facilities worked against the city's own objectives of promoting wholesome recreation and cutting down on juvenile delinquency.[38] In his remarks, Arai brought up Seattle's self-avowed reputation for tolerance to expose its hypocrisy for discriminating against Japanese and blacks. Because the Park Board had not upheld its own ethos of fairness, such people as Arai and Reiter took it upon themselves to invoke it and to remind the city that what it had condoned effectively amounted to a betrayal of American principles. "Other races have been proud of Seattle's tolerant and fair attitude," Arai said to the Park Board. "We have been proud of the fact that there are no 'Jim Crow' street cars in Seattle and that we all live as neighbors. We believe in a free America and seek to raise our children in this belief."[39]

These were powerful arguments, to which the city and Park Board officials had little to say in response. James A. Gibbs, the president of the Park Board, held to the earlier explanation that the pool had become overcrowded and added to this statement the unsubstantiated contention that white people had also been turned away. Ben Evans, the supervisor of the Parks Department, admitted that he ordered employees to deny entry to nonwhite pool users, although he insisted this practice was intended to be a temporary measure until the board came up with a formal solution for the overcrowding problem.[40] Evans vehemently denied any malicious intent to discriminate against anyone, and board members assured the aggrieved communities that the matter would be given "serious consideration."[41] Acting Mayor James Scavotto instructed the Park Board to "please discontinue practice at once, as all American citizens in this city will be accorded equal opportunities for all recreations owned, operated and maintained by taxation, regardless of race, color, or creed."[42]

City officials' denunciations of the incidents and their statements that such practices were a scourge on Seattle's reputation represented a public relations victory for Japanese Americans and blacks. The whole affair also brought the communities closer together in their struggles against racism. In practice, however, racial discrimination did not end in Seattle, or even at Colman pool. Despite the assurances that were made, it is not clear whether the city ever took decisive and permanent action to eliminate racism at Colman, because grumblings by black organizations about conditions there continued throughout the summer of 1941, and, according to historian Quintard Taylor, it was not truly integrated until 1944.[43] Moreover, after the hearings, the Park Board took no official action. In early August, the Parks Department continued to receive complaints of racial discrimination at the pool, and the chief clerk was directed to answer letters by simply stating that racial discrimination no longer occurred there. Mayor Earl Millikin also assured members of the Japanese and black communities in a letter that everyone would be treated fairly and that admission would proceed on an equal basis.

The controversy around the Colman pool incidents revealed a gap between rhetoric and reality in Seattle with regard to cultural diversity and racial equality. For much of its history, Seattle was a white city that also claimed to be cosmopolitan, requiring officials to pull off a tricky and often dubious balancing act. City leaders had touted Seattle's reputation for tolerance, which they claimed stemmed from its international orientation and heterogeneous cultural makeup. Along with other Seattleites, minority residents became believers in this discourse, but too many times, its shallowness was exposed in such episodes as the rejection of black and Japanese youths from the swimming pool at Colman. Yet because the city was invested in the image of racial and cultural tolerance, Park Board members knew they could not openly maintain a policy of segregation. The incident also underscored how crucial public spaces became sites of contestation over belonging and citizenship between minority communities and the city at large. Moreover, for the aggrieved Japanese and blacks, the Colman pool controversy proved to be an early instance of interracial political action. Being denied access to public space thrust them into the same arenas of protest against the white majority. Fighting fascism and Jim Crow and seeking equal protection were not goals specific to a single group but concerns blacks and Japanese shared. In turn, an acknowledgement of their shared grievances and experiences gave rise to broadly defined goals that would be further pursued after the war.

DASHED DREAMS OF A PEACEFUL PACIFIC

Through these two events in the summer of 1941, we can discern a subtle but decisive shift in Japanese Americans' strategies for civic belonging in Seattle. Unfortunately, the oncoming military conflict in the international arena gave them scarcely enough time to articulate a new vision and to put these strategies to effective use. Attaching themselves to United States–Japan relations and symbols of East-West friendship might have proven useful for Japanese Americans in Seattle during the early decades of the 1900s, but by the end of the 1930s, it was a losing proposition, merely a way to isolate and to marginalize themselves. By mid-1941, the United States was making increasingly assertive responses toward Japan and preparing itself for a Pacific war that appeared more and more likely.

It was not immediately clear what the freezing of Japanese assets in the United States, ordered in July 1941, meant in concrete terms, but it did throw life into limbo for Japanese Americans.[44] It was also vague as to what the policies effectively curbing commercial relations between the countries meant for liners already en route to the United States from Japan.[45] At the time, two Japanese banks operated in Seattle—Yokohama Specie, Ltd., and Sumitomo—as did three large commercial firms. These establishments continued to operate while awaiting interpretation of the government's action. Eventually, the banks were told they had to obtain licenses from the secretary of the Treasury to continue operation. Because the freezing of Japanese assets targeted Issei-run businesses, the Japanese American community was in effect financially paralyzed. Issei businessmen had to obtain authorization to release funds to pay for purchases and to complete other transactions, which made their day-to-day business operations highly onerous at best and impossible at worst.

The black press in Seattle was one of the most steadfast defenders of its Japanese American neighbors. In an article published on November 21, 1941, the *Northwest Enterprise* expressed its admiration for and solidarity with Seattle Japanese and urged readers not to be swayed against them because of events in Asia. "Seattle," the *Enterprise* stated, "should guard zealously against any unprovoked demonstrations against Japanese in this area because of strained relations between America and their fatherland." There was no credible evidence that they were a danger to national security or public safety. The Japanese of Seattle "seldom appear on police court records. They do not ask for help from the state or from individuals. They work hard and long on their farms from sun up in the summer and at twilight, they still will be, bent to their tasks."[46]

The morning of December 7, Japan launched its surprise bombing of Pearl Harbor and a few hours later invaded the Philippines. Seattle Japanese residents were reportedly "thunderstruck" by news of the air attack.[47] According to the *Great Northern Daily News,* the next day, business at Pike Place was slower than usual, because the Japanese merchants who ran most of the stalls there came to work late. They worried about a possible backlash against them and were, thus, reluctant to discuss the attack.[48] As Seattle and the rest of the nation sat stunned, federal authorities quickly descended upon the Japanese American community. Blackouts were scheduled for several days, requiring residents to turn off their lights from 11:00 P.M. until a half hour after daybreak.[49] People were also instructed not to telephone radio stations.

Initially, the Seattle press and Mayor's Office called for fair play toward Japanese Americans and urged citizens to behave with restraint. In a statement that was printed in the *Great Northern Daily News,* Mayor Millikin expressed his sympathy for the local Japanese American community and called for caution. "I cannot stress too much the importance of a spirit of tolerance for Seattle's Japanese," he said. "We must remember that nearly all of them are American born citizens."[50] As discussed in Chapter 4, the *Seattle Post-Intelligencer* printed a story titled "What's War to Friends?" on December 10 about Broadway High School and how friendships between white and Japanese students remained intact despite the outbreak of war.[51]

Events on the ground, however, indicated that feelings were much more mixed. Anti-Japanese incidents spiked in the immediate wake of Japan's attack, such as the beating of Harry Sato by a group of six Filipinos on Maynard and Weller.[52] After the Pearl Harbor bombing, the *Japanese-American Courier* and the *Great Northern Daily News* reported an increasing number of street brawls and assaults on Japanese people by non-Japanese assailants, often Filipinos, Chinese, or blacks. In December 1941 alone, the *Great Northern* reported three attacks on or burglaries of Japanese by blacks in Jackson Street.[53] In early 1942, the paper described a "race riot" involving two Filipinos and a Japanese hotel clerk at the Walden Hotel on Yesler Way. This fight was instigated by the Filipinos' allegedly shouting racial insults at the Japanese clerk.[54]

Japanese American leaders and writers tried to project an optimistic outlook, although this attitude was difficult to maintain in the face of uncertainty and likelihood that the United States would seek some form of retribution for the attack by Japan. On December 9, 1941, Richard Takeuchi, the editor of the *Great Northern Daily News,* thanked the mayor and asserted his faith in the United States to treat Japanese Americans fairly, but he also ominously predicted that "Christmas this year will be a memorable one, undoubtedly, not a merry occasion. Nor does the new year portend any happiness."[55] Indeed, the federal government had not hesitated to act, for on December 8, the day after the bombing, it declared German, Italian, and Japanese nationals to be enemy aliens. The attorney general gave authorities a blanket warrant to arrest those on the so-called ABC list, which the FBI had maintained to keep track of potential subversives prior to the outbreak of the war. The FBI arrested Issei and a few Nisei, among them Buddhist priests, Japanese-language teachers, and officials and leaders of community organizations. Throughout the West Coast, federal agents raided the homes of people on the ABC list, confiscating radios, cameras, and firearms. On December 9, the Immigration and Naturalization Service (INS) already had 1,792 enemy aliens in custody, of whom 1,212 were Japanese.[56] In Seattle, that number was 116.[57] Eleven days after the attack, 364 Japanese and 25 Italian "enemy aliens" were removed from Seattle and held at Fort Lincoln, North Dakota.[58] The Japanese contingent would later be sent to a detention center in Missoula, Montana, for the duration of the war.

The searches and arrests in effect removed the Japanese American leadership strata, thus, destabilizing the entire ethnic community.[59] ABC suspects made up 10 percent of the Japanese American population and included financiers, religious leaders, and key community figureheads.[60] Undermining the ethnic economy's financial viability was thoroughly disruptive to all Seattle Japanese. To carry out a nationwide ruling prohibiting the transfer of money and assets to Japanese nationals, the Federal Reserve Bank on December 10 ordered that Japanese-born domestic employees in Seattle clubs and homes should not be paid until further notice from the U.S. Treasury Department.[61] The Trading with the Enemy Act also forbade lodgers from paying rent to Issei landlords.[62] The Treasury Department canceled the licenses of all shipping companies that operated between Japan and the United States. Financial activities in Japanese America came to a grinding halt. Individual Issei business licenses were revoked, and their bank accounts blocked. Japanese Americans, and potentially all Asians, faced travel restrictions, as ticket sellers at the King Street train station were instructed to secure proof of citizenship from anyone who looked like they might be Japanese.[63] Japanese banks in the United States were shut down, and all Japanese investments were impounded. The economic stranglehold disrupted commerce on the West Coast, especially of fresh vegetables and other produce.

President Franklin D. Roosevelt's signing of Executive Order 9066 on February 19, 1942, and the government's subsequent announcement of plans to remove all persons of Japanese ancestry from the West Coast prompted a mass exodus of Japanese Americans from the workplace. At Gatewood School, for example, a group of local mothers claiming to have the support of the Parent-Teacher Association collected signatures for a petition demanding the resignation of Japanese clerks employed by the school. Before they could be forcibly removed, however, all the Japanese American employees voluntarily stepped down from their jobs.[64] These clerks, who just a decade or so earlier might have been singled out as exemplars of Seattle's cosmopolitan school system, made extraordinary sacrifices in the face of a tide of narrow, racialized patriotism in the wake of Pearl Harbor. In a group statement to the Seattle school board, the Japanese employees, all of whom were female, said they gave up their positions to prove their loyalty to the United States and to minimize any tension and possible disunity in the wider community. The assistant superintendent of the school district commended their actions. For other jobs vacated by Japanese Americans as evacuation loomed or got under way, workers waiting in the wings were immediately hired. As early as February 1942, at the Union Street train station, African Americans replaced Japanese porters, or "red caps," and similar patterns took hold in downtown hotels and restaurants.[65] At the nearby King Street station, employers hired Filipinos to replace the departing Japanese.

As a sense of social and economic uncertainty pervaded Japanese America throughout the West Coast, families, once the anchors of the ethnic community, were shaken to their core. Describing a scene that played out in Japanese American communities up and down the coast, Sone recalled FBI agents descending upon her neighborhood in Seattle, searching people's homes, and then spiriting away prominent ethnic leaders for detention, including her father. Not knowing when or whether the family would resume its normal life, Sone's father made arrangements for a neighbor to manage their hotel. The family packed their belongings, went to the Japanese Chamber of Commerce on Jackson Street to be inoculated against typhoid, and then reported to the assembly center at the Puyallup fairgrounds, the first stop before being taken by train further inland to Minidoka internment camp in Idaho.[66]

Not only were many male heads of households detained by the FBI, splitting up families in the process, but about twenty interethnic couples in which one spouse was Japanese also faced separation. Exemptions were initially granted to these families, but they were later revoked, according to the *Seattle Post-Intelligencer*.[67] Nellie Woo was a Nisei woman married to a Chinese man named Lum P. Woo, with whom she had two children. Because she and her daughters would have to leave Seattle, but Lum Woo was not required to, the family faced imminent separation. "There has been no official army ruling as to procedure in cases of such intermarriages," said the *Post-Intelligencer*, "but the Farm Security Administration locally says that the children generally remain with the mother."[68] For their protection, the girls wore buttons identifying them as Chinese, and the family placed a placard in front of their window that read "China." Desperate to avoid internment and to keep her family intact, Nellie sent a letter to John De-Witt, the military commander of the Western Defense Command, asking if an exception could be made in her case. She received a reply from the assistant adjutant general refusing the request.

On April 21, 1942, evacuation instructions were posted, notifying people of Japanese ancestry that they would be taken to the fairgrounds in Puyallup in three groups the following Tuesday, Thursday, and Friday.[69] For the most part, Japanese Americans in Seattle and the West Coast were compliant, saying and doing little to protest. Among the exceptions was Gordon Hirabayashi, a University of Washington law student who unsuccessfully challenged Japanese removal by violating the curfew order and refusing to report to the Civil Control Station for evacuation instructions.[70] James Sakamoto and the JACL, however, purporting to speak for the Japanese American population, committed their unqualified allegiance to the United States and pledged to demonstrate their loyalty by obeying the instructions of the government. The only objection that Sakamoto expressed on the removal policy was that it would not allow Japanese Americans to throw their full weight behind America's war effort. "Shops, hotels, stores, and farms must be attended," he said. "We desire to continue to do so, especially now when there is such a shortage of labor due to the demands of the defense industries, and every willing hand is a national asset."[71]

The forced exodus of Japanese Americans from the West Coast mirrored the shattering of Pacific Rim internationalism as a frame through which to comprehend Seattle's development and identity. With the United States and Japan at war with each other, the visions of friendship and commercial relations across the Pacific, once so prominent in the local urban imaginary, were now impossible hopes of a bygone past. Overnight, classrooms became much emptier. Once-bustling city blocks turned into rows of boarded-up storefronts (see Figure 6.1). Japanese youths disappeared from the scene at

Collins Park. The International Potlatch festival, discussed in Chapter 2, had its last run in the summer of 1942, on the heels of the Japanese removal. As an event that glorified and promoted United States–Japan relations, the Potlatch had become anachronistic, given the need for Americans to suspend their frivolities and to unite in a spirit of national sacrifice and the fact that these onetime friends of the Pacific world were now bitter enemies. The end of the International Potlatch, which for years had been a bold symbol of Seattle's cosmopolitan aspirations, also signaled broad transformations in the local and national cultures with the onset of World War II. Specifically, Americanism became much more rigid, as if hyperjingoistic patriotism were the only way to embody and to express U.S. nationalism and citizenship. Already subject to antiforeigner biases and racial prejudice and now linked to an enemy nation, Japanese Americans, noncitizens and citizens, would be figuratively and physically displaced from the West Coast as part of these transformations (see Figure 6.2).

By the spring of 1942, the rest of Seattle seemed resigned to its new realities, as little protest was raised as Japanese removal proceeded. One quarter from which dissenting voices continued to emerge was that of local African Americans. The evacuation and internment of Japanese Americans struck them as yet another example of the reprehensible treatment suffered by people of color in the United States. In a column titled "Life, Liberty, and the

Figure 6.1. An evacuation sale at a Japanese-owned store in Seattle, 1942. Prior to their removal, Japanese merchants had to scramble to dispose of their businesses or to make arrangements to have others oversee them.
(Source: Seattle Post-Intelligencer Collection, Museum of History and Industry.)

Figure 6.2. Vacant stores after the removal of Japanese Americans from Seattle, 1942. The removal left some blocks in the Jackson Street area a series of boarded-up storefronts. *(Source:* Seattle Post-Intelligencer *Collection, Museum of History and Industry.)*

Pursuit of Happiness," a writer for the *Northwest Enterprise* stated, "With the evacuation of the American-born Japanese, America's reputation for justice and equality no longer glistens. There is danger of our vaunted patriotism becoming the shield of unscrupulous and thoughtless persons, urged only by the flames of racial prejudice."[72] As the removal of Japanese threatened to tarnish "America's reputation for justice and equality," from another perspective, it would also deal a tremendous blow to Seattle's self-conception as the "gateway to the Orient," at least for the duration of the war.

CONCLUSION

From Washington State, a total of 12,892 persons of Japanese ancestry were interned. Seattle alone lost more than nine thousand of its residents. During the war years, Filipinos and blacks assumed a more prominent presence in the Jackson Street neighborhood, as they seized the new opportunities in housing and employment created by the departure of Japanese Americans. As the *Seattle Post-Intelligencer* related, the appearance of Filipinos and blacks into areas previously occupied by Japanese sustained Jackson Street's overall busy atmosphere and kept up the appearance that it was a "teeming quarter," despite the removal of what had been one of its largest communities.[73]

Providing one perspective on the changes in Jackson Street after the removal of Japanese Americans are wartime letters to James Sakamoto, written by his white friend and former neighbor Harold Schaffer. While Sakamoto was interned at Minidoka, Schaffer kept him updated on the changes that were transforming Seattle. In his letters, he would detail such mundane affairs as the rising prices of goods, the activities of other neighbors, and the work people were doing on their homes. He also told Sakamoto how much he missed his Japanese friends, especially the children, and that he looked forward to their return and life returning to normal. Overall, Schaffer conveyed consternation and bewilderment over the changes in Jackson Street and was especially bothered by the federal housing projects drawing new black residents to the area. As he wrote to Sakamoto in a letter dated July 20, 1944:

> You would hardly know Seattle it has grown so many out of town people here. People from all over the world. There is so much trash you wonder where they come from and the negroes are about to take over Seattle the way they are shipping them by the car load's in here it is really awful. They are getting pretty thick out here down on 14th ave and down by the Collins playfield they have built more houses on those vacant lots by Collins Playfield and they are all filled with negroes. Jackson st. is terrible now with them it is just black with them there is no market's on Jackson like when the Japanese were here they had such nice markets and now there is nothing and you can't get the fresh vegetables like when the Japanese gardeners were here now we have to raise our own to get fresh things.[74]

Shaffer's distinctly negative attitude regarding the changes in Jackson Street, which appear to owe largely to the Japanese absence and newly heightened black presence, signals among other things shifting perceptions of the neighborhood and race relations there. The comings and goings of people, once part of the overall dynamism of life in Jackson Street, took on a totally different meaning in the context of World War II. For Schaffer, the arrival of new black residents and the gains they made in employment and housing served to remind him of the losses suffered by his Japanese American friends who were forced out. Not long before these observations were made, the social and spatial circumstances facing blacks and Japanese in

Seattle held out the possibility for interracial cooperation around a number of issues. With the war, however, the trajectories of these communities went on vastly different courses, in Schaffer's view, linked only by the dynamics of displacement and succession.

Indeed, one of Seattle's most dramatic demographic transformations during the war was the growth of the city's African American population from just under thirty-eight hundred in 1940 to more than fifteen thousand by 1950.[75] Wartime jobs allowed black workers to break out of their dominant prewar employment patterns of being stuck in unskilled labor and domestic service and triggered the migration of many more from other parts of the country. Many African Americans, new and old, found work in ship construction; by the end of the war, 4,078 blacks were employed in Seattle shipyards, amounting to about 7 percent of the city's ship workers.[76] They also formed about 5 percent of nonmilitary federal employees in the city. African Americans were less prominent in the booming aircraft industry, making up just about 3 percent of aircraft construction workers at the end of the war, and far more black women than men were hired in this industry.[77] These gains in employment and numbers marked a new chapter in Seattle's and the Pacific Northwest's African American history, in which these citizens would emerge as the largest nonwhite group in the region.

Another notable change during the war was a dramatic makeover of Chinese Americans' image. This difference was apparent in prominent narratives of Chinese success and assimilation in America, which were in many ways precursors to the model minority stereotype that would become a dominant image of Asian Americans in later decades.[78] In Seattle during the war years, no single individual received more attention in this regard than Wing Luke, the student body president at Roosevelt High who went on to become a city councilmember during the 1960s. His election was deemed newsworthy by the *Seattle Post-Intelligencer,* which said, "The fact that Wing Luke, worker in his father's Chinese laundry, has been elected president of the largest high school student body in Seattle is a splendid tribute to the youth who attained this honor and to his fellow students, who made the honor possible."[79] Luke's achievements, which also included being elected to the district's Inter-School Student Council, were deemed by the paper to be "a tribute to an American school system, which has made it possible for this youth to attain an American education and which has inculcated in his fellow students a commendable breadth and tolerance," not to mention affirmation that "race is no barrier to being an American."[80]

This earnest and frankly over-the-top fawning over Luke is a window into some of the changes in racial politics in Seattle as well as shifting national alliances and ideologies during World War II. To those who celebrated him, the significance of Luke's leadership went beyond the halls of Roosevelt High and resonated with the broader meanings of the war itself, as he came to symbolize the triumph of the American spirit on the home front as well as U.S. interracial alliances with other countries and its victories over enemies abroad. "Hitler and Tojo will never get a toehold on America as long as young Americans continue to express their belief in democracy as a group of Seattle high school students did yesterday," stated the *Post-Intelligencer* in reference to Luke's election to the Inter-School Student Council.[81] Luke's appeal also had much to do with his Chinese ancestry in light of China's status as an American ally and the country's historical struggles against Japan: "It is in part a recognition of the regard which Americans feel for a heroic people, across the Pacific, who were victims of Japanese aggression for more than a decade before we experienced our Pearl Harbor, and are still fighting back bravely."[82]

Outside the picture and presumably beyond hope of redemption—signified by their physical removal from the West Coast—were Japanese Americans, whose internment has been extensively documented and analyzed.[83] Their resettlement in Seattle following Japan's surrender and the conclusion of the war in August 1945 would mark a new chapter in Japanese American history, filled with struggles to rebuild lives and to cope with the wartime ordeal and memories of it. In Seattle, Japanese Americans' postwar odyssey also saw the employment of new strategies for inclusion. These new strategies involved greater cooperation with blacks, Chinese, and Filipinos and reinvoked and repurposed cosmopolitanism, which, despite its problems and tenuousness, maintained its appeal in a city that was becoming even more diverse in the postwar era.

⇥╫╞⇤

Epilogue

In surveying conditions in the United States over the twentieth century, it has become all too trite to say that World War II changed everything. The wartime economic boom and postwar prosperity fostered improved standards of living and greater opportunities for mobility, availing an expanding suburban middle class of the "good life." The nation's ideological repudiation of white supremacy and the ascendancy of pluralism as the new orthodoxy for social relations presaged the coming modern civil rights movement and ushered in an era of "multiculturalism." Finally, the United States went from a rising nation in the global community to one of the preeminent world superpowers.

With respect to Japanese American history, for reasons that should be apparent, World War II likewise stands out as a watershed moment. Internment is regarded as an unfortunate, but perhaps inevitable, culmination of decades of anti-Asian xenophobia and U.S. imperial rivalry with Japan. Attitudes that had been simmering and building for some time finally exploded in the combustible international politics of the Pacific war. The watershed aspects of World War II for Japanese Americans became apparent by the mid-1950s, when they were increasingly praised in the media for their astonishing turnaround in fortunes. No longer unassimilable foreigners or despised enemies, they were now "model minorities" who put their harrowing ordeal behind them to thrive in the postwar era as productive, educated, and law-abiding middle-class citizens. This narrative—which was crafted with the input of Japanese Americans eager to rehabilitate their image—is representative of the postwar multicultural turn in the United States, but it also helped put to rest lingering worries that internees had resentments and psychological scars that would hinder their adjustment. In any case, the view that Japanese Americans' twentieth-century odyssey took them from being ostracized "others" to "model minorities" plays into the broader generalization that World War II was a crucial turning point in which the United States went from being an Anglo-centric nation to an avowedly multicultural one.

Such sanguine depictions that portrayed postwar Japanese American life as apolitical, upwardly striving, and integrated into the "mainstream" were one-sided at best. John Okada's 1957 novel, *No-No Boy*, discussed at the beginning of this book, paints an especially dark and haunting picture of postwar adjustment among Japanese Americans in Seattle. Born in Seattle in 1923, Okada and his family had been interned at Minidoka before he joined the U.S. Air Force and achieved the rank of sergeant. Along with thousands of other Nisei during the war, Okada sought to demonstrate his loyalty to the United States through military service. Although he followed this path, it caused him considerable turmoil and informed *No-No Boy's* depiction of the arduousness and uncertainty of resettlement. For the central character, Ichiro, the end of the war did not bring relief and redemption; instead, his inner strife intensified, his conflicts with other Japanese continued, and, under the weight of great stress and bitterness, his family disintegrated. Still unable to reconcile his identity as Japanese and American, Ichiro is tormented by this contradiction throughout the book, and it fuels his rage toward his Japan loyalist mother, magnifies his doubt over his decision to refuse serving in the U.S. military, and ultimately frustrates his search for peace and redemption.

The perceived clash and irreconcilability between the categories "Japanese" and "American," the crux of Ichiro's turmoil, has been a long-standing and confounding theme in Japanese American history and literature. This notion, stemming from the enduring assumption in Western thought that posits the "Orient" and "Occident" as opposites, informed the construction of white American identity in the nineteenth and twentieth centuries and underlay wrenching crises of identity among some Japanese Americans. Much of *No-No Boy's* poignancy draws from its focus on the postwar years, when the long-term consequences of wartime ideological rigidity could be observed at the level of individual people's lives. And although Ichiro does not romanticize or idealize his prewar life, we can infer that it was comparatively fluid with respect to politics and issues of national loyalty, certainly not having the kinds of consequences seen during and after the war.

In this book, by examining Japanese American experience against the backdrop of urbanization and Pacific Era discourse in early-twentieth-century Seattle, I have sought to depict a time and place when political, commercial, and geographic forces narrowed the perceived distance between the "Orient" and "Occident" and between Japan and the United States. In Seattle, Washington, a city at the proverbial edge of American frontier, booster enthusiasm, support for national expansion (and the city's role in this process), and pride in being a "gateway to the Orient" shaped the local ethos and culture. Imagining itself at the forefront of an exciting era in international relations and national growth, the city also embodied the contradictions of being part of the United States *and* the Pacific. As in other American cities, Seattle's social fabric reflected and reinforced white racial hegemony. But as a Pacific Rim locale, it extolled its cosmopolitan characteristics, pointing to proximity to and friendship with Japan and presence of immigrant communities from Europe and Asia. However, in this place, imagined as urban, cosmopolitan, and deeply vested in the Pacific world, the boundaries separating races and cultures were not blurred or erased, but rather highly magnified and fetishized. As Seattle came to be imagined as a place where East and West met in the interests of commerce, diplomacy, and exchange, certain "others" were incorporated into and acknowledged as integral to the local landscape, opening a small window of opportunity for these minorities to claim belonging.

For Japanese Americans in "cosmopolitan Seattle," life was full of contradictions. As a group, they faced widespread discrimination and xenophobia, but in some contexts—particularly in elite circles—being Japanese could be a source of cultural capital and symbolic power. White journalists, educators, and business leaders wrote of how their Japanese neighbors enhanced local conditions and validated Seattle's claims to international status, yet Japanese Americans remained a second-class population, as they were elsewhere in America. These contradictions notwithstanding, because of the prominence of Pacific Rim internationalism in Seattle's cultural and economic landscape during the early twentieth century, Japanese Americans could couch their claims to belonging in terms of cosmopolitanism and Americanism. Dominant notions of Americanism remained steeped in whiteness, and although cosmopolitanism fetishized difference, it was also premised on inclusiveness and respect for diversity. Furthermore, Japanese Americans found no shortage of white commentators willing to tout their presence in schools, public celebrations, and playgrounds as evidence of Seattle's image as a global city. And although Americanism was certainly alive and well as a discourse and objective in Japanese America, it was a fluid concept and deeply intertwined with cosmopolitanism; that is, being worldly, curious about and accepting of others, and conscious of the relationship of the United States to the rest of the world was part of being a "good American."

Once war broke out between Japan and the United States, the hyper-jingoistic atmosphere made it impossible, even in Seattle, to be both cosmopolitan and pro–United States; for similar reasons, Japanese Americans found it impossible to embrace their Japanese and American sides equally. And although wartime developments exposed the shallowness of cosmopolitanism as a practice, its core ideas were resurrected and repurposed in the late 1940s in a surprising incarnation. As Japanese Americans returned to Jackson Street and the ethnic community regrouped, residents invoked cosmopolitanism as a central ideal in the formation of the Jackson Street Community Council (JSCC) in 1946. Described by historian Quintard Taylor as a "model for interethnic cooperation," the JSCC was the first institutional link between the different racial and ethnic communities of the neighborhood.[1] Serving the area from Fourth to Twenty-third avenues and Dearborn to Jefferson, the JSCC took a self-help approach toward such issues as housing, neighborhood beautification, birth control, child care, nonviolent action, minority rights, interracial marriage, school segregation, police mistreatment, and employment. Its membership grew from 402 members in 1947 to 1,376 in 1949. Describing its constituents as a "cosmopolitan population of over 20,000," the JSCC sought to recapture a way of envisioning racial and cultural diversity in terms of worldly engagement and awareness.[2]

The JSCC was established at a time when the entire nation was adjusting to peacetime conditions, a period that brought particular challenges to America's cities. On the West Coast, new organizations and agencies were formed or expanded to specifically address issues stemming from black migration and Japanese resettlement.[3] Between 1940 and 1950, Seattle's black population nearly tripled, and beginning in January 1945, Japanese Americans began to return from the internment camps, with about forty-seven hundred resettled in the city by the end of the 1940s.[4] In 1944, the Mayor's Office initiated the formation of two organizations—the Central Seattle Community Council and the Civic Unity Committee—to assist new and newly returned residents as well as to facilitate discussions to promote peace and understanding between members of different communities. Along with these agencies, local churches and the Seattle branch of the Urban League played key roles in aiding new and needy Seattleites after the war.[5]

The JSCC was more autonomous than other organizations, because its authority did not derive from the Mayor's Office, nor did a national headquarters dictate or mediate its work. Because it was based in the neighborhood, officers had a close understanding of the community and its needs, enabling the organization to effectively collect data, to deliver services, and to tap into the morale of residents. The JSCC's main concerns usually involved improving conditions and standards in a neighborhood that had suffered from decades of neglect by the city. Studies undertaken by its Vital Statistics Committee highlighted challenges facing the community, such as poor infrastructure and other physical conditions compared to the rest of the city and a disproportionate concentration of unskilled seasonal workers and transients.[6] The research conducted by the Vital Statistics Committee affirmed much of what people already knew about the neighborhood, but it provided important impetus and justification for many of the JSCC's campaigns, such as a program to assist immigrants to register their declarations to become U.S. citizens, neighborhood cleanups, and child care services.

In addition to these and other community improvement and uplift campaigns, the JSCC was engaged in the work of molding a positive image of the neighborhood. Continuing its fight against the longtime association of the area with depressing slum conditions and poor, downtrodden residents, the organization turned to language from the past and took some of its core ideas but recast them to challenge Jackson Street's marginalization due to its high concentration of minorities. Describing the Jackson Street area as "cosmopolitan" brought attention to the interracial population in the area but made it a point of pride and rejected the prevailing idea that areas with large numbers of minorities were undesirable. In this regard, the organization saw itself at the forefront of race relations and progress in Seattle, claiming, for instance, that its greatest accomplishment was fostering "widespread cooperation in a city which is outstanding among the cities of the United States for its racial harmony."[7] In terms of how residents viewed the area, the JSCC found, based on a 1955 neighborhood study group, "There is loyalty in this community because they want outsiders to feel that this cosmopolitan area gets larger."[8] Additionally, when asked what they liked most about living in Jackson Street, the largest share of respondents cited the area's "cosmopolitan-international" characteristics, followed by friendship between all races. These qualities, the report explained, was "a good demonstration of the strength of the democratic tradition at work." Furthermore, because of the population's diversity, every child growing up in Jackson Street had "friends of all sorts."[9] Aware of its standing within the city, one respondent regretted that "[the] rest of Seattle looks down on us," with another observing, "I think there is a feeling that Seattle doesn't appreciate the importance of this international community."[10]

Occasionally, however, the JSCC did succeed in getting citywide attention. In 1958, a writer for the *Seattle Times* called the JSCC "one of Seattle's
most enterprising community organizations," noting members' success at
interracial cooperation: "[It is a] truly inspiring example of co-operation
between people of many races and faiths for the solution of mutual problems. It is a demonstration of democratic processes put into daily practice
seldom found even in communities whose people are more homogeneous
in origin. Seattle has reason to be proud of the council's accomplishments
and to hope for the realization of its plans for the future."[11] Remarkable for
its time, the JSCC showcased its multiracial orientation into its work and
rhetoric and strove especially to maintain an inclusive leadership and agenda. The board members included African Americans, Chinese Americans,
Japanese Americans, and Filipino Americans, and the officers served on a
rotating basis. Annual reports and other organization literature frequently
included the members' pictures to illustrate the organization's commitment
to interracial leadership.[12] Furthermore, affiliated and member organizations
included the Japanese Anti-Tuberculosis Committee, the Chong Wa Benevolent Association, the Alaska Fish Cannery Workers' Union, the Chinese
Merchants Club, the Filipino Community of Seattle, the JACL, and the
Booker T. Washington Post 188 of the American Legion.

Although the JSCC's channeling of cosmopolitanism had very different aims compared to those pursued by white Seattle elites prior to World
War II, both incarnations called for people to perform and to embody the
concept in highly visible ways. As mentioned above, underlining members'
racial and ethnic backgrounds as well as prominently displaying their pictures was a common aspect of this strategy. Also, to highlight the distinct
but similar histories of struggle linking the peoples of Jackson Street, the
JSCC included in its newsletters articles on such topics as the history of
anti-Chinese violence and black settlement in Seattle. Other examples were
more superficial, although in line with the idea that cosmopolitanism was
not just an idea but also something to be seen and experienced. For example, in the case of the JSCC's annual "international smorgasbord" dinner,
inaugurated in 1949, cosmopolitanism was something to be tasted and consumed. In 1950, the menu featured Japanese tempura, Chinese chow mein,
New Orleans lamb curry, Filipino sinigang and float cakes, Jewish kevtes
ovas macaron, and chopped chicken livers. Another annual event the JSCC
hosted was the International Free Style Rickshaw race, in which teams representing Chinese, Japanese, and Filipinos would compete to win a Golden
Rice Bowl.[13]

Its concerns may have been almost entirely local and focused on conditions in a single neighborhood, but the JSCC's conceptualization of cosmopolitan-ism echoed that of Seattleites during the early twentieth century in evoking and linking racial and cultural diversity, Americanism, and internationalism. For example, Victor Velasco, a JSCC member who also edited the newspaper *Filipino Forum,* described the organization as "A United Nations in Min-iature."[14] He lauded the JSCC for demonstrating "the possibility of greater accomplishment through cooperation among peoples even of diverse cultural background," thereby championing "the social philosophy of the universal brotherhood of man.[15]

Cementing Jackson Street's association with cosmopolitanism as a con-cept connecting local diversity and worldly engagement was the renaming of the western section of the area as the "International District." This change originated in 1951, when Mayor William Devin issued a proclamation for-mally naming the area bounded by Fourth and Fourteenth and Dearborn and Yesler the "International Center."[16] This proclamation, as well as the cre-ation of the *International Community News* and International Improvement Association shortly thereafter, institutionalized the new name. Eschewing identification with a particular ethnic group, the International District was broad, had a modern ring, and positioned itself as the center of "ethnic" Seattle. One of the traditions growing out of this new conceptualization that sought to reflect and to reinforce the sense of community and solidarity among the minority communities under the banner of "internationalism" was the International Carnival, organized by the JSCC and the Internation-al Improvement Association and held during Seafair.[17] Seafair was an annual summer festival inaugurated in 1950 on the occasion of the centennial of the city's founding. Inclusive of all the major racial and ethnic communities in the area, the culmination of the International Carnival was the crowning of four queens—Japanese, Filipina, African American, and Chinese—shar-ing the title "Miss International Center" (see Figure E.1).

The naming of the "International Center" signaled a crystallizing of a bottom-up incarnation of cosmopolitanism in the Jackson Street neighbor-hood that began with the formation of the JSCC. James Sakamoto, who had been a prominent figure in prewar Japanese American affairs, returned to Seattle after internment to resume being an important voice in local affairs. In an article he wrote for the *International Community News,* he sought to explain the ways in which the neighborhood represented not just interracial understanding but also good internationalism. The article, which appeared on January 1, 1953, was in fact titled "Good Internationalism." In the post-war era, Sakamoto intoned, it was more important than ever that Americans cultivate awareness of the world and be mindful of the connections between

International
Centennial
Festival   1952

———————AUGUST 6-7-8-9———————

FOUR QUEENS OF SEATTLE'S INTERNATIONAL CENTER

Some of the loveliest girls in Seattle are members of the International Community. This year's winners—beauties, all—are (left to right) Sumi Mitsui, Japanese queen; Ranita de Leon, queen of the Filipino community of Seattle and the Puget Sound Area; Adaia Avery, Negro queen and Miss International Center of 1952; and Fonn Woo, Miss Chinatown. All four take part in the International Festival, and also serve as princesses in the Greater Seattle Centennial Seafair.

Figure E.1. The cover of the International Centennial Festival program, 1952. The four queens of Seattle's International Center were selected to represent the neighborhood's ethnic diversity. *(Source: University of Washington Libraries, Special Collections, Elmer Ogawa Papers, Acc 1383 Box 8/10.)*

their own lives and the city, country, and world at large. As a model of a community that combined "good Americanism" with "good internationalism," he looked no further than his own neighborhood: "The district of the Seattle community often designated as the International Settlement, is laudably following the national pattern. There are groups here whose backgrounds stretch out to the near and far corners of the earth. Despite this fact it is good to know that where the interest and welfare of their community, state or nation are involved, they take precedence over individual or racial concern."[18]

As uplifting and galvanizing as these ideas might have been for the people of a neighborhood routinely disparaged by outsiders, disputes within the JSCC revealed discrepancies between the image and reality of the community as well as the divergent, at times conflicting, agendas of members. For example, as early as 1953, organizers of the International Carnival, purportedly a showcase of diversity and interracial harmony, became divided over its purpose and whether it was even worth continuing. Although Velasco thought it was an effective means of promoting intercultural and international good will, others saw it as an embarrassing, overcommercialized, and "objectionable" spectacle that did nothing to help the community's image or material well-being.[19] African American member Arthur Solomon said that the festival had never been truly "international" and was furthermore not even popular with locals. Such debates underscored a constant concern among JSCC leaders regarding whether sustained interethnic harmony and cooperation was possible or would give way to intergroup rivalry and self-interest. A survey undertaken by the organization in 1955 revealed that residents felt pride in the neighborhood's "international" characteristics but also perceived divisions in the community along racial lines. It "appears that each race has its own social strata with like stratas [sic] or layers getting along better with each other," the report concluded. Although some felt that "racial unity and spirit [were] better than average [in the] community," a greater number of respondents said that cliques based on race existed. The survey also reported that "distinct and deeply rooted social barriers [kept] people apart and thus [robbed] them of their full potential for democratic action and community development." Evidence of racial stereotypes also surfaced, as one resident stated, "The Negro element carries a chip on its shoulder," and another said, "The Chinese usually act superior."[20]

Into the 1960s, neighborhood activists devoted stronger efforts toward addressing the issue of Asian-black relations. For example, in January 1965, a local Seattle television station aired a half-hour program called *Viewpoint*, which delved into the subject of Japanese-black relations. Later that year, a series of six meetings with the theme "Misunderstandings between Negroes and Japanese" was held, resulting from discussions among members of the Congress of Racial Equality (CORE), the Central Area Citizens' Council, the JACL, and the JSCC.[21] Whether Asians should become actively involved in the civil rights movement was the topic of discussion at a forum held at the Eastside YMCA on December 14, 1965. In 1966, the JACL Human Rights Division sponsored a meeting to discuss the same topic.[22] Commenting on the issue, the JSCC newsletter stated that "the attitude of Oriental Americans toward the racial struggle has been a puzzle to most Negroes and many educators. Many Negroes resent the attitude of Orientals believing they benefit from gains made but take no active part in the struggle."[23]

Just as circumstances pointed to a greater need for Asians and blacks to examine their relationship with one another, the impulse among locals to focus on interethnic relations and to strengthen ties between communities showed signs of weakening and giving way to individual group concerns. For one, the naming of the International Center highlighted the Asian character of the area, and, increasingly, the "Central District" or "Central Area" denoted the part of Jackson Street where blacks tended to concentrate. Thus, Asians and blacks came to see themselves as increasingly separate in spatial as well as social terms. In 1967, the Jackson Street Community Council merged with the Central Seattle Community Council and from there ceased to be a distinct voice championing the neighborhood once touted as the center of "cosmopolitan Seattle." Although a long, robust, and uninterrupted intraminority organizing tradition has largely eluded Seattle's Asian American and black communities, the ideal of interethnic coexistence and cooperation remains powerful and is often foregrounded in representations of the International District's history. For instance, the Wing Luke Asian Museum, which is located in the heart of the old Nihonmachi and is named after the former Roosevelt High student body president who went on to become the first Asian American elected to office in the Pacific Northwest, distinguishes the neighborhood as "perhaps the only area in the continental United States where Chinese, Japanese, Filipinos, African Americans, Vietnamese, Koreans, and Cambodians settled together and built one neighborhood."[24]

The quotation above also illustrates the appeal of cosmopolitan tropes for describing local populations and conditions. It is a stretch to say, after all, that "Chinese, Japanese, Filipinos, African Americans, Vietnamese, Koreans, and Cambodians" settled the International District "together," yet the neighborhood's multiethnic past and present grant the depiction some plausibility. Further, it is not difficult to understand why museum curators would want to portray the district in such terms. When used to characterize communities and places, cosmopolitanism drives the point that diversity strengthens rather than weakens a collective body, while depicting local diversity as a phenomenon of connections to the larger world. Furthermore, people emerge from such communities better off for it, as more enlightened, compassionate, and worldly actors. In cosmopolitan settings, everyone, whether the newly arrived or long established, is a potential member and can, thus, lay claim to the community. These aspects of cosmopolitanism—its unboundedness and unlimited potential for belonging—also raised the hopes of Japanese Americans in Seattle during the early twentieth century. Because elites' construction of cosmopolitan Seattle proposed viewing the city as a "gateway to the Orient" connecting the United States and Japan, Japanese residents could articulate especially persuasive claims to the city and spaces within it. Yet the promises of inclusion and equality that cosmopolitanism implied belied the racial power dynamics shaping the material conditions of life in Seattle and maintaining inequalities in its population. Everyone in "cosmopolitan Seattle" theoretically had a place, and the differences among people were, furthermore, not merely appreciated but magnified. Yet not everyone had an equal voice or share in accessing power.

Despite its contradictions as a concept and shortcomings as a practice, cosmopolitanism retained its appeal among Seattleites after World War II.

That it has such enduring interest, in Seattle and elsewhere, then and now, perhaps reveals more about *our* hopes than it does about the materiality of the places and communities we seek to describe. Attempts to relate the bigness of the world to local conditions reflect our awareness of interconnections across the globe, appreciation of the vastness of human diversity, and desire to build a society where each and every person is worthy of membership—all encouraging points, to be sure. At a time when our differences continue to provoke anxiety, suspicion, and violence, there is something very hopeful about a vision in which not only anyone can belong but also any place can be home, and this outlook can inspire action to make those visions a reality. But who wields that vision and why matters too, as do the terms by which people gain entry and the limits on their membership.

꙰

Notes

INTRODUCTION

1. John Okada, *No-No Boy*, 8th ed. (Seattle: University of Washington Press, 1993), 1.

2. Ibid.

3. Ibid., 2.

4. Ibid., 5.

5. Ibid.

6. Ibid., 51.

7. "South End Grows into 'Far East' of Seattle City," *Japanese-American Courier*, March 22, 1930. South End was another name for the area I refer to as Jackson Street.

8. Eiichiro Azuma, *Between Two Empires: Race, History, and Transnationalism in Japanese America* (New York: Oxford University Press, 2005), 22–23, 81, 101; Akira Iriye, *Pacific Estrangement: Japanese and American Expansion, 1897–1911* (Cambridge, MA: Harvard University Press, 1972), 84–90.

9. Arif Dirlik, ed., *What Is in a Rim? Critical Perspectives on the Pacific Region Idea*, 2nd ed. (Lanham, MD: Rowman and Littlefield Publishers, 1998), 6.

10. Arif Dirlik, "The Asia-Pacific Idea: Reality and Representation in the Invention of a Regional Structure," in Dirlik, *What Is in a Rim?* 16.

11. Yong Chen, *Chinese San Francisco, 1850–1943: A Trans-Pacific Community* (Stanford, CA: Stanford University Press, 2000); Dorothy Fujita-Rony, *American Workers, Colonial Power: Philippine Seattle and the Transpacific West, 1919–1941* (Berkeley: University of California Press, 2003); Azuma, *Between Two Empires*.

12. Quoted in Gail M. Nomura, "Significant Lives: Asia and Asian Americans in the U.S. West," in *A New Significance: Re-envisioning the History of the American West*, ed. Clyde A. Milner (Oxford: Oxford University Press, 1996), 137.

13. Ibid., 138.

14. Ibid.

15. John Tchen, *New York before Chinatown: Orientalism and the Shaping of American Culture, 1776–1882* (Baltimore: Johns Hopkins University Press, 1999); Vijay Prashad, *The Karma of Brown Folk* (Minneapolis: University of Minnesota Press, 2000).

16. In his study of Isaiah Bowman, the geographer for Presidents Theodore Roosevelt and Woodrow Wilson, Neil Smith argues that globalism became the principle around which the United States justified its actions. Neil Smith, *American Empire: Roosevelt's Geographer and the Prelude to Globalization* (Berkeley: University of California Press, 2003).

17. Ibid., 22. Also see William Appleman Williams, *The Tragedy of American Diplomacy* (1959; repr., New York: W. W. Norton, 1988).

18. Akira Iriye, *Cultural Internationalism and World Order* (Baltimore: Johns Hopkins University Press, 1997), 62.

19. Akira Iriye, *From Nationalism to Internationalism: U.S. Foreign Policy to 1914* (London: Routledge and Kegan Paul, 1977), chap. 1.

20. Ibid., 72.

21. Jon Thares Davidann, "'Colossal Illusions': U.S.-Japanese Relations in the Institute of Pacific Relations, 1919–1938," *Journal of World History* 12, no. 1 (2001): 155–182; Eiichiro Azuma, "'The Pacific Era Has Arrived': Transnational Education among Japanese Americans, 1932–1941," *History of Education Quarterly* 42, no. 1 (2003): 39–73.

22. Smith, *American Empire;* Iriye, *From Nationalism to Internationalism,* chap. 5.

23. Charles Bright and Michael Geyer, "Where in the World Is America? The History of the United States in the Global Age," in *Rethinking American History in a Global Age,* ed. Thomas Bender (Berkeley: University of California Press, 2002), 67.

24. Azuma, *Between Two Empires;* Fujita-Rony, *American Workers, Colonial Power.*

25. "The Orient Masters Steel, Steam and Electricity," *Japanese-American Courier,* January 1, 1935.

26. David Hollinger, *Postethnic America: Beyond Multiculturalism* (New York: Basic Books, 1995), 85–86.

27. Kwame Anthony Appiah, *Cosmopolitanism: Ethics in a World of Strangers* (New York: W. W. Norton, 2006).

28. Randolph Bourne, "Trans-National America," *Atlantic Monthly* 118, no. 18 (1916): 86–97. Also see Leslie J. Vaughn, "Cosmopolitanism, Ethnicity and American Identity: Randolph Bourne's 'Trans-National America,'" *Journal of American Studies* 25, no. 3 (1991): 443–459.

29. David Palumbo-Liu, *Asian/American: Historical Crossings of a Racial Frontier* (Stanford, CA: Stanford University Press, 1999), 20.

30. Iriye, *Cultural Internationalism and World Order,* 82.

31. From after World War II until the 1980s, much of the scholarship on Japanese in America focused on some aspect of internment—either discrimination, the experience itself, or its legacy. Examples of these studies include Roger Daniels, *Concentration Camps USA: Japanese Americans and World War II* (New York: Holt, Rinehart and Winston, 1972); Audrey Girdner and Anne Loftis, *The Great Betrayal: The Evacuation of the Japanese Americans during World War II* (New York: Macmillan, 1969); Bill Hosokawa, *Nisei: The Quiet Americans* (New York: Morrow, 1969); Toru Matsumoto, *Beyond Prejudice: A Story of the Church and Japanese Americans* (New York: Friendship Press, 1946); Jacobus Ten Broek, *Prejudice, War, and the Constitution* (Berkeley: University of California Press, 1958); Michi Weglyn, *Years of Infamy: The Untold Story of America's Concentration Camps* (New York: Morrow, 1976).

32. Sylvia Junko Yanagisako, *Transforming the Past: Tradition and Kinship among Japanese Americans* (Stanford, CA: Stanford University Press, 1985); Yuji Ichioka, *The Issei: The World of the First Generation of Japanese Americans, 1885–1924* (New York: Free

Press, 1988); Valerie Matsumoto, *Farming the Homeplace: A Japanese American Community in California, 1919–1982* (Ithaca, NY: Cornell University Press, 1993); Evelyn Nakano Glenn, *Issei, Nisei, War Bride: Three Generations of Japanese American Women in Domestic Service* (Philadelphia: Temple University Press, 1986); Linda Tamura, *The Hood River Issei: An Oral History of Japanese Settlers in Oregon's Hood River Valley* (Urbana: University of Illinois Press, 1993); Paul Spickard, *Japanese Americans: The Formation and Transformations of an Ethnic Group* (New York: Twayne Publishers, 1996).

33. Shotaro Frank Miyamoto, *Social Solidarity among the Japanese in Seattle* (1939; repr., Seattle: University of Washington Press, 1984), 3.

34. Azuma, *Between Two Empires;* David Yoo, *Growing Up Nisei: Race, Generation, and Culture among Japanese Americans of California, 1924–49* (Urbana: University of Illinois Press, 2000); Brian Hayashi, *For the Sake of Our Japanese Brethren: Assimilation, Nationalism, and Protestantism among the Japanese of Los Angeles, 1895–1942* (Stanford, CA: Stanford University Press, 1995); Lon Kurashige, *Japanese American Celebration and Conflict: A History of Ethnic Identity and Festival, 1934–1990* (Berkeley: University of California Press, 2002); Gordon H. Chang, *Morning Glory, Evening Shadow: Yamato Ichihashi and His Internment Writings* (Stanford, CA: Stanford University Press, 1999).

35. Some recent exceptions include Fujita-Rony, *American Workers, Colonial Power;* Chris Friday, *Organizing Asian American Labor: The Pacific Coast Canned-Salmon Industry, 1870–1942* (Philadelphia: Temple University Press, 1994); Huping Ling, *Chinese St. Louis: From Enclave to Cultural Community* (Philadelphia: Temple University Press, 2004); Mary Ting Yi Lui, *The Chinatown Trunk Murder Mystery: Murder, Miscegenation, and Other Dangerous Encounters in Turn-of-the-Century New York* (Princeton, NJ: Princeton University Press, 2005); Moon-Ho Jung, *Coolies and Cane: Race, Labor, and Sugar in the Age of Emancipation* (Baltimore: Johns Hopkins University Press, 2006).

36. Gabriela Arredondo, *Mexican Chicago: Race, Identity, and Nation, 1916–39* (Urbana: University of Illinois Press, 2008); Coll Thrush, *Native Seattle: Histories from the Crossing-Over Place* (Seattle: University of Washington Press, 2007); Robert Self, *American Babylon: Race and the Struggle for Postwar Oakland* (Princeton, NJ: Princeton University Press, 2003); Scott Kurashige, *The Shifting Grounds of Race: Black and Japanese Americans in the Making of Multiethnic Los Angeles* (Princeton, NJ: Princeton University Press, 2008).

CHAPTER 1

1. Monica Sone, *Nisei Daughter,* 4th ed. (Seattle: University of Washington Press, 1987), 15.

2. Ibid., 18.

3. Ibid.

4. Carlos Bulosan, *America Is in the Heart: A Personal History* (New York: Harcourt Brace, 1946), 153.

5. Scott Kurashige, *The Shifting Grounds of Race: Black and Japanese Americans in the Making of Multiethnic Los Angeles* (Princeton, NJ: Princeton University Press, 2008); Mark Wild, *Street Meeting: Multiethnic Neighborhoods in Early Twentieth-Century Los Angeles* (Berkeley: University of California Press, 2005); Allison Varzally, *Making a Non-white America: Californians Coloring outside Ethnic Lines, 1925–1955* (Berkeley: University of California Press, 2008).

6. Dorothy Fujita-Rony, *American Workers, Colonial Power: Philippine Seattle and the Transpacific West, 1919–1941* (Berkeley: University of California Press, 2003); Kornel

Chang, "Enforcing Transnational White Solidarity: Asian Migration and the Formation of the U.S.-Canadian Boundary," *American Quarterly* 60, no. 3 (2008): 671–696.

7. Quintard Taylor, *In Search of the Racial Frontier: African Americans in the American West, 1528–1990* (New York: W. W. Norton, 1998); Richard White, "Race Relations in the West," *American Quarterly* 38, no. 3 (1986): 396–416.

8. Susan Johnson, *Roaring Camp: The Social World of the California Gold Rush* (New York: W. W. Norton, 2000), chap. 1.

9. Murray Morgan, *Skid Road: An Informal Portrait of Seattle* (New York: Viking Press, 1951), 4.

10. The name Seattle was a variation on a local Indian leader's name, Sealth. Matthew Klingle, *Emerald City: An Environmental History of Seattle* (New Haven, CT: Yale University Press, 2007), 28.

11. On railroads in Seattle, see Richard Berner, *Seattle in the Twentieth Century 1900–1920: From Boomtown, Urban Turbulence, to Restoration* (Seattle: Charles Press, 1991); Frank Leonard, "'Wise, Swift, and Sure'? The Great Northern Entry into Seattle," *Pacific Northwest Quarterly* 92, no. 2 (2001): 81–90.

12. Berner, *Seattle in the Twentieth Century 1900–1920*, 60.

13. Jorgen Dahlie, "Old World Paths in the New: Scandinavians Find a Familiar Home in Washington," in *Experiences in a Promised Land: Essays in Pacific Northwest History*, ed. G. Thomas Edwards and Carlos Schwantes (Seattle: University of Washington Press, 1986), 99–108; Roger Sale, *Seattle Past to Present: An Interpretation of the Foremost City in the Pacific Northwest* (Seattle: University of Washington Press, 1976), 60.

14. Coll Thrush, *Native Seattle: Histories from the Crossing-Over Place* (Seattle: University of Washington Press, 2007), 3.

15. Ibid., 54.

16. Sale, *Seattle Past to Present*, 62.

17. Ibid., 57.

18. Ibid., 37.

19. Ibid., 57–58.

20. Ibid.

21. Berner, *Seattle in the Twentieth Century 1900–1920*, 61.

22. Doug Chin and Peter Bacho, "The History of the International District: Early Chinese Immigration," *International Examiner*, October 17, 1984; Ron Chew, ed., *Reflections of Seattle's Chinese Americans: The First 100 Years* (Seattle: University of Washington Press, Wing Luke Asian Museum, 1994); Doug Chin and Art Chin, *Up Hill: The Settlement and Diffusion of the Chinese in Seattle, Washington* (Seattle: Shorey Book Store, 1973).

23. Chew, *Reflections of Seattle's Chinese Americans*, 126.

24. Chin and Chin, *Up Hill*, 11.

25. For a brief background on Chinese immigration during the nineteenth century, see Ronald Takaki, *Strangers from a Different Shore: A History of Asian Americans* (Boston: Little Brown, 1989), chap. 3; Sucheng Chan, *Asian Americans: An Interpretive History* (Boston: Twayne, 1991), chaps. 1 and 2.

26. Erika Lee, *At America's Gates: Chinese Immigration during the Exclusion Era, 1882–1943* (Chapel Hill: University of North Carolina Press, 2003), 238.

27. Richard White, *It's Your Misfortune and None of My Own: A New History of the American West* (Norman: University of Oklahoma Press, 1991), 283. On Chinese participation in other industries in the canned-salmon industry in the American West, see Chris Friday, *Organizing Asian American Labor: The Pacific Coast Canned-Salmon Industry, 1870–1942* (Philadelphia: Temple University Press, 1994).

28. Chin and Chin, *Up Hill.*

29. On anti-Chinese violence and politics in the West during the nineteenth century, see Alexander Saxton, *The Indispensable Enemy: Labor and the Anti-Chinese Movement in California* (Berkeley: University of California Press, 1975); Liping Zhu, *A Chinaman's Chance: The Chinese on the Rocky Mountain Frontier* (Niwot, CO: University Press of Colorado, 1997); Jean Pfaelzer, *Driven Out: The Forgotten War against Chinese Americans* (Berkeley: University of California Press, 2008).

30. Officials in Taishan County erected a statue in Chin Gee Hee's honor in 1984. Madeline Yuan-Yin Hsu, *Dreaming of Gold, Dreaming of Home: Transnationalism and Migration between the United States and South China, 1882–1943* (Stanford, CA: Stanford University Press, 2000), 1.

31. Ibid., 160.

32. Mary Ting Yi Lui, *The Chinatown Trunk Murder Mystery: Murder, Miscegenation, and Other Dangerous Encounters in Turn-of-the-Century New York City* (Princeton, NJ: Princeton University Press, 2005), chaps. 1 and 2.

33. For a comparative background on racism and exclusion in the West, see Tomas Almaguer, *Racial Fault Lines: The Historical Origins of White Supremacy in California* (Berkeley: University of California Press, 1994); Ronald Takaki, *Iron Cages: Race and Culture in 19th-Century America* (New York: Knopf, 1979); Natalia Molina, *Fit to Be Citizens? Public Health and Race in Los Angeles, 1879–1939* (Berkeley: University of California Press, 2006).

34. James A. Halseth and Bruce A. Glasrud, "Anti-Chinese Movements in Washington, 1885–1886: A Reconsideration," in *The Northwest Mosaic: Minority Conflicts in Pacific Northwest History,* ed. James A. Halseth and Bruce A. Glasrud (Boulder, CO: Pruett Publishing, 1977), 116–139.

35. On the anti-Chinese movement in the Rocky Mountain states, see Liping Zhu, *Chinaman's Chance.*

36. Morgan, *Skid Road,* 95.

37. Ibid., 93; George Kinnear, *Anti-Chinese Riots at Seattle, Wn., February 8th, 1886* (Seattle: Privately Printed, 1911).

38. Morgan, *Skid Road,* 95–106.

39. Ibid., 95.

40. Chin and Chin, *Up Hill,* 36.

41. Morgan, *Skid Road,* 105.

42. Ibid., 106.

43. Chan, *Asian Americans,* 37.

44. In 1908, six hundred of the three thousand railroad workers in Washington, or 20 percent, were Japanese. Berner, *Seattle in the Twentieth Century 1900–1920,* 67.

45. On picture brides, see Chan, *Asian Americans,* 107–109.

46. On the second-generation dilemma among Japanese Americans, see Yuji Ichioka, *The Issei: The World of the First Generation of Japanese Americans, 1885–1924* (New York: Free Press, 1988), 196–210, 53–54; Jere Takahashi, *Nisei Sansei: Shifting Japanese American Identities and Politics* (Philadelphia: Temple University Press, 1997), chap. 3; David Yoo, *Growing Up Nisei: Race, Generation, and Culture among Japanese Americans of California, 1924–49* (Urbana: University of Illinois Press, 2000), 61–62; Lon Kurashige, *Japanese American Celebration and Conflict: A History of Ethnic Identity and Festival, 1934–1990* (Berkeley: University of California Press, 2002), 2–3; Valerie Matsumoto, "Desperately Seeking 'Dierdre': Gender Roles, Multicultural Relations, and Nisei Women Writers of the 1930s," *Frontiers* 12, no. 1 (1991): 19–32.

47. On Japanese in Seattle, see David Takami, *Divided Destiny: A History of Japanese Americans in Seattle* (Seattle: University of Washington Press, 1999).

48. The Japanese Association reported the Japanese population in 1920 was 9,066, which is more than 1,000 more than U.S. Census reported for that year. According to the 1930 Census, 8,448 Japanese lived in Seattle. Katherine Jane Lentz, "Japanese-American Relations in Seattle" (master's thesis, University of Washington, 1924), 1; Shotaro Frank Miyamoto, *Social Solidarity among the Japanese in Seattle* (1939; repr., Seattle: University of Washington Press, 1984), 14.

49. Mary Ota Higa, interview by Tom Ikeda, December 17, 2004, Densho Visual History Collection, Densho.

50. Ibid.

51. "Historically Speaking: Bailey Gatzert, Seattle's First and Only Jewish Mayor," *Jewish Transcript,* December 10, 1987.

52. Lentz, "Japanese-American Relations in Seattle," 22.

53. Miyamoto, *Social Solidarity among the Japanese in Seattle,* 16.

54. Kazuo Ito, *Issei: A History of Japanese Immigrants in North America,* trans. Shinchiro Nakamura and Jean S. Gerard (Seattle: Executive Committee for Publication of *Issei: A History of Japanese Immigrants in North America,* 1973), 519–520.

55. Ibid., 150.

56. Miyamoto, *Social Solidarity among the Japanese in Seattle,* 3.

57. Ibid., 21.

58. The Aeolian Society was a popular Japanese American group that supported eclectic musical interests among Japanese residents. In May 1932, the group met to discuss black spirituals. "Negro Spiritual Explained," *Japanese-American Courier,* May 21, 1932.

59. On the Japanese American Citizens League, see Paul R. Spickard, "The Nisei Assume Power: The Japanese American Citizens League, 1941–1942," *Pacific Historical Review* 52, no. 2 (1983): 147–174; Yuji Ichioka, "A Study in Dualism: James Yoshinori Sakamoto and the *Japanese-American Courier,* 1928–1942," *Amerasia* 13, no. 2 (1986–1987): 49–81.

60. Ito, *Issei,* 137.

61. Ibid., 137–138.

62. Ibid., 138.

63. On the anti-Japanese movement, see Roger Daniels, *The Politics of Prejudice: The Anti-Japanese Movement in California and the Struggle for Japanese Exclusion* (Berkeley: University of California, 1962).

64. Ito, *Issei,* 153.

65. Ibid, 151.

66. In one case, Matsuta Miyake and Kazuo Okazaki, two Japanese immigrants who ran the Togo Junk Company in Seattle, sued the city when it refused to renew their business license in 1919. They sued on the grounds that refusing to renew their license violated the Japan–United States Treaty of Commerce, which stated that Japanese could freely enter and travel and reside in the United States and could lease or own houses, factories, warehouses, and shops, they invoked the U.S. Constitution's equal protection clause, the Washington state constitution, and freedom of property rights. The Judge of King County Supreme Court ruled in Miyake and Okazaki's favor. The case showed that Japanese business owners were vulnerable to these kinds of attacks, but it also showed that Japanese found ways to overcome these challenges. Ibid., 170.

67. Ibid., 98.

68. Ibid., 97.

69. Ibid., 98.

70. Quintard Taylor, *The Forging of a Black Community: Seattle's Central District from 1870 through the Civil Rights Era* (Seattle: University of Washington Press, 1994), 52.

71. Taylor, *In Search of the Racial Frontier*, 192.

72. Ibid.

73. Taylor, *Forging of a Black Community*, 43.

74. Kurashige, *Shifting Grounds of Race;* Wild, *Street Meeting;* Taylor, *Forging of a Black Community*, chap. 4.

75. Aki Kurose, interview by Matt Emery, July 17, 1997, Densho Visual History Collection, Densho. Also on Aki Kurose, see Gail M. Nomura, "'Peace Empowers': The Testimony of Aki Kurose, a Woman of Color in the Pacific Northwest," *Frontiers: A Journal of Women Studies* 22, no. 3 (2001): 75–92.

76. Kurose interview. Evidence suggests that Evelyn Whistler may have herself graduated from the Kokugo Gakko, as a 1934 article in the *Northwest Enterprise* indicates. "Colored Girl Graduate of Japanese School," *Northwest Enterprise*, September 20, 1934.

77. Taylor, *In Search of the Racial Frontier*, 249. On the Seattle jazz scene during the 1940s and 1950s, see Paul DeBarros and Eduardo Calderon, *Jackson Street after Hours: The Roots of Jazz in Seattle* (Seattle: Sasquatch Books, 1993).

78. Taylor, *Forging of a Black Community*, 130.

79. Fujita-Rony, *American Workers, Colonial Power*, 99.

80. On "migratory communities" composing Filipino America, see Rick Baldoz, *The Third Asiatic Invasion: Race, Class, and Conflict in Filipino America, 1898–1946* (New York: New York University Press, 2010); Linda España-Maram, *Creating Masculinity in Los Angeles's Little Manila: Working Class Filipinos and Popular Culture, 1920s–1950s* (New York: Columbia University Press, 2006).

81. Fujita-Rony, *American Workers, Colonial Power*. For a perspective on how Los Angeles emerged as such a node, see España-Maram, *Creating Masculinity in Los Angeles's Little Manila*, chap. 1.

82. Fujita-Rony, *American Workers, Colonial Power*, chap. 2.

83. Ibid., 62.

84. *Garfield Messenger*, April 14, 1926.

85. Chew, *Reflections of Seattle's Chinese Americans*, 57.

86. "Jackson Street Is Quiet Thoroughfare on Sunday," *Northwest Enterprise*, October 12, 1933.

87. Ito, *Issei*, 803.

88. Ibid.

89. "A Dangerous Corner," *Japanese-American Courier*, May 5, 1928.

90. Some of these columns can be found in the following issues: "Down Main Street," *Japanese-American Courier*, March 17, 1928; March 31, 1928; May 12, 1928; May 19, 1928; June 2, 1928; September 29, 1928; October 20, 1928; December 29, 1928; August 3, 1929; January 1, 1931.

91. "Down Main Street," *Japanese-American Courier*, September 29, 1928.

92. "Down Main Street," *Japanese-American Courier*, March 17, 1928.

93. "Jackson Street Is Quiet Thoroughfare on Sunday."

94. Ibid.

95. Kurose interview.

96. "Chinese Help Jim Crow," *Northwest Enterprise*, March 14, 1935.

97. James Sakamoto Papers (hereafter Sakamoto Papers), Box 16, Folder 18, Manuscripts, Special Collections and University Archives (hereafter MSCUA), University of Washington.

98. "Japanese Are Studious," *Northwest Enterprise,* April 25, 1941.

99. "Cayton, Candidate for Representative Submits Platform," *Japanese-American Courier,* September 1, 1928.

100. "C.T. Arai Wages Election Drive," *Japanese-American Courier,* August 25, 1934.

101. "Prominent Men behind C.T. Arai," *Japanese-American Courier,* August 12, 1933; "Colored Friends Boost Clarence Arai for Representative in 37th," *Northwest Enterprise,* August 23, 1934.

CHAPTER 2

1. Lancaster Pollard, "Cosmopolitan Seattle," *Town Crier,* September 1936. The other installments appeared in October 1936, November 1936, and January 1937.

2. Pollard, "Cosmopolitan Seattle," September 1936.

3. Ibid.

4. Pollard, "Cosmopolitan Seattle," *Town Crier,* November 1936.

5. David Glassberg, *Sense of History: The Place of the Past in American Life* (Amherst: University of Massachusetts Press, 2001), chap. 7; William Deverell, *Whitewashed Adobe: The Rise of Los Angeles and the Remaking of Its Mexican Past* (Berkeley: University of California Press, 2004); Phoebe Kropp, *California Vieja: Culture and Memory in a Modern American Place* (Berkeley: University of California Press, 2006).

6. Kropp, *California Vieja,* 7.

7. W. A. Powell, "Will Tacoma Be the Metropolis of the American Occident?" *Northwest Magazine* 20, no. 3 (1902): 22.

8. Ibid.

9. Murray Morgan, *Skid Road: An Informal Portrait of Seattle* (New York: Viking Press, 1951), 69.

10. Roger Sale, *Seattle Past to Present: An Interpretation of the Foremost City in the Pacific Northwest* (Seattle: University of Washington Press, 1976), 54; Lisa Mighetto and Marcia Montgomery, *Hard Drive to the Klondike: Promoting Seattle during the Gold Rush* (Seattle: Northwest Interpretive Association in association with University of Washington Press, 2002).

11. Vancouver is about a hundred miles closer, Portland about fifty miles farther, and San Francisco about three hundred miles farther. Richard Berner, *Seattle in the Twentieth Century 1900–1920: From Boomtown, Urban Turbulence, to Restoration* (Seattle: Charles Press, 1991), 30.

12. Morgan, *Skid Road,* 106.

13. Berner, *Seattle in the Twentieth Century, 1900–1920,* 10.

14. Ibid.

15. Ibid., 31.

16. Matthew Klingle, *Emerald City: An Environmental History of Seattle* (New Haven, CT: Yale University Press, 2007), 154. Also on the A-Y-P and its relationship to Seattle urban identity, see Shelley S. Lee, "The Contradictions of Cosmopolitanism: Consuming the Orient at the Alaska-Yukon-Pacific Exposition and International Potlatch Festival," *Western Historical Quarterly* 38, no. 3 (2007): 277–302; John M. Findlay, "Fair City: Seattle as Host of the 1909 Alaska-Yukon-Pacific Exposition," *Pacific Northwest Quarterly* 100, no. 1 (2008–2009): 3–11; Richard H. Engeman, "The 'Seattle Spirit' Meets *The Alaskan:* A Story of Business, Boosterism, and the Arts," *Pacific Northwest Quarterly* 81, no. 2 (1990): 54–66; George A. Frykman, "The Alaska-Yukon-Pacific Exposition, 1909," *Pacific Northwest Quarterly* (July 1962): 89–99.

17. Frykman, "The Alaska-Yukon-Pacific Exposition, 1909"; Janet A. Northam and Jack W. Berryman, "Sport and Urban Boosterism in the Pacific Northwest: Seattle's Alaska-Yukon-Pacific Exposition, 1909," *Journal of the West* 17, no. 3 (1978): 53–60; Robert Rydell, *All the World's a Fair: Visions of Empire at American International Expositions, 1876–1916* (Chicago: University of Chicago Press 1984), chap. 7; and Matthew Klingle, *Emerald City,* chap. 5.

18. Quoted in Frykman, "The Alaska-Yukon-Pacific Exposition, 1909," 90.

19. Coll Thrush, *Native Seattle: Histories from the Crossing-Over Place* (Seattle: University of Washington Press, 2007), 119.

20. "Indian Festivities for Seattle Day," *Seattle Post-Intelligencer,* August 13, 1909. Newspaper clipping from the Alaska-Yukon-Pacific Exposition Pamphlet File (hereafter, A-Y-P file), MSCUA, University of Washington.

21. "Seattle Is Planning Another Exposition Designed to Bring the Orient Nearer America," *New York Times,* November 4, 1906.

22. "Foreign Participation Alaska-Yukon-Pacific," newspaper clipping from A-Y-P file.

23. Frank Merrick, publicity material, p. 5, A-Y-P file.

24. Japan first took part in an international exposition in Vienna in 1873. Its first American exposition was Philadelphia's in 1876. Rydell, *All the World's a Fair,* 49.

25. Quoted in ibid., 48.

26. Handwritten note, n.d., A-Y-P file.

27. "Japan's Day Marks New Era," *Seattle Times,* September 4, 1909. Newspaper clipping from A-Y-P file.

28. Thomas Burke Papers, Folder 32–5, MSCUA, University of Washington.

29. "Valuable Japanese Vase the Most Pretentious of Many Gifts Accepted," *Seattle Post-Intelligencer,* October 1, 1909.

30. "With Glad Hand Japanese Guests Come to Visit," *Seattle Post-Intelligencer,* September 1, 1909. Newspaper clipping from A-Y-P file.

31. "Welcome Japan's Masters of Trade," *Seattle Post-Intelligencer,* September 2, 1909. Newspaper clipping from A-Y-P file.

32. "Japan Plans Elaborate Program," *Seattle Times,* August 18, 1909. Newspaper clipping from A-Y-P file.

33. "Japan's Day Marks New Era"; "Japanese Day at Seattle Brings Host of Orientals," *Los Angeles Times,* September 5, 1909.

34. "Japanese Day at Seattle Brings Host of Orientals."

35. "Japs Are Preparing Elaborate Display," *Seattle Star,* August 30, 1909. Newspaper clipping from A-Y-P file.

36. Rydell, *All the World's a Fair;* Thrush, *Native Seattle,* chap. 7.

37. Akira Iriye, *Pacific Estrangement: Japanese and American Expansion, 1897–1911* (Cambridge, MA: Harvard University Press, 1972); Eiichiro Azuma, *Between Two Empires: Race, History, and Transnationalism in Japanese America* (New York: Oxford University Press, 2005).

38. Fair Guidebook, A-Y-P file.

39. "Colors of Orient and Occident Are Mingled at Fair," *Seattle Post-Intelligencer,* September 5, 1909.

40. "Japan's Day Marks New Era."

41. "Local Japanese to Print Book on Fair," *Seattle Post-Intelligencer,* n.d. Newspaper clipping from A-Y-P file.

42. "Igorrote Village 'Needs No Boosting'—P-I: Great Exhibit of Wild People from the Philippine Islands," n.d. From A-Y-P file.

43. Rydell, *All the World's a Fair*, 203.

44. On Chinese at the World's Fair, see ibid., 228.

45. Ibid., 181.

46. Quoted in ibid., 205.

47. J. H. McGraw, "Coast in Arms," *Chicago Chronicle*, December 6, 1906. Newspaper clipping from A-Y-P file.

48. Rydell, *All the World's a Fair*, 205.

49. Mighetto and Montgomery, *Hard Drive to the Klondike*, 59.

50. R. S. Jones, "What the Visitor Sees at the Seattle Fair," *American Review of Reviews* 40 (July 1909): 66.

51. Dana Frank, *Purchasing Power: Consumer Organizing, Gender, and the Seattle Labor Movement, 1919–1929* (Cambridge, UK: Cambridge University Press, 1994), chap. 4.

52. Port of Seattle, *Bulletin: Sailings and Shipping Information* (Seattle: Port of Seattle, 1923); Port of Seattle, *Bulletin: Sailings and Shipping Information* (Seattle: Port of Seattle, 1928).

53. Richard Berner, *Seattle 1921–1940: From Boom to Bust* (Seattle: Charles Press, 1992), 154.

54. Ibid., 154–155.

55. Port of Seattle, *Bulletin: Sailings and Shipping Information* (Seattle: Port of Seattle, 1924).

56. Ole Kay Moe, "An Analytical Study of the Foreign Trade through the Port of Seattle" (master's thesis, University of Washington, 1932), 32. In terms of imports, silk was the main commodity Americans wanted, but Seattle imported tea, camphor, porcelain, toys, vegetable oil, wool, furs, and skins. Also see Berner, *Seattle 1921–1940*, 54.

57. Berner, *Seattle 1921–1940*, 154.

58. "U.S. and Japan Need Each Other in Trade," *Great Northern Daily News*, January 1, 1935.

59. "Nihonjin Shokun!" *Town Crier*, October 19, 1918.

60. Mayumi Tsutakawa, *Kanreki: The 60th Anniversary History of the Japan-America Society of the State of Washington, 1923–1983* (Seattle: Japan-America Society of the State of Washington 1983), 6.

61. Ibid.

62. "Seattle, Orient Gateway, Scene for Convention," *Japanese-American Courier*, July 6, 1935.

63. "Japanese Enact Perry Incident," *Japanese-American Courier*, July 4, 1936.

64. Quoted in "Seattle Is Mindful of Japanese Aid to City Welfare," *Japanese-American Courier*, January 1, 1931.

65. Letter from King Dykeman to James Sakamoto, June 17, 1931, James Sakamoto Papers, Box 1, Folder 16, MSCUA, University of Washington.

66. Yuji Ichioka, "A Study in Dualism: James Yoshinori Sakamoto and the *Japanese-American Courier*, 1928–1942," *Amerasia* 13, no. 2 (1986–1987): 49–81.

67. "Growing Seattle," *Japanese-American Courier*, December 12, 1938.

68. For examples, see Thomas Arai, "Seattle Is the Gateway to the Orient," *Japanese-American Courier*, January 7, 1928; Thomas Arai, "Port of Seattle High in Ranking in Foreign Trade," *Japanese-American Courier*, March 17, 1928.

69. "The Pacific Melting Pot," *Japanese-American Courier*, October 4, 1928.

70. Ibid.

71. "The Fusing of Cultures," *Japanese-American Courier*, December 15, 1928.

72. Clarence Arai, "Orientals Played Prominent Part in Building of West-Arai," *Great Northern Daily News,* January 4, 1938.

73. Izumi Hirobe, *Japanese Pride, American Prejudice: Modifying the Exclusion Clause of the 1924 Immigration Act* (Stanford, CA: Stanford University Press, 2001), chap. 5.

74. Berner, *Seattle 1921–1940,* 36.

75. Hirobe, *Japanese Pride, American Prejudice,* 131.

76. "Seattle's Week at Home," *Town Crier,* July 12, 1913.

77. "Sound Truths around the Merriment," *Town Crier,* July 29, 1911.

78. Ibid.

79. "Again the Round-Up," *Town Crier,* March 29, 1913.

80. 1934 Official Potlatch Program, Seattle-International Potlatch Pamphlet File (hereafter Potlatch file), MSCUA, University of Washington.

81. Ibid.

82. Ibid.

83. In 1885, the Canadian government outlawed the potlatch. The practice was not outlawed in the United States. Douglas Cole and Ira Chaikin, *An Iron Hand upon the People: The Law against the Potlatch on the Northwest Coast* (Seattle: University of Washington Press, 1990), 175. On the demise of the potlatch in the Northwest Coast, see Alexandra Harmon, *Indians in the Making: Ethnic Relations and Indian Identities around Puget Sound* (Berkeley: University of California Press, 1998), chap. 4.

84. Thrush, *Native Seattle,* chap. 7.

85. Ibid., 3.

86. 1934 Official Potlatch Program.

87. Ibid.

88. "The International Potlatch," *Town Crier,* August 15, 1934.

89. 1934 Official Potlatch Program.

90. Letter from Clifton Pease, executive secretary of Seattle Chamber of Commerce, to S. Hara, executive secretary of Japanese Chamber of Commerce, August 30, 1934, Japanese Association of North America papers (hereafter JANA), Box 4, Folder 56, MSCUA, University of Washington.

91. Monica Sone, *Nisei Daughter,* 4th ed. (Seattle: University of Washington Press, 1987), 60.

92. Letter from Clifton Pease to S. Hara.

93. Letter from Mayor Charles Smith to Buehi Nakasone, executive secretary of Japanese Chamber of Commerce, March 27, 1935; letter from Alfred Lundin, executive chairman of Seattle Chamber of Commerce, to Chusaburo Ito, president of Japanese Chamber of Commerce, October 9, 1934, JANA, Box 4, Folder 56, MSCUA, University of Washington.

94. Letter from Dorothy Denee Snowden to G. Mihara, president of the Japanese Chamber of Commerce, July 17, 1935, JANA, Box 4, Folder 67, MSCUA, University of Washington.

95. "2-Hour Parade Brings Throng for Potlatch," *Seattle Times* July 28, 1940.

96. "Japanese Participate in Potlatch Events," *Great Northern Daily News,* July 26, 1935.

97. "Japanese Float Wins Potlatch Fete Prize," *Great Northern Daily News,* August 3, 1935. Japanese American floats also won prizes in 1938 and 1941.

98. "Japanese to Present Potlatch Odori Show," *Great Northern Daily News,* July 30, 1935.

99. "Dawning Participation," *Japanese-American Courier,* July 27, 1935.
100. "Main Street," *Great Northern Daily News,* June 5, 1941.
101. Ibid.

CHAPTER 3

1. Quoted in *Notan: Bulletin of the Seattle Camera Club,* July 8, 1927.
2. Ibid.
3. SCC is my abbreviation, not theirs.
4. "The Pictorial Photographic Workers of the Pacific Northwest and Their Relation to the Art of Pictorial Photography, *Notan,* September 13, 1929.
5. In his history of Seattle, historian Richard Berner comments that Seattle arts did not flourish until after World War II, when New Deal federal support for artists and wartime infusions of people, dollars, and infrastructure began to bear fruit. The decade has also been obscured in part because the most famous group of painters from the Pacific Northwest, the "Northwest School," among them Mark Tobey, first gained attention during the 1930s and 1940s. Richard Berner, *Seattle in the Twentieth Century 1900–1920: From Boomtown, Urban Turbulence, to Restoration* (Seattle: Charles Press, 1991), 251.
6. The Seattle Camera Club is also examined in the following: Robert D. Monroe, "Light and Shade: Pictorial Photography in Seattle, 1920–1940, and the Seattle Camera Club," in *Turning Shadows into Light: Art and Culture of the Northwest's Early Asian/Pacific Community,* ed. Mayumi Tsutakawa and Alan Chong Lau (Seattle: Young Pine Press, 1982): 8–32; David F. Martin, "Painted with Light: Photographs by the Seattle Camera Club," *American Art Review* 12, no. 1 (2000): 164–169; Carol Zabilski, "Dr. Kyo Koike, 1878–1947: Physician, Poet, Photographer," *Pacific Northwest Quarterly* 68, no. 2 (1977): 73–78.
7. Joel Eisinger, *Trace and Transformation: American Criticism of Photography in the Modern Period* (Albuquerque: University of New Mexico Press, 1995).
8. Lawrence W. Levine, *Highbrow/Lowbrow: The Emergence of Cultural Hierarchy in America* (Cambridge, MA: Harvard University Press, 1988), 161.
9. Alfred Stieglitz is often credited with bringing pictorialism to America. After taking part in European salons, Stieglitz bemoaned American photography's lagging development and dedicated himself to raising the quality of the craft in the United States. He returned to the United States in 1890, founded and edited *Camera Work* magazine, and provided the guiding force behind the Photo-Secession movement. The Photo-Secession, a cadre of American pictorial photographers based in New York, dominated American pictorialism from about the turn of the twentieth century to the 1920s. Although tightly controlled and elitist, the movement helped raise the popularity and respectability of pictorialism as an art form in the United States. Eisinger, *Trace and Transformation.*
10. Arthur H. Farrow, "The Lack of Interest in Photographic Magazines—Who or What Is to Blame?" *Photo-Era Magazine* 58, no. 1 (1927): 14.
11. Christian A. Peterson, *After the Photo-Secession: American Pictorial Photography, 1910–1955* (London: Minneapolis Institute of Art in Association with W. W. Norton, 1997), 140.
12. *Notan,* March 26, 1926.
13. Roger Sale, *Seattle Past to Present: An Interpretation of the Foremost City in the Pacific Northwest* (Seattle: University of Washington Press, 1976), 149.

14. Richard Berner, *Seattle 1921–1940: From Boom to Bust* (Seattle: Charles Press, 1992), 251.

15. Sale, *Seattle Past to Present,* 161–163.

16. In 1924, Kunishige staged a showing of his catalog of seventy prints at the Seattle Commercial Club, located at Maynard and Washington.

17. According to *Notan,* the club had fifty-eight charter members, while Robert Monroe says it had thirty-nine. Monroe, "Light and Shade," 8.

18. Kyo Koike, "The Seattle Camera Club," *Photo-Era Magazine* 55, no. 4 (1925): 184.

19. Ibid., 182.

20. Dennis Reed, *Japanese Photography in America, 1920–1940* (Los Angeles: George J. Doizaki Gallery, Japanese American Cultural and Community Center, 1985), 23.

21. *Notan,* January 11, 1929.

22. Fellow SCC member Himoru Kira wrote for the series in 1930, and other writers included William Zerbe, Louis Bucher, Max Thorek, and William Woodburn.

23. Dennis Reed, "The Wind Came from the East: Asian American Photography, 1850–1965," in *Asian American Art: A History, 1850–1970,* ed. Gordon H. Chang, Mark Dean Johnson, and Paul J. Karlstrom, 141–168 (Stanford, CA: Stanford University Press, 2008); *Toyo Miyatake: Infinite Shades of Gray,* VHS, directed by Robert A. Nakamura (Los Angeles: Japanese American National Museum, 2001).

24. Henry Hall, letter, Notan, November 13, 1925.

25. John Bodnar, *The Transplanted: A History of Immigrants in Urban America* (Bloomington: Indiana University Press, 1985), 184.

26. Shotaro Frank Miyamoto, *Social Solidarity among the Japanese in Seattle* (1939; repr., Seattle: University of Washington Press, 1984), 67–68.

27. Ibid.

28. Peterson, *After the Photo-Secession,* 130. Kyo Koike and Iwao Matsushita struck up a friendship that lasted from 1920 until Koike's death in 1947. See Louis Fiset, *Imprisoned Apart: The World War II Correspondence of an Issei Couple* (Seattle: University of Washington Press, 1997), 15–24.

29. "To the Seattle Photographers, Amateur and Professional," *Notan,* March 11, 1927.

30. *Notan,* April 8, 1927.

31. Reed, *Japanese Photography in America, 1920–1940,* 19.

32. Kyo Koike, "Why I Am a Pictorial Photographer," *Photo-Era Magazine* 61, no. 3 (1928): 123.

33. Mary Ting Yi Lui, *The Chinatown Trunk Mystery: Murder, Miscegenation, and Other Dangerous Encounters in Turn-of-the-Century New York* (Princeton, NJ: Princeton University Press, 2005).

34. *Notan,* September 11, 1925.

35. *Notan,* July 7, 1927.

36. *Notan,* January 13, 1928.

37. *Notan,* December 11, 1925.

38. *Notan,* December 10, 1926; Notan, June 11, 1926.

39. "The Publisher's Corner," *Photo-Era* 57, no. 4 (1926): 228.

40. "Here, There, and Everywhere," *Photo-Era* 57, no. 5 (1926): 283.

41. *Notan,* June 11, 1926.

42. *Notan,* May 14, 1926.

43. *Notan,* March 8, 1929.

44. *Notan,* July 12, 1929.

45. *Notan,* June 14, 1929.

46. *Notan,* February 14, 1927.

47. William Taylor, *In Pursuit of Gotham* (New York: Oxford University Press, 1992), 17.

48. Kyo Koike, "Mount Rainier," *Camera Craft* 33, no. 3 (1926): 117–123.

49. "To the Seattle Photographers, Amateur and Professional."

50. *Notan,* September 11, 1925.

51. "To the Seattle Photographers, Amateur and Professional."

52. Ibid.

53. Ibid.

54. Zabilski, "Dr. Kyo Koike, 1878–1947," 75.

55. Koike, "The Seattle Camera Club," 188.

56. *Notan,* June 12, 1925.

57. *Notan,* February 11, 1927.

58. "The Pictorial Photographic Workers of the Pacific Northwest and Their Relation to the Art of Pictorial Photography."

59. Zabilski, "Dr. Kyo Koike, 1878–1947," 77.

60. Quoted in *Notan,* October 10, 1929.

61. Sigismund Blumann, "What Our Japanese Pictorialists Might Do," *Notan,* April 10, 1925.

62. Ibid.

63. *Notan,* April 29, 1926.

64. Reed, *Japanese Photography in America, 1920–1940,* 57.

65. *Notan,* August 9, 1929.

66. Ibid.

67. According to Christian Peterson, Haz was born in Hungary. See Peterson, *After the Photo-Secession,* 34.

68. Kyo Koike, "Japanese Work in Pictorial Photographic Field," *Notan,* August 9, 1929.

69. *Notan,* September 13, 1929.

70. Ibid.

71. Zabilski, "Dr. Kyo Koike, 1878–1947," 77.

72. "To the Seattle Photographers, Amateur and Professional."

73. Ibid.

74. Ibid.

75. *Notan,* February 8, 1929.

76. *Notan,* October 11, 1929.

77. "Dr. Koike to Exhibit in International Salon," *Great Northern Daily News,* February 8, 1935.

78. "Grocer-Photographer Awarded New Honors in Bristol Exhibition," *Great Northern Daily News,* May 22, 1935; "Honors from All Parts of the Globe Come to Grocer-Photographer," *Great Northern Daily News,* February 4, 1935.

79. "Furuya Camera Club Sponsors Contest," *Japanese-American Courier,* May 4, 1930.

80. "Japanese Surrender Equipment" *Seattle Times,* December 29, 1941.

81. "Japs Turn in Cameras Here" *Seattle Post-Intelligencer,* December 29, 1941.

82. Monroe, "Light and Shade."

CHAPTER 4

1. This is the legend of how, when asked by his father if he chopped down a cherry tree in the family orchard, young George Washington replied, "I cannot tell a lie," and confessed, thus mythologizing his image of honesty and humility.

2. Quoted in Ruth Grenier, "Seattle's Japanese George Washington," 1924, Survey of Race Relations, Box 27, Folder 164, Hoover Institution Archives, Stanford University. According to Grenier, the reporter did not actually make it on time to witness the performance for himself. The original article appeared as "Seattle's George Washington," *Seattle Star*, February 22, 1924.

3. Grenier, "Seattle's Japanese George Washington," 3.

4. Ibid., 6.

5. Ibid., 5.

6. Ibid., 4.

7. Ibid., 8.

8. Mark Wild, *Street Meeting: Multiethnic Neighborhoods in Early Twentieth-Century Los Angeles* (Berkeley: University of California Press, 2005), chap. 4.

9. Eiichiro Azuma, "'The Pacific Era Has Arrived': Transnational Education among Japanese Americans, 1932–1941," *History of Education Quarterly* 42, no. 1 (2003): 39–73; Yoon K. Pak, *Wherever I Go, I Will Always Be a Loyal American: Schooling Seattle's Japanese Americans during World War II* (New York: RoutledgeFalmer, 2002); David Yoo, *Growing Up Nisei: Race, Generation, and Culture among Japanese Americans of California, 1924–49* (Urbana: University of Illinois Press, 2000).

10. For an overview of the expansion of public education in American cities, see David B. Tyack, *One Best System: A History of American Urban Education* (Cambridge, MA: Harvard University Press, 1974); Paula Fass, *Outside In: Minorities and the Transformation of American Education* (New York: Oxford University Press, 1989), chaps. 1 and 2.

11. See Frank Van Nuys, *Americanizing the West: Race, Immigrants, and Citizenship, 1890–1930* (Lawrence: University of Kansas Press, 2002), 33–41. For a more general discussion of Progressivism and other reforms of that era, see Robert Wiebe, *The Search for Order, 1877–1920* (New York: Hill and Wang, 1967).

12. Van Nuys, *Americanizing the West*, 41–69; George Sanchez, *Becoming Mexican American: Ethnicity, Culture, and Identity in Chicano Los Angeles, 1900–1945* (New York: Oxford University Press, 1993), 94–96; Keith A. Murray, "The Charles Niederhauer Case: Patriotism in the Seattle Schools, 1919," *Pacific Northwest Quarterly* 74, no. 1 (1983): 11–17.

13. Worth McClure, "America's Melting Pot," *Seattle Grade Club Magazine* (May 1932): 8.

14. Doris Hinson Pieroth, *Seattle's Women Teachers of the Interwar Years: Shapers of a Livable City* (Seattle: University of Washington Press, 2004), 15.

15. Bryce E. Nelson, "Frank B. Cooper: Seattle's Progressive School Superintendent, 1901–1922," *Pacific Northwest Quarterly* 74, no. 4 (1983): 167–177.

16. Ibid., 5.

17. Pieroth, *Seattle's Women Teachers of the Interwar Years*, 131.

18. Ironically, one of the reasons Seattle Schools did not establish a separate school for Asians was that a white resident of the neighborhood of the proposed site protested the school would bring down property values. Minutes from the Meetings of the Board of Directors, Pacific School, January 6, 1922, Record no. 18, p. 224, Seattle Public Schools Archives and Records Management Center (hereafter SPSARMC).

19. Roger Sale, *Seattle Past to Present: An Interpretation of the Foremost City in the Pacific Northwest* (Seattle: University of Washington Press, 1976), 141.

20. Ibid., 142.

21. Ibid., 141–142.

22. "Fifty-three Japanese Students Graduate From University and Seattle High Schools This June," *Japanese-American Courier*, June 16, 1928.

23. "Twenty Three Nisei Enter Garfield High," *Great Northern Daily News*, February 11, 1935.

24. Pak, *Wherever I Go, I Will Always Be a Loyal American*, 38.

25. Shigeko Sese Uno, interview by Beth Kawahara and Alice Ito, September 18, 1998, Densho Visual History Collection, Densho.

26. May Namba, interview by Alice Ito, October 21, 2004, Densho Visual History Collection, Densho.

27. Sharon Tanagi Aburano, interview by Tom Ikeda and Megan Asaka, March 25, 2008, Densho Visual History Collection, Densho.

28. Louise Kashino, interview by Alice Ito, March 15, 1998, Densho Visual History Collection, Densho.

29. Mits Takahashi, interview by Tom Ikeda, March 20, 1998, Densho Visual History Collection, Densho.

30. Yuji Ichioka, *The Issei: The World of the First Generation of Japanese Americans, 1885–1924* (New York: Free Press, 1988), 206; Kazuo Ito, *Issei: A History of Japanese Immigrants in North America*, trans. Shinchiro Nakamura and Jean S. Gerard (Seattle: Executive Committee for Publication of *Issei: A History of Japanese Immigrants in North America*, 1973), 599.

31. Ito, *Issei*, 590.

32. Seiko Edamatsu, interview by Megan Asaka, June 7, 2006, Densho Visual History Collection, Densho.

33. In 1921, the California state legislature passed a law regulating the certification of teachers and content of instructional materials in private schools that was later nullified. Ichioka, *Issei*, 207. Also see Noriko Asato, "Ousting Japanese Language Schools: Americanization and Cultural Maintenance in Washington State, 1919–1927," *Pacific Northwest Quarterly* 94, no. 3 (2003): 140–150; Noriko Asato, *Teaching Mikadoism: The Attack on Japanese Language Schools in Hawaii, California, and Washington, 1919–1927* (Honolulu: University of Hawaii Press, 2005).

34. Ichioka, *Issei*, 199.

35. *Seattle Grade Club Magazine* (October 1923).

36. "Americanization in the Seattle Grade Schools," *Seattle Grade Club Magazine* (October 1928): 12.

37. McClure, "America's Melting Pot," 8.

38. "Americanization in the Seattle Grade Schools," 12.

39. Mark Wild, "'So Many Children at Once and So Many Kinds': Schools and Ethno-racial Boundaries in Early-Twentieth Century Los Angeles," *Western Historical Quarterly* 33, no. 4 (2002): 462.

40. *Seattle Grade Club Magazine* (May 1932).

41. "Americanization in the Seattle Grade Schools," 13.

42. Ibid.

43. McClure, "America's Melting Pot," 8.

44. Ibid. Yoon K. Pak explains that Seattle Schools' approach to Americanization, which she calls "interculturalism," solidified during the 1930s. As she explains, interculturalism

was a modification of Americanization, from relative uniformity to greater tolerance and "intercultural education. Pak, *Wherever I Go, I Will Always Be a Loyal American,* chap. 4.

45. Dorothy Rutherford, "Cosmopolitan Christmas," *Seattle Grade Club Magazine* (December 1935): 13–14.

46. *Seattle Grade Club Magazine* (December 1931).

47. Richard Berner, *Seattle 1921–1940: From Boom to Bust* (Seattle: Charles Press, 1992), 226.

48. Ibid.

49. Ibid.

50. "Move for Japan Courses in High Schools Begins," *Japanese-American Courier,* April 18, 1931.

51. "Japanese Seeks Language Credit," *Franklin Tolo,* September 27, 1933.

52. "Teach Japanese in High Schools," *Japanese-American Courier,* March 8, 1930.

53. "Move for Japan Courses in High Schools Begins."

54. "Japanese Consul Talks on Far East Situation at Meet," *Franklin Tolo,* April 4, 1935.

55. In separate visits, Kenji Ito, a Japanese American, spoke on the Japanese point of view, and Lawrence Lew Kay, a Chinese American, gave a speech titled, "The Sino-Japanese Situation from the Chinese Standpoint"; "Chinese Debater at U.W. Will Speak to Broadway Students," *Great Northern Daily News,* October 16, 1937.

56. "Japan Awakens to New Ideas," *Franklin Tolo,* October 6, 1920.

57. *Successful Living* (Seattle: Seattle Public Schools, 1935), 56–57.

58. "Franklin Debate Seems Doubtful," *Franklin Tolo,* February 17, 1926.

59. These included Katherine Lentz, Charlotte Bianza, Kathleen Cowan, Marian White, Ada Mahon, and Edward Stafford. Katherine Lentz, who had visited Japan, China, and Korea, taught a course titled "The Pacific Rim"; *Franklin Tolo,* August 19, 1928. Charlotte Bianza, an art teacher also at Franklin, went on a world tour, stopping in Japan to study Japanese art; "Popular Teacher in Japan Soon," *Japanese-American Courier,* April 28, 1928. Also see "Teachers to Go on Japan Visit," *Japanese-American Courier,* May 18, 1929; "Seattle Teachers on Oriental Tour," *Seattle Star,* July 4, 1939. Additionally, in 1935, the Japanese Association and Chamber of Commerce voted to finance a tour of Japan for a group of Northwest college students and educators who wanted to learn about the customs, arts, and systems of Japan; "Japanese Association to Finance Oriental Trip of NW Educators," *Great Northern Daily News,* September 20, 1935.

60. "Parents to Honor School Principal," *Japanese-American Courier,* May 10, 1930.

61. Ibid.

62. "Differences in Education and Environment Causes for Breach between Young and Old Japanese," *Japanese-American Courier,* June 20, 1928; "Association to Invite Educators for Meet," *Great Northern Daily News,* September 20, 1935.

63. "Japanese Grads' List Biggest Yet," *Japanese-American Courier,* May 23, 1936.

64. "41 Listed on Franklin High School Honor List," *Great Northern Daily News,* October 16, 1937.

65. "Association to Invite Educators for Meet."

66. "Better Americans Aimed by Schools," *Japanese-American Courier,* November 9, 1929.

67. Ibid.

68. "Dr Howard Martin Opens Public Forum at Bailey Gatzert School, Ada J. Mahon Presides," *Great Northern Daily News,* January 28, 1937.

69. *Franklin Tolo,* October 6, 1920.

70. "Garfield a Good Example of How Various Nationalities Can Be Welded into a Group" *Garfield Messenger,* May 12, 1926.

71. Editorial, *Garfield Messenger,* February 17, 1933.

72. *Garfield Arrow* Annual, 1938.

73. Ibid.

74. "Educational 'Melting Pot,'" *Seattle Sunday Times,* December 24, 1939.

75. "William Yamaguchi Asset to Franklin," *Franklin Tolo,* April 10, 1936.

76. Tanagi Aburano interview.

77. Mits Takahashi interview, March 20, 2008.

78. Yae Aihara, interview by Megan Asaka, July 4, 2008, Densho Visual History Collection, Densho.

79. May Y. Namba interview, October 21, 2004.

80. Victor Ikeda, interview by Richard Potashin, November 6, 2007, Manzanar National Historic Site Collection, Densho.

81. "My Contact with Orientals by Miss Lentz, Teacher at Franklin," Survey of Race Relations, Box 27, Folder 165, Hoover Institution Archives, Stanford University.

82. Ibid.

83. "Report of Survey Interviews for State of Washington," 5, Survey of Race Relations, Box 18, Folder 15, Hoover Institution Archives, Stanford University.

84. *Seattle Principal's Exchange,* November 1938, Seattle Public School Archives; School Board Minutes, Bailey Gatzert, January 31, 1941, Record no. 37, p. 216, SPSARMC.

85. Mahon began working for the school district in 1901, teaching at Denny and Horace Mann before going to Bailey Gatzert in 1910 to serve as vice principal; "Beloved Teacher Passes," *Seattle Post-Intelligencer,* June 18, 1951.

86. *Japanese-American Courier,* June 28, 1939.

87. Frank Miyamoto, interview by Stephen Fugita, February 26, 1998, Densho Visual History Collection, Densho.

88. Sharon Tanagi Aburano interview, April 3, 2008, by Tom Ikeda and Megan Asaka, Densho Visual History Collection, Densho.

89. Ibid.

90. Sharon Tanagi Aburano, interview by Tom Ikeda and Megan Asaka, March 25, 2008, Densho Visual History Collection, Densho; George Yoshida, interview by Alice Ito and John Pai, February 18, 2002, Densho Visual History Collection, Densho.

91. George Yoshida interview, February 18, 2002.

92. Nile Thompson and Carolyn J. Marr, *Building for Learning: Seattle Public School Histories, 1862–2000,* Unpublished School Histories, 2002, Seattle School District No. 1, SPSARMC.

93. Minutes from Meetings of the Board of Directors of Seattle School District, Bailey Gatzert, December 2, 1921, Record no. 18, p. 196, SPSARMC.

94. Ada J. Mahon, "Intimate Glimpses of Japan," *Seattle Grade Club Magazine* (October 1931): 13.

95. "From the Address of Jiuji G. Kasai," *Seattle Grade Club Magazine* (May 1929): 31.

96. Ibid., 32.

97. Letter from Ada Mahon to Seattle Japanese Chamber of Commerce and Japanese Association of North America, March 22, 1935, JANA, Box 9, Folder 21, MSCUA, University of Washington. Also see letter from Ada Mahon to Seattle Japanese Chamber of Commerce and Japanese Association of North America, April 22, 1938, JANA, Box 9, Folder 23, MSCUA, University of Washington.

98. "Miss Mahon," *Japanese-American Courier,* June 30, 1928.

99. Mahon, "Intimate Glimpses of Japan," 12.

100. "Report of the Survey Interviews for State of Washington," 5, Survey of Race Relations, Box 18, Folder 15, Hoover Institution Archives, Stanford University.

101. According to Ruth Grenier, Kimura graduated and delivered an address that one attendee remembered to be deeply impressive and drawing a prolonged applause. Ruth Grenier, "The Japanese Valedictorian of Franklin High School," 1924, Survey of Race Relations, Box 25, Folder 82, Hoover Institution Archives, Stanford University.

102. "Will Mr. Coolidge Listen? Proud Americans to Hear Japanese Boy Deliver Valedictory at Franklin Hi School," *Seattle Star,* May 15, 1924 (reprinted in Grenier, "The Japanese Valedictorian of Franklin High School").

103. Ibid.

104. Ibid.

105. Grenier, "The Japanese Valedictorian of Franklin High School," 3.

106. Quoted in ibid., 4.

107. Quoted in ibid.

108. Ibid., 6.

109. Ibid., 5.

110. Ibid., 5–6.

111. Kay Matsuoka, interview by Alice Ito, December 29–30, 1999, Densho Visual History Collection, Densho.

112. Namba interview.

113. Ibid.; Takahashi interview; Ruby Inouye, interview by Alice Ito and Dee Goto, April 3–4, 2003, Densho Visual History Collection, Densho; Yae Aihara, interview by Megan Asaka, July 4, 2008, Densho Visual History Collection, Densho.

114. "Can They Teach Us?" *Franklin Tolo,* November 8, 1933.

115. "Garfield's Sons of Samurai Participate in Courier Ball," *Garfield Messenger,* January 22, 1937.

116. *Franklin Tolo* Annual, 1924.

117. *Franklin Tolo* Annual, 1931.

118. *Garfield Messenger,* January 21, 1938.

119. *Franklin Tolo,* April 16, 1936.

120. *Franklin Tolo,* April 21, 1939.

121. "Myself, as an American Citizen," *Great Northern Daily News,* December 11, 1937.

122. "War No Barrier to Friendship at High School," *Great Northern Daily News,* December 11, 1941.

123. Quoted in Pak, *Wherever I Go, I Will Always Be a Loyal American,* 102–103.

124. *Garfield Messenger,* May 1, 1942.

125. Ibid.

CHAPTER 5

1. The address was reprinted in an issue of the *Japanese-American Courier;* George Okada, "Taiyo Teaches High Principles," *Japanese-American Courier,* March 17, 1934.

2. Albert G. Spalding, *America's National Game: Historic Facts Concerning the Beginning, Evolution, Development and Popularity of Base Ball* (Lincoln: University of Nebraska Press, 1992), 533.

3. Ibid.

4. Okada, "Taiyo Teaches High Principles."

5. *Japanese-American Courier,* July 22, 1939.

6. On Japanese and baseball, see Gail M. Nomura, "Beyond the Playing Field: The Significance of Pre–World War II Japanese American Baseball in the Yakima Valley," in *Bearing Dreams, Shaping Visions: Asian Pacific American Perspectives,* ed. Linda A. Revilla, Gail M. Nomura, Shawn Wong, and Shirley Hune (Pullman: Washington State University Press, 1993), 15–31; Samuel O. Regalado, "Incarcerated Sport: Nisei Women's Softball and Athletics during Japanese American Internment," *Journal of Sport History* 27, no. 3 (2000): 431–444; Samuel O. Regalado, "'Play Ball!': Baseball and Seattle's Japanese-American Courier League, 1928–1941," *Pacific Northwest Quarterly* 97, no. 1 (1995–1996): 29–37; Samuel O. Regalado, "Sport and Community in California's Japanese American 'Yamato Colony,' 1930–1945," *Journal of Sport History* 19, no. 2 (1992): 130–143.

7. For background on the development of a national sporting culture, see Peter Levine, *A. G. Spalding and the Rise of Baseball: The Promise of American Sport* (New York: Oxford University Press, 1985), chap. 6. On the development of a sporting culture in Seattle, I used Janet A. Northam and Jack W. Berryman, "Sport and Urban Boosterism in the Pacific Northwest: Seattle's Alaska-Yukon-Pacific Exposition, 1909," *Journal of the West* 17, no. 3 (1978): 53–60. Also see S. W. Pope, *Patriotic Games: Sporting Traditions in the American Imagination, 1876–1926* (New York: Oxford University Press, 1997).

8. Matthew Klingle, *Emerald City: An Environmental History of Seattle* (New Haven, CT: Yale University Press, 2007), chap. 4. Also on the promotion of Seattle as a recreation city, see Janet Northam Russell and Jack W. Berryman, "Parks, Boulevards, and Outdoor Recreation: The Promotion of Seattle as an Ideal Residential City and Summer Resort, 1890–1910," *Journal of the West* 26, no. 1 (1987): 5–17.

9. On Jewish American athletes, Peter Levine has shown that playing Western sports reinforced the ethnic component of personal and community identity. In 1854, Jews formed the Young Men's Hebrew Association, which sponsored a wide range of sporting activities, from swimming to basketball. For the individual athletes, participation in these activities was a way to challenge stereotypes of Jewish aversion to sports and also provided a critical meeting point where majority and minority people intersected. Athletics were also an area of life that they had control over. In sports, Jewish American athletes adapted traditional practices to new American settings and made their American experience compatible with "ethnic" ways. Peter Levine, *Ellis Island to Ebbet's Field: Sport and the American-Jewish Experience* (New York: Oxford University Press, 1992).

10. Mayumi Tsutakawa, "Memories of Nisei Sports Clubs," *Journal of the International District* 3, no. 7 (1976): 1.

11. Nomura, "Beyond the Playing Field," 16.

12. Frank Miyamoto, interview by Stephen Fugita, February 26, 1998, Densho Visual History Collection, Densho.

13. Toshio Ito, interview by Alice Ito, May 21, 1998, Densho Visual History Collection, Densho.

14. Ibid.

15. Tsutakawa, "Memories of Nisei Sports Clubs," 1.

16. "A Warning," *Japanese-American Courier,* January 28, 1928.

17. "Sport Scope: A Public Benefactor," *Japanese-American Courier,* March 3, 1928. Also see Nomura, "Beyond the Playing Field," 31; Regalado, "'Play Ball!'"

18. Bill Hosokawa, "Hangovers," *Japanese-American Courier,* June 15, 1935.

19. "Sport Scope: A Public Benefactor," *Japanese-American Courier,* March 3, 1928.

20. Ibid.

21. The most thorough treatment of Japanese American baseball in the Courier League can be found in Regalado, "'Play Ball!'"

22. "A Warning."

23. Yuji Ichioka, "A Study in Dualism: James Yoshinori Sakamoto and the *Japanese-American Courier,* 1928–1942," *Amerasia* 13, no. 2 (1986–1987): 49–81.

24. "Sport Scope," *Japanese-American Courier,* January 2, 1928. The Courier League also sponsored other sports, such as basketball and football, and by the 1940–1941 season, it comprised five hundred athletes and fifty-five teams in all sports.

25. "Sport Scope: A Public Benefactor," *Japanese-American Courier,* March 3, 1928.

26. Regalado, "'Play Ball!'"

27. "Coast-wide . . ." *Japanese-American Courier,* February 26, 1938.

28. Quoted in Regalado, "'Play Ball!'" 34.

29. Bill Hosokawa, "Curtain Falls on Most Disastrous Baseball Season; Will Try New Strategy Next Year," *Japanese-American Courier,* September 28, 1935.

30. Budd Fukei, "Budd's Banter," *Great Northern Daily News,* January 1, 1938.

31. "Lil' Tokyo Series to Be Held Next Year," *Great Northern Daily News,* October 5, 1937.

32. *Japanese-American Courier,* September 24, 1938.

33. Ryoichi Shibazaki, "Seattle and the Japanese-United States Baseball Connection, 1905–1926" (master's thesis, University of Washington, 1981), 7.

34. "Kwansei's Championship Caliber," *Japanese-American Courier,* July 28, 1928.

35. Ibid.

36. "Keio Sportsmanship," *Japanese-American Courier,* June 9, 1929; "Wapato Team Has Strong Lineup; Set to Meet Tokio Pros," *Japanese-American Courier,* April 27, 1935.

37. Robert J. Sinclair, "Baseball's Rising Sun: American Interwar Baseball Diplomacy and Japan," *Canadian Journal of History of Sport* 16, no. 2 (1985): 46. Also on the relationship between sports and American national identity, see Alan Bairner, *Sport, Nationalization, and Globalization* (Albany: State University of New York Press, 2001); Pope, *Patriotic Games.*

38. Levine, *A. G. Spalding and the Rise of Baseball,* 100.

39. Richard C. Crepeau, "Pearl Harbor: A Failure of Baseball?" *Journal of Popular Culture* 15, no. 4 (1982): 67. Also see Regalado, "Sport and Community in California's Japanese American 'Yamato Colony,' 1930–1945," 132; and for discussion of compatibility of Japanese values and baseball, see Sinclair, "Baseball's Rising Sun," 46.

40. "Sports Scope," *Japanese-American Courier,* December 25, 1928.

41. Sinclair, "Baseball's Rising Sun," 47.

42. "Sport Slants," *Great Northern Daily News,* July 3, 1935. According to Samuel Regalado, this tournament was also sponsored by the Courier League. Regalado, "'Play Ball!'"

43. "Intermission Numbers Set for League Event," *Great Northern Daily News,* July 3, 1935.

44. In the team's early days, its principal competition came from Japanese teams from Victoria, but Harry Miyasaki, the Asahis' manager from 1922 to 1929, wanted to create a team capable of competing against the "bigger, harder hitting Occidental teams and to win the Terminal League Championship" of Vancouver, of which they were the only Japanese team. See Pat Adachi, *Asahi: A Legend in Baseball* (Etobicoke, Ontario, Canada: Asahi Baseball Organization, 1992), 53. He recruited the most talented players, not all of them Japanese, from around the city and nearby suburbs, and by the late 1920s, the Asahis became a top attraction in the Vancouver Japanese community and a major player

in British Columbia semiprofessional baseball. Team members included "Occidentals" Joe Brown and Ernie Papke from the 1921 team. They were champions of the International League in 1919, the Terminal League in 1926 and 1930, and the Burrard League between 1938 and 1940.

45. Adachi, *Asahi*.

46. "Same Old Story: Vancouver Asahi Tossers Defeat Fife Nippon, 10–5," *Great Northern Daily News,* July 24, 1939; "Giants Set for Canadians," *Great Northern Daily News,* August 21, 1940.

47. "Nippons Are Ready for Vancouver Clash; Close Battle Expected," *Great Northern Daily News,* August 10, 1935.

48. "Vancouver Asahis Shut Out Nippons in Close Contest," *Japanese-American Courier,* September 28, 1928.

49. Adachi, *Asahi,* 125.

50. "Vancouver Asahis Take Doubleheader, Series from Taiyo," *Japanese-American Courier,* September 8, 1934.

51. Budd Fukei, "Budd's Banter," *Great Northern Daily News,* July 8, 1941.

52. Ibid.

53. Tsutakawa, "Memories of Nisei Sports Clubs."

54. George Ishihara, "We Oldsters," *Great Northern Daily News,* January 1, 1938.

55. "N.A.C. Wins Tilts 9–0 over Royal Colored Giants," *Japanese-American Courier,* April 12, 1930.

56. "Canadians . . ." *Japanese-American Courier,* July 30, 1938.

57. "Four Races Seen in Mixed Bouts on Fight Card at Crystal Pool," *Northwest Enterprise,* March 5, 1931.

58. "Harold Hoshino Scores Technical Knockout Win over Nationalista," *Great Northern Daily News,* November 16, 1938.

59. Eiichiro Azuma, "Interethnic Conflict Under Racial Subordination: Japanese Immigrants and their Asian Neighbors in Walnut Grove, California, 1909–1941," *Amerasia Journal* 20, no. 2 (1994): 27–56.

60. Ibid., 47.

61. Ibid., 43.

62. Eiichiro Azuma, "Racial Struggle, Immigrant Nationalism, and Ethnic Identity: Japanese and Filipinos in the California Delta, 1930–1941," *Pacific Historical Review* 67 (May 1998): 163–199; Chris Friday, *Organizing Asian American Labor: The Pacific Coast Canned-Salmon Industry, 1870–1942* (Philadelphia: Temple University Press, 1994), 130–131.

63. "Beware of Romance with Filipinos," *Great Northern Daily News,* August 8, 1940.

64. "Arai Bowls Self into Big League Company with 200; Match On," *Great Northern Daily News,* January 5, 1935.

65. "Barber Shop Team Favored to Win over Japanese All-Stars," *Great Northern Daily News,* November 10, 1934.

66. "Filipino Barber Four Give New Trimming to Japanese Bowlers," *Great Northern Daily News,* November 27, 1934.

67. "Filipino Barber Four Beat Japanese Pinmen," *Great Northern Daily News,* November 19, 1934.

68. "Arai Bowls Self into Big League Company with 200; Match On," *Great Northern Daily News,* January 5, 1935.

69. Chris Friday, "Recasting Identities: American-Born Chinese and Nisei in the Era of the Pacific War," in *Power and Place in the North American West,* ed. Richard White and John M. Findlay (Seattle: University of Washington Press, 1999), 145.

70. Ibid., 153.

71. "Hangovers," *Japanese-American Courier,* February 13, 1937.

72. "Sport Scope: Buck Lai, Wonder Boy," *Japanese-American Courier,* February 11, 1928. For more on the Hawaiian team that Lai played for, see "Chinese Tour Revives Memories," *Japanese-American Courier,* April 27, 1925.

73. "Hangovers," *Japanese-American Courier,* January 24, 1937.

74. On Chinese American basketball, see Kathleen Yep, *Outside the Paint: When Basketball Ruled at the Chinese Playground* (Philadelphia: Temple University Press, 2009).

75. "Hangovers," *Japanese-American Courier,* November 16, 1935.

76. "Seven Straight Won by Chinese," *Japanese-American Courier,* February 2, 1929.

77. "China Club to Meet Hi-Stars," *Japanese-American Courier,* March 16, 1929.

78. "Lil' Tokyo Series to Be Held Next Year," *Great Northern Daily News,* October 5, 1937.

79. "China Club to Meet Hi-Stars," *Japanese-American Courier,* March 16, 1929.

80. "Sports Dusts," *Great Northern Daily News,* November 25, 1940.

81. "Oriental Hoopers Will Clash Tonight," *Japanese-American Courier,* March 3, 1929.

82. "Comedy Marks First Oriental Grid Meet," *Japanese-American Courier,* October 31, 1931.

83. Ibid.

84. Eddie Luke, "Hangovers," *Japanese-American Courier,* November 28, 1936.

85. "China Club Downs Black Hawks 21–14," *Great Northern Daily News,* January 10, 1935.

86. "Nisei and Chinese Play Together for Victory Says P-I Writer," *Great Northern Daily News,* February 4, 1941.

87. "Hangovers," *Japanese-American Courier,* September 24, 1938.

88. Eddie Luke, "Hangovers," *Japanese-American Courier,* November 28, 1936.

89. "Hangovers," *Japanese-American Courier,* June 19, 1937.

90. "Nice Going Gals," *Japanese-American Courier,* July 22, 1939.

91. "No Color Line," *Japanese-American Courier,* November 20, 1937.

92. Editorial, "Sportsmanship and Loyalty," *Northwest Enterprise,* August 14, 1936.

93. Of the forty-one bouts for which results are known, his record is thirty-six wins, three losses, and two draws. Because twenty-nine of these victories were by knockout, Hoshino became known as the Japanese Sandman or Homicide Hal and a hero to the Nisei of the Pacific Coast. Joseph R. Svinth, "Harold Hoshino, the Japanese Sandman," *Journal of Combative Sport,* June 2002, available at http://ejmas.com/jcs/jcsframe.htm (accessed August 8, 2007).

94. *Japanese-American Courier,* November 20, 1938.

95. Linda España-Maram, *Creating Masculinity in Los Angeles's Little Manila: Working-Class Filipinos and Popular Culture, 1920s–1950s* (New York: Columbia University Press, 2006), 81, 94.

96. Bud Fukei, "Budd's Banter," *Great Northern Daily News,* January 18, 1941.

97. Shibazaki, "Seattle and the Japanese-United States Baseball Connection, 1905–1926," 7, 23–24.

98. "Sport Scope," *Japanese-American Courier,* January 21, 1928.

99. Ibid.

100. Frank Sugiyama, "Sport Scope: Baseball and International Peace," *Japanese-American Courier,* April 27, 1929.

101. Quoted in "Japan Owes America Debt in Teaching Sports and Spirit of Sportsmanship," *Japanese-American Courier,* October 21, 1933.

102. "Prince Says Baseball Bridge of Friendship between U.S., Japan," *Great Northern Daily News,* November 16, 1934.

103. "Hangovers," *Japanese-American Courier,* August 19, 1939.

104. James Shinkai, "Sport Scope: Democracy in Action," *Japanese-American Courier,* December 23, 1933.

105. "Japanese Nines Promotes Respect among Fandom," *Japanese-American Courier,* January 14, 1932.

106. Ibid.

107. "No Color Line."

108. Memo, September 27, 1929, Ben Evans Recreation Program Collection (hereafter Evans Collection), Box 5, Folder 5, Seattle Municipal Archives (hereafter SMA).

109. Pearl Powell, Playfield Report, Summer 1931, Evans Collection, Box 41, Folder 14, SMA.

110. Petition, Evans Collection, Box 5, Folder 5, SMA.

111. Ibid.

112. "Playfield Needed Plea Voiced by General Public," *Japanese-American Courier,* January 7, 1928.

113. "Biography of H. S. Boy," Survey of Race Relations, Box 27, Folder 151.

114. Alice M. Lopp, "Report of the Activities Carried On at the Collins Field House," October 1932–April 1933, Evans Collection, Box 5, Folder 6, SMA.

115. Nobuko Yamaguchi, Playground Report to Ben Evans, 1930, Evans Collection, Box 41, Folder 14, SMA.

116. Pearl Powell, Playfield Report, Summer 1931, Evans Collection, Box 41, Folder 14, SMA.

117. "68 Japanese Play for Collins Fives," *Japanese-American Courier,* November 21, 1936.

118. *Seattle Post-Intelligencer,* February 28, 1949; "2 Collins Teams Win to Take Leadership," *Japanese-American Courier,* December 26, 1931.

119. "Vince O'Keefe: And Now, Time Off for Just Fishin'," *Seattle Times,* January 21, 1972.

120. Phil Taylor, "Collins Kids—One World: Boyd's Cagers Form United Nations," *Seattle Times,* January 27, 1948.

121. Letter from James Sakamoto to Don Evans, January 13, 1942, Evans Collection, Box 5, Folder 6, SMA.

122. Crepeau, "Pearl Harbor," 72.

123. Ibid.

CHAPTER 6

1. Eiichiro Azuma, "'The Pacific Era Has Arrived': Transnational Education among Japanese Americans, 1932–1941," *History of Education Quarterly* 42, no. 1 (2003): 62.

2. For background on the events leading to the Pacific War, I relied on Akira Iriye, *Power and Culture: The Japanese-American War, 1941–1945* (Cambridge, MA: Harvard University Press, 1981), chap. 1; Walter Lafeber, *The Clash: A History of U.S.-Japan Relations* (New York: W. W. Norton, 1997), chap. 7; Herbert Feis, *The Road to Pearl Harbor: The Coming War between the United States and Japan* (Princeton, NJ: Princeton University Press, 1950).

3. Lafeber, *Clash,* 166.

4. David Kennedy, *Freedom from Fear: The American People in Depression and War, 1929–1945* (New York: Oxford University Press, 1999), 515.

5. Tetsuden Kashima, *Judgment without Trial: Japanese American Imprisonment during World War II* (Seattle: University of Washington Press, 2003), 23; Greg Robinson, *By Order of the President: FDR and the Internment of Japanese Americans* (Cambridge, MA: Harvard University Press, 2001), 61; Louis Fiset, *Imprisoned Apart: The World War II Correspondence of an Issei Couple* (Seattle: University of Washington Press, 1997), 28.

6. Fiset, *Imprisoned Apart,* 28.

7. Ibid. Category A consisted of known dangerous persons who had been subjects of individual investigations. They required constant observation and included fishermen, produce distributors, priests, influential businessmen, and consulate members—in other words, people in strategic locations or situations where sabotage was likely. Category B consisted of potentially dangerous but not fully investigated individuals. Category C consisted of people with pro-Japanese leanings.

8. "Sino-Japanese Situation to be a Topic at Forum," *North American Times,* November 7, 1936.

9. "Extra-Territoriality," *Japanese-American Courier,* April 19, 1930.

10. "Takashi Matsui Scores Triumph in Oratorical Contest on Sino-Japanese Issue; 300 Attend Speech," *Great Northern Daily News,* February 12, 1938. Part of the speech was printed in the same issue of the newspaper. Takashi Matsui, "Significance of Sino-Japanese Conflict," *Great Northern Daily News,* February 12, 1938.

11. "Boycott Is Unjust to Those Japanese Living in America," *Great Northern Daily News,* November 5, 1937. This article originally appeared in the *Pacific Citizen.*

12. Yong Chen, *Chinese San Francisco, 1850–1943: A Trans-Pacific Community* (Stanford, CA: Stanford University Press, 2000), 234.

13. Monica Sone, *Nisei Daughter,* 4th ed. (Seattle: University of Washington Press, 1987), 118.

14. Ibid., 119.

15. Ibid.

16. Ibid.

17. "Japanese Unwitting Cause of Chinese Jackson St. Brawl," *Great Northern Daily News,* January 9, 1939.

18. "Nisei Fights with Chinese Boys over Stolen Bicycle of Friend," *Great Northern Daily News,* July 8, 1940.

19. Howard Imazaki, "Nisei Girl Is Attacked by Chinese," *Great Northern Daily News,* October 23, 1937.

20. Ibid.

21. "Japanese Unwitting Cause of Chinese Jackson St. Brawl."

22. "Odd Friendship to Occidentals," *Great Northern Daily News,* January 1, 1938.

23. Ibid.

24. "Chinese, Japanese Pastors Change Pulpits," *Great Northern Daily News,* October 30, 1940.

25. Daniel Widener, "'Perhaps the Japanese Are to Be Thanked?' Asia, Asian Americans, and the Construction of Black California," *positions* 11, no. 1 (2003): 135–181.

26. W. A. Domingo, the president of the Inter-racial Forum, agreed that Japan could not be counted on to defend "colored" races; as an example, he pointed out that Japan had not taken a stand on the persecution of the "Scottsboro boys," nine African American youths accused of raping two white women in Alabama in 1931, while England, France, and Germany had made demonstrations. "Japanese Are No Friend to Negro Say the Chinese," *Northwest Enterprise,* April 26, 1934.

27. Ibid.

28. Quoted in "Japanese Plan to Play One Race against Another," *Northwest Enterprise*, February 21, 1935.

29. "Japanese Heads Group to Fight for Colored Races," *Northwest Enterprise*, January 10, 1935.

30. Richard Berner, *Seattle Transformed: World War II to Cold War* (Seattle: Charles Press, 1999), 44–46.

31. Letter to S. Hara from A. E. Harding, May 19, 1941, Seattle Hotel Operators Domeikai, Roll 1, MSCUA, University of Washington.

32. "Japanese Hotels Refusing to Keep Negroes," *Northwest Enterprise*, May 9, 1941.

33. "Main Street," *Great Northern Daily News*, May 10, 1941.

34. "Delegation Waits on Park Board in Discrimination," *Northwest Enterprise*, July 25, 1941.

35. "Mayor Millikin Halts Pool Bias," *Northwest Enterprise*, August 1, 1941.

36. Ibid.

37. "Just to Remind You," *Northwest Enterprise*, July 23, 1941.

38. *Great Northern Daily News*, July 25, 1941.

39. Ibid.

40. Ibid.

41. Seattle Park Board Minutes, July 24, 1941, SMA.

42. James Scavotto to Members of Seattle Park Board, July 11, 1941, Sherwood History Collection, Box 35, Folder 20, SMA.

43. Quintard Taylor, *The Forging of a Black Community: Seattle's Central District from 1870 through the Civil Rights Era* (Seattle: University of Washington Press, 1994), 168.

44. "Nipponese Here Planning Business as Usual—Almost," *Seattle Times*, July 27, 1941.

45. Ibid. When the executive order was issued, a steamer from the Nippon Yusen Kaisha line carrying a large quantity of silk was headed to Seattle. Over the past year, shipments between Seattle and Japan had been nonmilitary; scraps had stopped about a year earlier, and main exports were lumber, logs, pulp, flour, wheat. The Seattle manager of the company expressed uncertainty as to what would happen but hoped that the two countries would work out some arrangement in which Japanese vessels could complete their voyage.

46. "All Japanese Here Win Our Respect," *Northwest Enterprise*, November 21, 1941.

47. "Japanese Here Thunderstruck by Air Attack," *Seattle Times*, December 8, 1941.

48. "'Business as Usual' at Pike Place Market," *Great Northern Daily News*, December 9, 1941.

49. "Blackout for Seattle Held Again Tonight," *Great Northern Daily News*, December 9, 1941; Bill Hosokawa, "The Uprooting of Seattle," in *Japanese Americans, from Relocation to Redress*, ed. Roger Daniels, Sandra C. Taylor, and Harry H. L. Kitano (Seattle: University of Washington Press, 1991), 19.

50. Editorial, *Great Northern Daily News*, December 9, 1941.

51. "What's War to Friends?" *Seattle Post-Intelligencer*, December 10, 1941.

52. "Japanese Beaten Up by 6 Filipinos Yesterday," *Great Northern Daily News*, December 11, 1941.

53. "Two Negroes Beat Up Elderly Japanese in Nihonmachi Hotel," *Great Northern Daily News*, December 26, 1941; "Negro Chokes, Slugs Issei Woman in Local Nihonmachi Robbery; Escapes with $36," *Great Northern Daily News*, December 7, 1941; "Well-Dressed Negro Walks out of Japanese Office with 80 Dollars," *Great Northern Daily News*, December 12, 1941.

54. "Filipino Swings; Japanese Ducks; Second Filipino Smacked on Nose," *Great Northern Daily News*, January 26, 1942.

55. Editorial, *Great Northern Daily News*, December 9, 1941.

56. Fiset, *Imprisoned Apart*, 31.

57. Ibid., 32.

58. Ibid., 36.

59. Ibid., 30; Berner, *Seattle Transformed*, 23; Sucheng Chan, *Asian Americans: An Interpretive History* (Boston: Twayne, 1991), 123.

60. Fiset, *Imprisoned Apart*, 32.

61. "Issei Domestic Help Cannot Be Compensated," *Great Northern Daily News*, December 11, 1941.

62. Fiset, *Imprisoned Apart*, 33.

63. Ibid.

64. "Japanese Clerks in Schools Hit," *Seattle Star*, February 24, 1942; "27 Japanese Girls Leave School Jobs," *Seattle Post-Intelligencer*, February 26, 1942. This episode is also discussed in Berner, *Seattle Transformed*, 31–32.

65. "Japanese Replaced by Negroes as 'Redcaps,'" *Great Northern Daily News*, February 27, 1942.

66. Sone, *Nisei Daughter*, 152–157.

67. "Japs Wed to Non-Nipponese Must Leave," *Seattle Post-Intelligencer*, May 9, 1942.

68. "Evacuation to Part Chinese, Jap Family," *Seattle Post-Intelligencer*, April 4, 1942.

69. Sone, *Nisei Daughter*, 166; Berner, *Seattle Transformed*, 39.

70. Many accounts discuss Hirabayashi's quest for justice and *Hirabayashi v. United States*, 320 U.S. 81 (1943). For a concise treatment, see Roger Daniels, *Prisoners without Trial: Japanese Americans in World War II* (New York: Hill and Wang, 1993), 59–62.

71. "Best Interest of Nation Cannot Be Served by Evacuation Says Sakamoto," *Great Northern Daily News*, January 22, 1942.

72. "Life, Liberty and the Pursuit of Happiness," *Northwest Enterprise*, April 3, 1942.

73. "Oriental Quarter Still a Teeming District," *Seattle Post-Intelligencer*, June 6, 1942.

74. Harold Schaffer to James Sakamoto, May 21, 1944, Sakamoto Papers, Box 2, Folder 35.

75. Taylor, *Forging of a Black Community*, 159.

76. Ibid., 161.

77. Of the 329 blacks working at Boeing in 1943, 86 percent were women. Ibid., 164.

78. Xiaojian Zhao, *Remaking Chinese America: Immigration, Family, and Community, 1940–1965* (New Brunswick, NJ: Rutgers University Press, 2002), 55–56; K. Scott Wong, *Americans First: Chinese Americans and the Second World War* (Cambridge, MA: Harvard University Press, 2005), chap. 5.

79. "Wing Luke," *Seattle Post-Intelligencer*, May 8, 1943.

80. Ibid.

81. "Chinese Youth Student Head," *Seattle Post-Intelligencer*, September 9, 1943.

82. Ibid.

83. It would take a great deal of space to provide an exhaustive list of studies on Japanese internment, so I will list some of the most recent notable books on different aspects of the subject: Brian Hayashi, *Democratizing the Enemy: The Japanese American Internment* (Princeton, NJ: Princeton University Press, 2004); Allan W. Austin, *From Concentration Camp to Campus: Japanese American Students and World War II* (Urbana: University of Illinois Press, 2004); Eric Muller, *American Inquisition: The Hunt for Japanese American Disloyalty during World War II* (Chapel Hill: University of North Carolina Press, 2007); Alice Yang Murray, *Historical Memories of the Japanese American Internment and the Struggle for Redress* (Stanford, CA: Stanford University Press, 2008); Greg Robinson, *Tragedy of Democracy: Japanese Confinement in North America* (New York: Columbia University Press, 2009).

EPILOGUE

1. Quintard Taylor, *The Forging of a Black Community: Seattle's Central District from 1870 through the Civil Rights Era* (Seattle: University of Washington Press, 1994), 174.

2. Elmer Ogawa Papers (hereafter Ogawa Papers), Box 8, Folder 4, MSCUA, University of Washington. However, according to Peter Chin and Peter Bacho, Jackson Street's population was 4,800. Doug Chin and Peter Bacho, "The Origins of the International District," *International Examiner*, November 21, 1984.

3. Howard Droker, "Seattle Race Relations during the Second World War," in *Experiences in a Promised Land: Essays in Pacific Northwest History*, ed. G. Thomas Edwards and Carlos A. Schwantes (Seattle: University of Washington Press, 1986), 359–366.

4. Robert W. O'Brien, "Seattle: Race Relations Frontier, 1949," *Common Ground* (1949): 18–23; S. Frank Miyamoto and Robert W. O'Brien, "A Survey of Some Changes in the Seattle Japanese Community Resulting from the Evacuation," 1947 or 1948, Central Seattle Community Council Records (hereafter CSCC), Box 35, Folder 7, MSCUA, University of Washington.

5. Taylor, *Forging of a Black Community*, 167–168; Richard Berner, *Seattle Transformed: World War II to Cold War* (Seattle: Charles Press, 1999), 118–134.

6. The Vital Statistics Committee found that in 1950, 77.1 percent of Jackson Street residents did not own the homes they lived in, compared to 41.8 percent in Seattle. Owners occupied 17.3 percent of homes in Jackson Street, and in Seattle overall, 54.3 percent. The unemployment rate in Jackson Street was 24.1 percent among men and 10.6 percent for women, compared to 9.2 percent for men and 5.9 percent for women in the rest of Seattle. Ogawa Papers, Box 8, Folder 6.

7. Ogawa Papers, Box 8, Folder 4.

8. The report was based on a survey of seventy-two people who attended a meeting on January 13, 1955. "A Survey of Attitudes and Opinions in the Jackson Street Community Study Area," January 13, 1955, Part II, Ogawa Papers, Box 8, Folder 2.

9. Other important events named in the survey were the Jackson Street Council Dinner, Bon Odori, Chinese New Year, Christmas, Clean-up Campaign, Japanese Bazaar, Washington Jr. High International Dinner, Little League Athletics, Neighborhood House Carnival, Moon Festival, and Washington Trade Fair. Ibid.

10. Ibid.

11. Matthew O'Connor," Jackson Street Community Council: Group Including Many Races Hasn't Single Racial Problem," *Seattle Times*, May 19, 1958.

12. Ogawa Papers, Box 8, Folder 3.

13. Ogawa Papers, Box 7, Folder 17.

14. *Filipino Forum*, April 1951, Ogawa Papers, Box 4, Folder 9.

15. Ogawa Papers, Box 4, Folder 9.

16. Ogawa Papers, Box 8, Folder 10.

17. Ogawa Papers, Box 4, Folder 10.

18. James Sakamoto, "Good Internationalism," *International Community News*, January 1, 1953.

19. Ogawa Papers, Box 7, Folder 12.

20. Ibid.

21. CSCC Records, Box 35, Folder 8.

22. Ogawa Papers, Box 8, Folder 6.

23. January 1966 newsletter, Ogawa Papers, Box 8, Folder 8.

24. Wing Luke Asian Museum, available at www.wingluke.org/district.htm (accessed October 31, 2009).

꙳║╠꙳

Selected Bibliography

MANUSCRIPT AND ARCHIVAL COLLECTIONS

Alaska-Yukon-Pacific Exposition Pamphlet File. Manuscripts, Special Collections, and University Archives. University of Washington.

Ben Evans Recreation Program Collection. Seattle Municipal Archives.

Civic Unity Committee of Seattle Records. Manuscripts, Special Collections, and University Archives. University of Washington.

Densho: The Japanese American Legacy Project. Digital archive of videotaped interviews, photographs, documents, and other materials relating to the Japanese American experience. www.densho.org.

Don Sherwood Parks History Collection. Seattle Municipal Archives.

Elmer Ogawa Papers. Manuscripts, Special Collections, and University Archives. University of Washington.

Frank Fukuda Scrapbooks. Manuscripts, Special Collections, and University Archives. University of Washington.

James Sakamoto Papers. Manuscripts, Special Collections, and University Archives. University of Washington.

Japanese American Citizens League Records. Manuscripts, Special Collections, and University Archives. University of Washington.

Japanese Association of North America Records. Manuscripts, Special Collections, and University Archives. University of Washington.

Japanese Students Club of the University of Washington Records. Manuscripts, Special Collections, and University Archives. University of Washington.

Kyo Koike Papers. Manuscripts, Special Collections, and University Archives. University of Washington.

Pacific Northwest—Japanese 1925—Present Pamphlet File. Manuscripts, Special Collections, and University Archives. University of Washington.

Seattle Hotel Operators Domeikai. Manuscripts, Special Collections, and University Archives. University of Washington.

Seattle—Minority Groups Pamphlet File. Manuscripts, Special Collections, and University Archives. University of Washington.

Seattle Urban League Records. Special Collections, and University Archives Manuscripts and Special Collections. University of Washington.

Survey of Race Relations. Hoover Institution Archives. Stanford University.

World's Fair Pamphlet File. Manuscripts, Special Collections, and University Archives. University of Washington.

NEWSPAPERS, YEARBOOKS, AND SERIALS

Bulletin: Sailings and Shipping Information. Port of Seattle.
Camera Craft
Franklin Tolo
Garfield Arrow
Great Northern Daily News
International Community News
International Examiner
Japanese-American Courier
Northwest Enterprise
Northwest Magazine
Notan: Bulletin of the Seattle Camera Club
Photo-Era Magazine
Seattle Argus
Seattle Grade Club Magazine
Seattle Post-Intelligencer
Seattle Star
Seattle Times
Town Crier

SELECTED PUBLISHED PRIMARY SOURCES

Bourne, Randolph. "Trans-National America." *Atlantic Monthly* 118, no. 18 (July 1916): 86–97.

Bulosan, Carlos. *America Is in the Heart: A Personal History.* New York: Harcourt Brace, 1946.

Kallen, Horace M. *Culture and Democracy in the United States.* New York: Boni and Liveright, 1924.

Okada, John. *No-No Boy.* 8th ed. Seattle: University of Washington Press, 1993.

Park, Robert E. "Human Migration and the Marginal Man." *American Journal of Sociology* 33, no. 6 (1928): 881–893.

Sone, Monica. *Nisei Daughter.* 4th ed. Seattle: University of Washington Press, 1987.

UNPUBLISHED SOURCES

Successful Living. Seattle: Seattle Public Schools, 1935.

Thompson, Nile, and Carolyn Marr. *Building for Learning: Seattle Public School Histories, 1862–2000.* Seattle Public Schools Archives and Records Management Center, 2002.

SELECTED SECONDARY SOURCES

Adachi, Pat. *Asahi: A Legend in Baseball*. Etobicoke, Ontario, Canada: Asahi Baseball Organization, 1992.

Almaguer, Tomas. *Racial Fault Lines: The Historical Origins of White Supremacy in California*. Berkeley: University of California Press, 1994.

Arredondo, Gabriela F. *Mexican Chicago: Race, Identity, and Nation, 1916–39*. Urbana: University of Illinois Press, 2008.

Asato, Noriko. "Ousting Japanese Language Schools: Americanization and Cultural Maintenance in Washington State, 1919–1927." *Pacific Northwest Quarterly* 94, no. 3 (2003): 140–150.

_____. *Teaching Mikadoism: The Attack on Japanese Language Schools in Hawaii, California, and Washington, 1919–1927*. Honolulu: University of Hawaii Press, 2005.

Azuma, Eiichiro. *Between Two Empires: Race, History, and Transnationalim in Japanese America*. New York: Oxford University Press, 2005.

_____. "Interethnic Conflict under Racial Subordination: Japanese Immigrants and Their Asian Neighbors in Walnut Grove, California, 1909–1941." *Amerasia Journal* 20, no. 2 (1994): 27–56.

_____. "'The Pacific Era Has Arrived': Transnational Education among Japanese Americans, 1932–1941." *History of Education Quarterly* 42, no. 1 (2003): 39–73.

_____. "Racial Struggle, Immigrant Nationalism, and Ethnic Identity: Japanese and Filipinos in the California Delta, 1930–1941," *Pacific Historical Review* 67 (May 1998): 163–199.

Baldoz, Rick. *The Third Asiatic Invasion: Race, Class, and Conflict in Filipino America, 1898–1946*. New York: New York University Press, 2010.

Berner, Richard. *Seattle in the Twentieth Century 1900–1920: From Boomtown, Urban Turbulence, to Restoration*. Seattle: Charles Press, 1991.

_____. *Seattle Transformed: World War II to Cold War*. Seattle: Charles Press, 1999.

Blackford, Mansel G. "Reform Politics during the Progressive Era, 1902–1916." *Pacific Northwest Quarterly* 59, no. 4 (October 1968): 177–185.

Bogue, Allan G. "The Course of Western History's First Century." In *A New Significance: Re-envisioning the History of the American West,* edited by Clyde A. Milner, 3–28. Oxford: Oxford University Press, 1996.

Brechin, Gray. *Imperial San Francisco: Urban Power, Earthly Ruin*. Berkeley: University of California Press, 1999.

Bright, Charles, and Michael Geyer. "Where in the World Is America? The History of the United States in the Global Age." In *Rethinking American History in a Global Age,* edited by Thomas Bender, 63–99. Berkeley: University of California Press, 2002.

Burke, Padraic. "Struggle for Public Ownership: The Early History of the Port of Seattle." *Pacific Northwest Quarterly* 68, no. 2 (April 1977): 60–71.

Chan, Sucheng. *Asian Americans: An Interpretive History*. Boston: Twayne, 1991.

Chen, Yong. *Chinese San Francisco, 1850–1943: A Trans-Pacific Community*. Stanford, CA: Stanford University Press, 2000.

Chew, Ron, ed. *Reflections of Seattle's Chinese Americans: The First 100 Years*. Seattle: University of Washington Press, Wing Luke Asian Museum, 1994.

Chin, Doug, and Peter Bacho. "The History of the International District: Early Chinese Immigration." *International Examiner,* October 17, 1984.

_____. "The Origins of the International District." *International Examiner,* November 21, 1984.

Chin, Doug, and Art Chin. *Up Hill: The Settlement and Diffusion of the Chinese in Seattle, Washington.* Seattle: Shorey Book Store, 1973.

Clarke, David. "Teng Baiye and Mark Tobey: Interactions between Chinese and American Art in Shanghai and Seattle." *Pacific Northwest Quarterly* 93, no. 4 (Fall 2002): 171–179.

Coates, Kenneth S. "A Matter of Context: The Pacific Northwest in World History." In *Terra Pacifica: People and Place in the Northwest States and Western Canada,* edited by Paul W. Hirt, 109–133. Pullman: Washington State University Press, 1998.

Crepeau, Richard C. "Pearl Harbor: A Failure of Baseball?" *Journal of Popular Culture* 15, no. 4 (1982): 67–74.

Dahlie, Jorgen. "Old World Paths in the New: Scandinavians Find a Familiar Home in Washington." In *Experiences in a Promised Land: Essays in Pacific Northwest History,* edited by G. Thomas Edwards and Carlos Schwantes, 99–108. Seattle: University of Washington Press, 1986.

Daniels, Roger. *Concentration Camps USA: Japanese Americans and World War II.* New York: Holt, Rinehart and Winston, 1972.

_____. *The Politics of Prejudice: The Anti-Japanese Movement in California and the Struggle for Japanese Exclusion.* Berkeley: University of California Press, 1962.

Davidann, Jon Thares. "'Colossal Illusions': U.S.-Japanese Relations in the Institute of Pacific Relations, 1919–1938." *Journal of World History* 12, no. 1 (2001): 155–182.

DeBarros, Paul, and Eduardo Calderon. *Jackson Street after Hours: The Roots of Jazz in Seattle.* Seattle: Sasquatch Books, 1993.

Deloria, Philip J. *Playing Indian.* New Haven, CT: Yale University Press, 1998.

Deverell, William. *Whitewashed Adobe: The Rise of Los Angeles and the Remaking of Its Mexican Past.* Berkeley: University of California Press, 2004.

Dirlik, Arif. "Asians on the Rim: Transnational Capital and Local Community in the Making of Contemporary Asian America." *Amerasia* 22, no. 3 (1996): 1–24.

_____, ed. "The Asia-Pacific Idea: Reality and Representation in the Invention of a Regional Structure." In *What Is in a Rim? Critical Perspectives on the Pacific Region Idea,* 15–36. Lanham, MD: Rowman and Littlefield Publishers, 1998.

Droker, Howard. "The Seattle Civic Unity Committee and the Civil Rights Movement, 1944–1964." Ph.D. diss., University of Washington, 1974.

_____. "Seattle Race Relations during the Second World War." In *Experiences in a Promised Land: Essays in Pacific Northwest History,* edited by G. Thomas Edwards and Carlos Schwantes, 353–368. Seattle: University of Washington Press, 1986.

Dubrow, Gail Lee. *Sento and Sixth at Main: Preserving Landmarks of Japanese American Heritage.* Seattle: Seattle Arts Commission, 2002.

Dye, Douglas. "For the Sake of Seattle's Soul: The Seattle Council of Churches, the Nikkei Community, and World War II." *Pacific Northwest Quarterly* 93, no. 2 (Summer 2002): 127–136.

Eisinger, Joel. *Trace and Transformation: American Criticism of Photography in the Modern Period.* Albuquerque: University of New Mexico Press, 1995.

Engeman, Richard H. "The 'Seattle Spirit' Meets *The Alaskan*: A Story of Business, Boosterism, and the Arts." *Pacific Northwest Quarterly* 81, no. 2 (1990): 54–66.

España-Maram, Linda. *Creating Masculinity in Los Angeles's Little Manila: Working Class Filipinos and Popular Culture, 1920s–1950s.* New York: Columbia University Press, 2006.

Findlay, John M. "Fair City: Seattle as Host of the 1909 Alaska-Yukon-Pacific Exposition." *Pacific Northwest Quarterly* 100, no. 1 (2008–2009): 3–11.

Fiset, Louis. *Imprisoned Apart: The World War II Correspondence of an Issei Couple.* Seattle: University of Washington Press, 1997.

———. "Nikkei Life in the Northwest: Photographic Impressions, 1912–1954." *Pacific Northwest Quarterly* 91, no. 1 (Winter 1999–2000): 25–41.

Forssblad, Marianne. "Scandinavians in King County: Excerpts from Ballard's Oral History Project." In *More Voices, New Stories: King County, Washington's First 150 Years,* edited by Mary C. Wright, 133–154. Seattle: University of Washington Press, 2002.

Frank, Dana. *Purchasing Power: Consumer Organizing, Gender, and the Seattle Labor Movement, 1919–1929.* Cambridge, UK: Cambridge University Press, 1994.

Friday, Chris. *Organizing Asian American Labor: The Pacific Coast Canned-Salmon Industry, 1870–1942.* Philadelphia: Temple University Press, 1994.

———. "Recasting Identities: American-Born Chinese and Nisei in the Era of the Pacific War." In *Power and Place in the North American West,* edited by Richard White and John M. Findlay, 144–173. Seattle: University of Washington Press, 1999.

Friesen, Gerald. "From 54° 40° to Free Trade: Relations between the American Northwest and Western Canada." In *Terra Pacifica: People and Place in the Northwest States and Western Canada,* edited by Paul W. Hirt, 93–108. Pullman: Washington State University Press, 1998.

Frykman, George A. "The Alaska-Yukon-Pacific Exposition, 1909." *Pacific Northwest Quarterly* (July 1962): 89–99.

Fujita-Rony, Dorothy B. *American Workers, Colonial Power: Philippine Seattle and the Transpacific West, 1919–1941.* Berkeley: University of California Press, 2003.

Girdner, Audrey, and Anne Loftis. *The Great Betrayal: The Evacuation of the Japanese Americans during World War II.* New York: Macmillan, 1969.

Glassberg, David. *Sense of History: The Place of the Past in American Life.* Amherst: University of Massachusetts Press, 2001.

Halseth, James A., and Bruce A. Glasrud, eds. "Anti-Chinese Movements in Washington, 1885–1886: A Reconsideration." In *The Northwest Mosaic: Minority Conflicts in Pacific Northwest History,* 116–139. Boulder, CO: Pruett Publishing, 1977.

Hannerz, Ulf. "Cosmopolitans and Locals in a World Culture." In *Global Culture: Nationalism, Globalization and Modernity,* edited by Mike Featherstone, 237–252. London: Sage Publications, 1990.

Harmon, Alexandra. *Indians in the Making: Ethnic Relations and Indian Identities around Puget Sound.* Berkeley: University of California Press, 1998.

Hayashi, Brian Masaru. *Democratizing the Enemy: The Japanese American Internment.* Princeton, NJ: Princeton University Press, 2004.

———. *For the Sake of Our Japanese Brethren: Assimilation, Nationalism, and Protestantism among the Japanese of Los Angeles, 1895–1942.* Stanford, CA: Stanford University Press, 1995.

Hill, D. G. "The Negro as a Political and Social Issue in the Oregon Country." In *The Northwest Mosaic: Minority Conflicts in Pacific Northwest History,* edited by James A. Halseth and Bruce A. Glasrud, 27–40. Boulder, CO: Pruett Publishing, 1977.

Hirobe, Izumi. *Japanese Pride, American Prejudice: Modifying the Exclusion Clause of the 1924 Immigration Act.* Stanford, CA: Stanford University Press, 2001.

Hirt, Paul W., ed. *Terra Pacifica: People and Place in the Northwest States and Western Canada.* Pullman: Washington State University Press, 1998.

Hollinger, David A. *Postethnic America: Beyond Multiculturalism.* New York: Basic Books, 1995.

Hosokawa, Bill. *Nisei: The Quiet Americans.* New York: Morrow, 1969.
_____. *Out of the Frying Pan: Reflections of a Japanese American.* Boulder: University Press of Colorado, 1998.
_____. "The Uprooting of Seattle." In *Japanese Americans: From Relocation to Redress,* edited by Roger Daniels, Sandra C. Taylor, and Harry H. L. Kitano, 18–20. Seattle: University of Washington Press, 1991.
Hsu, Madeline Yuan-Yin. *Dreaming of Gold, Dreaming of Home: Transnationalism and Migration between the United States and South China, 1882–1943.* Stanford, CA: Stanford University Press, 2000.
Ichioka, Yuji. *The Issei: The World of the First Generation of Japanese Americans, 1885–1924.* New York: Free Press, 1988.
_____. "Japanese Immigrant Nationalism: The Issei and the Sino-Japanese War, 1937–1941." *California History* 69, no. 3 (Fall 1990): 260–275.
_____. "A Study in Dualism: James Yoshinori Sakamoto and the *Japanese American Courier,* 1928–1942." *Amerasia* 13, no. 2 (1986–1987): 49–81.
Iriye, Akira. *Cultural Internationalism and World Order.* Baltimore: Johns Hopkins University Press, 1997.
_____. *From Nationalism to Internationalism: U.S. Foreign Policy to 1914.* London: Routledge and Kegan Paul, 1977.
_____. "Internationalizing International History." In *Rethinking American History in a Global Age,* edited by Thomas Bender, 47–62. Berkeley: University of California Press, 2002.
_____. *Pacific Estrangement: Japanese and American Expansion, 1897–1911.* Cambridge, MA: Harvard University Press, 1972.
Ito, Kazuo. *Issei: A History of Japanese Immigrants in North America.* Translated by Shinchiro Nakamura and Jean S. Gerard. Seattle: Executive Committee for Publication of *Issei: A History of Japanese Immigrants in North America,* 1973.
Johnson, Susan Lee. *Roaring Camp: The Social World of the California Gold Rush.* New York: W. W. Norton, 2000.
Johnston, Norman J. "The Olmsted Brothers and the Alaska-Yukon-Pacific Exposition: 'Eternal Loveliness.'" *Pacific Northwest Quarterly* 75, no. 2 (1984): 50–61.
Kessler, Lauren. "Spacious Dreams: A Japanese American Family Comes to the Pacific Northwest." *Oregon Historical Quarterly* (Summer–Fall 1993): 141–165.
Klingle, Matthew. *Emerald City: An Environmental History of Seattle.* New Haven, CT: Yale University Press, 2007.
Kropp, Phoebe. *California Vieja: Culture and Memory in a Modern American Place.* Berkeley: University of California Press, 2006.
Kurashige, Lon. *Japanese American Celebration and Conflict: A History of Ethnic Identity and Festival, 1934–1990.* Berkeley: University of California Press, 2002.
Kurashige, Scott. *The Shifting Grounds of Race: Black and Japanese Americans in the Making of Multiethnic Los Angeles.* Princeton, NJ: Princeton University Press, 2008.
Lee, Shelley S. "The Contradictions of Cosmopolitanism: Consuming the Orient at the Alaska-Yukon-Pacific Exposition and International Potlatch Festival." *Western Historical Quarterly* 38, no. 3 (2007): 277–302.
_____. "'Good American Subjects Done through Japanese Eyes': Race, Nationality, and the Seattle Camera Club, 1924–1929." *Pacific Northwest Quarterly* 96, no. 1 (2004–2005): 24–34.
Lentz, Katharine Jane. "Japanese-American Relations in Seattle." Master's thesis, University of Washington, 1924.

Leonard, Frank. "'Wise, Swift, and Sure'? The Great Northern Entry into Seattle." *Pacific Northwest Quarterly* 92, no. 2 (2001): 81–90.

Levine, Lawrence W. *Highbrow/Lowbrow: The Emergence of Cultural Hierarchy in America.* Cambridge, MA: Harvard University Press, 1988.

Levine, Peter. *A. G. Spalding and the Rise of Baseball: The Promise of American Sport.* New York: Oxford University Press, 1985.

_____. *Ellis Island to Ebbet's Field: Sport and the American-Jewish Experience.* New York: Oxford University Press, 1992.

Loy, Edward. "Editorial Opinion and American Imperialism: Two Northwest Newspapers." *Oregon Historical Quarterly* 72, no. 3 (1971): 209–227.

Lui, Mary Ting Yi. *The Chinatown Trunk Murder Mystery: Murder, Miscegenation, and Other Dangerous Encounters in Turn-of-the-Century New York.* Princeton, NJ: Princeton University Press, 2005.

MacDonald, Norbert. *Distant Neighbors: A Comparative History of Seattle and Vancouver.* Lincoln: University of Nebraska Press, 1987.

Martin, David F. "Painted with Light: Photographs by the Seattle Camera Club." *American Art Review* 12, no. 1 (2000): 164–169.

Matsumoto, Toru. *Beyond Prejudice: A Story of the Church and Japanese Americans.* New York: Friendship Press, 1946.

Matsumoto, Valerie. "Desperately Seeking 'Dierdre': Gender Roles, Multicultural Relations, and Nisei Women Writers of the 1930s." *Frontiers* 12, no. 1 (1991): 19–32.

_____. *Farming the Homeplace: A Japanese American Community in California, 1919–1982.* Ithaca, NY: Cornell University Press, 1993.

Mighetto, Lisa, and Marcia Montgomery. *Hard Drive to the Klondike: Promoting Seattle during the Gold Rush.* Seattle: Northwest Interpretive Association in association with University of Washington Press, 2002.

Mirel, Jeffrey. "Urban Schools as Contested Terrain." *Journal of Urban Studies* 19, no. 1 (1992): 111–126.

Miyamoto, Shotaro Frank. "An Immigrant Community in Seattle." In *The Northwest Mosaic: Minority Conflicts in Pacific Northwest History,* edited by James A. Halseth and Bruce A. Glasrud, 245–273. Boulder, CO: Pruett Publishing, 1977.

_____. *Social Solidarity among the Japanese in Seattle.* 1939. Reprinted with new introduction. Seattle: University of Washington Press, 1984.

Moe, Ole Kay. "An Analytical Study of the Foreign Trade through the Port of Seattle." Master's thesis, University of Washington, 1932.

Monroe, Robert D. "Light and Shade: Pictorial Photography in Seattle, 1920–1940, and the Seattle Camera Club." In *Turning Shadows into Light: Art and Culture of the Northwest's Early Asian/Pacific Community,* edited by Mayumi Tsutakawa and Alan Chong Lau, 8–32. Seattle: Young Pine Press, 1982.

Morgan, Murray. *Skid Road: An Informal Portrait of Seattle.* New York: Viking Press, 1951.

Murray, Keith A. "The Charles Niederhauer Case: Patriotism in the Seattle Schools, 1919." *Pacific Northwest Quarterly* 74, no. 1 (1983): 11–17.

Neil, J. M. "Paris or New York? The Shaping of Downtown Seattle, 1903–14." *Pacific Northwest Quarterly* 75, no. 1 (1984): 22–33.

Nelson, Bryce E. "Frank B. Cooper: Seattle's Progressive School Superintendent, 1901–1922." *Pacific Northwest Quarterly* 74, no. 4 (1983): 167–177.

Nomura, Gail M. "Beyond the Playing Field: The Significance of Pre–World War II Japanese American Baseball in the Yakima Valley." In *Bearing Dreams, Shaping Visions:*

Asian Pacific American Perspectives, edited by Linda A. Revilla, Gail M. Nomura, Shawn Wong, and Shirley Hune, 15–32. Pullman: Washington State University Press, 1993.

———. "'Peace Empowers': The Testimony of Aki Kurose, a Woman of Color in the Pacific Northwest. *Frontiers: A Journal of Women Studies* 22, no. 3 (2001): 75–92.

———. "Significant Lives: Asia and Asian Americans in the U.S. West." In *A New Significance: Re-envisioning the History of the American West,* edited by Clyde A. Milner, 135–157. Oxford: Oxford University Press, 1996.

Northam, Janet A., and Jack W. Berryman. "Sport and Urban Boosterism in the Pacific Northwest: Seattle's Alaska-Yukon-Pacific Exposition, 1909." *Journal of the West* 17, no. 3 (1978): 53–60.

Northam Russell, Janet, and Jack W. Berryman. "Parks, Boulevards, and Outdoor Recreation: The Promotion of Seattle as an Ideal Residential City and Summer Resort, 1890–1910." *Journal of the West* 26, no. 1 (1987): 5–17.

O'Brien, Kenneth B., Jr. "Education, Americanization and the Supreme Court: The 1920s." *American Quarterly* 13, no. 2 (1961): 161–171.

O'Brien, Robert W. "Seattle: Race Relations Frontier, 1949." *Common Ground* (1949): 18–23.

Okihiro, Gary Y. *Margins and Mainstreams: Asians in American History and Culture.* Seattle: University of Washington Press, 1994.

Pak, Yoon K. *Wherever I Go, I Will Always Be a Loyal American: Schooling Seattle's Japanese Americans during World War II.* New York: RoutledgeFalmer, 2002.

Peterson, Christian A. *After the Photo-Secession: American Pictorial Photography, 1910–1955.* London: Minneapolis Institute of Art in Association with W. W. Norton, 1997.

———. *Index to the Annuals of the Pictorial Photographers of America.* Minneapolis: Privately Printed, 1993.

Pieroth, Doris Hinson. *Seattle's Women Teachers of the Interwar Years: Shapers of a Livable City.* Seattle: University of Washington Press, 2004.

Pope, S. W., ed. *The New American Sport History: Recent Approaches and Perspectives,* Urbana: University of Illinois Press, 1997.

———. *Patriotic Games: Sporting Traditions in the American Imagination, 1876–1926.* New York: Oxford University Press, 1997.

Prashad, Vijay. *The Karma of Brown Folk.* Minneapolis: University of Minnesota Press, 2000.

Reed, Dennis. *Japanese Photography in America, 1920–1940.* Los Angeles: George J. Doizaki Gallery, Japanese American Cultural and Community Center, 1985.

Regalado, Samuel O. "Baseball along the Columbia: The Nisei, Their Community, Their Sport in Northern Oregon." In *Sports Matters: Race, Recreation, and Culture,* edited by John Bloom and Nevin Willard, 75–85. New York: New York University Press, 2002.

———. "Incarcerated Sport: Nisei Women's Softball and Athletics during Japanese American Internment." *Journal of Sport History* 27, no. 3 (2000): 431–444.

———. "'Play Ball!': Baseball and Seattle's Japanese-American Courier League, 1928–1941." *Pacific Northwest Quarterly* 97, no. 1 (1995–1996): 29–37.

———. "Sport and Community in California's Japanese American 'Yamato Colony,' 1930–1945." *Journal of Sport History* 19, no. 2 (1992): 130–143.

———. *Viva Baseball! Latin Major Leaguers and Their Special Hunger.* Urbana: University of Illinois Press, 1998.

Rydell, Robert. *All the World's a Fair: Visions of Empire at American International Expositions, 1876–1916.* Chicago: University of Chicago Press, 1984.

———. "Visions of Empire: International Expositions in Portland and Seattle, 1905–1909." *Pacific Historical Review* 52, no. 1 (1983): 37–65.

Sale, Roger. *Seattle Past to Present: An Interpretation of the Foremost City in the Pacific Northwest.* Seattle: University of Washington Press, 1976.

Schmid, Calvin F. *Social Trends in Seattle.* Vol. 14, *University of Washington Publications in the Social Sciences.* Seattle: University of Washington Press, 1944.

Schmid, Calvin F., Sanford M. Dornbusch, and Vincent A. Miller. *Population Growth and Distribution State of Washington.* Seattle: Washington State Census Board, 1955.

Schmid, Calvin F., Charles E. Noble, and Arlene E. Mitchell. *Nonwhite Races: State of Washington.* Olympia: Washington State Planning and Community Affairs Agency, 1968.

Schwantes, Carlos. *The Pacific Northwest: An Interpretive History.* Lincoln: University of Nebraska Press, 1989.

Shibazaki, Ryoichi. "Seattle and the Japanese–United States Baseball Connection, 1905–1926." Master's thesis, University of Washington, 1981.

Sinclair, Robert J. "Baseball's Rising Sun: American Interwar Baseball Diplomacy and Japan." *Canadian Journal of History of Sport* 16, no. 2 (1985): 44–53.

Smith, Neil. *American Empire: Roosevelt's Geographer and the Prelude to Globalization.* Berkeley: University of California Press, 2003.

Spalding, Albert G. *America's National Game: Historic Facts Concerning the Beginning, Evolution, Development and Popularity of Base Ball.* Lincoln: University of Nebraska Press, 1992.

Spickard, Paul. *Japanese Americans: The Formation and Transformations of an Ethnic Group.* New York: Twayne Publishers, 1996.

_____. "The Nisei Assume Power: The Japanese American Citizens League, 1941–1942." *Pacific Historical Review* 52, no. 2 (1983): 147–174.

Sugimoto, Howard Hiroshi. *Japanese Immigration, the Vancouver Riots, and Canadian Diplomacy.* New York: Arno Press, 1978.

Takahashi, Jere. *Nisei Sansei: Shifting Japanese American Identities and Politics.* Philadelphia: Temple University Press, 1997.

Takaki, Ronald. *Strangers from a Different Shore: A History of Asian Americans.* Boston: Little, Brown, 1989.

Takami, David. *Divided Destiny: A History of Japanese Americans in Seattle.* Seattle: University of Washington Press, 1999.

Tamura, Linda. *The Hood River Issei: An Oral History of Japanese Settlers in Oregon's Hood River Valley.* Urbana: University of Illinois Press, 1993.

Taylor, Quintard. *The Forging of a Black Community: Seattle's Central District from 1870 through the Civil Rights Era.* Seattle: University of Washington Press, 1994.

_____. *In Search of the Racial Frontier: African Americans in the American West, 1528–1990.* New York: W. W. Norton, 1998.

_____. "'There Was No Better Place to Go'—The Transformation Thesis Revisited: African-American Migration to the Pacific Northwest, 1940–1950." In *Terra Pacifica: People and Place in the Northwest States and Western Canada,* edited by Paul W. Hirt, 206–217. Pullman: Washington State University Press, 1998.

Taylor, William. *In Pursuit of Gotham.* New York: Oxford University Press, 1992.

Tchen, John. *New York before Chinatown: Orientalism and the Shaping of American Culture, 1776–1882.* Baltimore: Johns Hopkins Press, 1999.

Ten Broek, Jacobus. *Prejudice, War, and the Constitution.* Berkeley: University of California Press, 1958.

Thrush, Coll. *Native Seattle: Histories from the Crossing-over Place.* Seattle: University of Washington Press, 2007.

Tsutakawa, Mayumi. *Kanreki: The 60th Anniversary History of the Japan-America Society of the State of Washington, 1923–1983*. Seattle: Japan-America Society of the State of Washington, 1983.

———. "Memories of Nisei Sports Clubs." *Journal of the International District* 3, no. 7 (1976): 1, 5.

Tyack, David B. *One Best System: A History of American Urban Education*. Cambridge, MA: Harvard University Press, 1974.

———. "The Perils of Pluralism: The Background of the Pierce Case." *American Historical Review* 74, no. 1 (1968): 74–98.

Varzally, Allison. *Making a Non-white America: Californians Coloring outside Ethnic Lines, 1925–1955*. Berkeley: University of California Press, 2008.

Vaughan, Leslie J. "Cosmopolitanism, Ethnicity and American Identity: Randolph Bourne's 'Trans-National America.'" *Journal of American Studies* 25, no. 3 (1991): 443–459.

Wacker, Fred R. "Assimilation and Cultural Pluralism in American Social Thought." *Phylon* 40, no. 4 (1979): 325–353.

Weglyn, Michi. *Years of Infamy: The Untold Story of America's Concentration Camps*. New York: Morrow, 1976.

White, Richard. *It's Your Misfortune and None of My Own: A New History of the American West*. Norman: University of Oklahoma Press, 1991.

———. "Race Relations in the West." *American Quarterly* 38, no. 3 (1986): 396–416.

Widener, Daniel. "'Perhaps the Japanese Are to Be Thanked?' Asia, Asian Americans, and the Construction of Black California." *positions* 11, no. 1 (2003): 135–181.

Wiebe, Robert. *The Search for Order, 1877–1920*. New York: Hill and Wang, 1967.

Wild, Mark. "'So Many Children at Once and So Many Kinds': Schools and Ethno-racial Boundaries in Early Twentieth Century Los Angeles." *Western Historical Quarterly* 33, no. 4 (2002): 453–476.

———. *Street Meeting: Multiethnic Neighborhoods in Early Twentieth-Century Los Angeles*. Berkeley: University of California, 2005.

Williams, William Appleman. *The Tragedy of American Diplomacy*. Cleveland: World Publishing, 1959. New York: W. W. Norton, 1988. Reprint.

Wong, K. Scott. *Americans First: Chinese Americans and the Second World War*. Cambridge, MA: Harvard University Press, 2005.

Woodside, Alexander. "The Asia-Pacific Idea as a Mobilization Myth." In *What Is in a Rim? Critical Perspectives on the Pacific Region Idea,* edited by Arif Dirlik, 36–52. Lanham, MD: Rowman and Littlefield Publishers, 1998.

Yanagisako, Sylvia Junko. *Transforming the Past: Tradition and Kinship among Japanese Americans*. Stanford, CA: Stanford University Press, 1985.

Yoo, David. *Growing Up Nisei: Race, Generation, and Culture among Japanese Americans of California, 1924–49*. Urbana: University of Illinois Press, 2000.

———. "'Read All about It': Race, Generation and the Japanese American Ethnic Press, 1925–1941." *Amerasia Journal* 19, no. 1 (1993): 69–92.

Zabilski, Carol. "Dr. Kyo Koike, 1878–1947: Physician, Poet, Photographer." *Pacific Northwest Quarterly* 68, no. 2 (1977): 73–78.

Zhao, Xiaojian. *Remaking Chinese America: Immigration, Family, and Community, 1940–1965*. New Brunswick, NJ: Rutgers University Press, 2002.

Zhu, Liping, *A Chinaman's Chance: The Chinese on the Rocky Mountain Frontier*. Niwot, CO: University Press of Colorado, 1997.

Index

SHELLEY SANG-HEE LEE is an Associate Professor of Comparative American Studies and History at Oberlin College.

Also in the series *Asian American History and Culture*:

Martin F. Manalansan IV, ed., *Cultural Compass: Ethnographic Explorations of Asian America*

Ko-lin Chin, *Smuggled Chinese: Clandestine Immigration to the United States*

Evelyn Hu-DeHart, ed., *Across the Pacific: Asian Americans and Globalization*

Soo-Young Chin, *Doing What Had to Be Done: The Life Narrative of Dora Yum Kim*

Robert G. Lee, *Orientals: Asian Americans in Popular Culture*

David L. Eng and Alice Y. Hom, eds., *Q & A: Queer in Asian America*

K. Scott Wong and Sucheng Chan, eds., *Claiming America: Constructing Chinese American Identities during the Exclusion Era*

Lavina Dhingra Shankar and Rajini Srikanth, eds., *A Part, Yet Apart: South Asians in Asian America*

Jere Takahashi, *Nisei/Sansei: Shifting Japanese American Identities and Politics*

Velina Hasu Houston, ed., *But Still, Like Air, I'll Rise: New Asian American Plays*

Josephine Lee, *Performing Asian America: Race and Ethnicity on the Contemporary Stage*

Deepika Bahri and Mary Vasudeva, eds., *Between the Lines: South Asians and Postcoloniality*

E. San Juan, Jr., *The Philippine Temptation: Dialectics of Philippines–U.S. Literary Relations*

Carlos Bulosan and E. San Juan, Jr., eds., *The Cry and the Dedication*

Carlos Bulosan and E. San Juan, Jr., eds., *On Becoming Filipino: Selected Writings of Carlos Bulosan*

Vicente L. Rafael, ed., *Discrepant Histories: Translocal Essays on Filipino Cultures*

Yen Le Espiritu, *Filipino American Lives*

Paul Ong, Edna Bonacich, and Lucie Cheng, eds., *The New Asian Immigration in Los Angeles and Global Restructuring*

Chris Friday, *Organizing Asian American Labor: The Pacific Coast Canned-Salmon Industry, 1870–1942*

Sucheng Chan, ed., *Hmong Means Free: Life in Laos and America*

Timothy P. Fong, *The First Suburban Chinatown: The Remaking of Monterey Park, California*

William Wei, *The Asian American Movement*

Yen Le Espiritu, *Asian American Panethnicity*

Velina Hasu Houston, ed., *The Politics of Life*

Renqiu Yu, *To Save China, To Save Ourselves: The Chinese Hand Laundry Alliance of New York*

Shirley Geok-lin Lim and Amy Ling, eds., *Reading the Literatures of Asian America*

Karen Isaksen Leonard, *Making Ethnic Choices: California's Punjabi Mexican Americans*

Gary Y. Okihiro, *Cane Fires: The Anti-Japanese Movement in Hawaii, 1865–1945*

Sucheng Chan, *Entry Denied: Exclusion and the Chinese Community in America, 1882–1943*